P9-BJA-246

Children's Literature in Canada

Twayne's World Authors Series
Children's Literature

Ruth K. MacDonald, Editor

TWAS 823

Children's Literature in Canada

Elizabeth Waterston

University of Guelph, Ontario

Twayne Publishers • New York
Maxwell Macmillan Canada • *Toronto*
Maxwell Macmillan International • *New York   Oxford   Singapore   Sydney*

Children's Literature in Canada
Elizabeth Waterston

Copyright 1992 by Twayne Publishers.

Twayne Publishers
Macmillan Publishing Company
866 Third Avenue
New York, New York 10022

Maxwell Macmillan Canada Inc.
1200 Eglinton Avenue East
Suite 200
Don Mills, Ontario M3C 3N1

Macmillan Publishing Company is a member of the Maxwell Communication Group of Companies.

Library of Congress Cataloging-in-Publication Data

Waterston, Elizabeth, 1922-
    Children's literature in Canada / Elizabeth Waterston.
        p.   cm. — (Twayne's world authors series. Children's
    literature ; TWAS 823)
    Includes bibliographical references and index.
    ISBN 0-8057-8264-8 (alk. paper)
    1. Children's literature, Canadian—History and criticism.
    2. Children's literature, French-Canadian—History and criticism.
    3. Children—Canada—Books and reading.   I. Title.   II. Series.
    PR9193.9.W37 1992
    810.9'9282—dc20   92-24079
                                                             CIP

10 9 8 7 6 5 4 3 2 1

Printed and bound in the United States of America.

Contents

List of Illustrations

Preface

Children's literature in Canada is as rich and varied as the history of the country and the dreams and experiences of childhood. From pemmican to pizza, from pabulum to popsicles, a wide variety of food has been offered to Canadian children in different periods of Canadian history and at different stages of childhood. A wide range of literature has been offered to Canadian children too: from Eskimo legends to stories of immigrant problems, from nursery rhymes about snowflakes to romances about the Royal Canadian Mounties. In 1788, one rickety printing press in Halifax published a little hymn for children; in 1990 some 65 publishing houses rolled out over 450 titles, part of an always increasing mass.

Precious examples of the earliest books are cached in libraries from Newfoundland to Vancouver Island. Librarians across the country have helped me examine them and I have enjoyed sharing their pleasure in the rare books they preserve. Most of the current productions come across the desk of *Canadian Children's Literature (CCL)*, a journal of criticism and review of which I am coeditor. I have depended heavily on the reviews and articles in *CCL*, by scholars, teachers, librarians, and parents all across the country, for help in selecting particular books for emphasis. My graduate and undergraduate students and my children and grandchildren have also had a major influence on my choices.

The perspective of children and young people is essential in assessing books designed for them. This study is organized to emphasize the changing tastes, perspectives, and capabilities of the child who moves from one genre to the next, from hearing nursery rhymes as a baby to reading science fiction and occult romance as a young adult. But each chapter in the study also emphasizes the two other terms, "Canadian" and "literature." I have brought the critical approaches by which we discriminate excellence in adult literature to bear on the children's books, and I have considered books and genres in the context of Canadian national development and interests.

Geographically, Canada is huge; socially, it is relatively small, and its literary community is tightly interconnected. Our best contemporary women novelists, Margaret Atwood and Alice Munro, grew up reading *Anne of Green Gables;* our best new poets have read Dennis Lee's *Alligator Pie* to their children. All know and echo each other's work. The connections among critics, authors, and readers are also strong. As a student I took classes from Cyrus Macmillan, whose 1920 pioneer work in collecting and retelling Indian legends I had read as a child; I once taught Mordecai Richler, whose *Jacob Two-Two Meets the Hooded Fang* now delights my grandchildren; those same grandchildren have been in preschool classes run by Robert Munsch, author of *The Paper Bag Princess* and other delights.

But connections with American, British, and other traditions are also very strong in Canadian literature and criticism, especially in the children's field. My professional interest began in the United States, when at Bryn Mawr I encountered the legend of Cornelia Meigs and her work of assembling a critical history of children's literature, and I am now annotating the British poems in *A Child's Garden of Verses,* that classic Scottish contribution to the universe of children's reading. Canadian children's literature is a region within that universe which is worth exploring. I hope this book will open its borders to more travelers.

Acknowledgments

Librarians from Charlottetown to Vancouver have helped me locate and examine early examples of Canadian children's literature; I acknowledge their kindness and offer particular thanks to Irene Aubrey, head of the Children's Division of the National Library of Canada, and Margaret Maloney, curator of the Osborne and Lillian H. Smith Collections, Boys and Girls House, Toronto Public Library, and her assistants, Jill Shefrin and bibliographer Dana Tenny. John Hayes of Stratford showed me his excellent private collection of children's books. I am also grateful to colleagues at *Canadian Children's Literature* in Guelph, Barbara Conolly, François Paré, and in particular Mary Rubio, who offered valuable criticism of my manuscript. Glenys Stow suggested effective changes in my handling of books by or about Indians and Inuit. My husband and our son and daughters, as always, supported my research efforts; I am particularly indebted to Charlotte Waterston, who teaches second-grade French immersion, and Christy Waterston Beaver, who teaches fifth grade, for updating my understanding of theories about reading and child development. I appreciate the encouragement of Ruth K. MacDonald and the helpful editorial work of Barbara Sulton, Liz Fowler and Lesley Poliner.

I gratefully acknowledge the kindess of authors, artists, and publishers in granting permission to reproduce illustrative materials. Quotations from *Up in the Tree* are used by permission of the Canadian Publishers, McClelland & Stewart, Toronto; reprinted by permission of Margaret Atwood. "Lake St. Clair", part iv of "The Great Lakes Suite," copyright by James Reaney, is reprinted by permission of the author. Published in *The Red Heart & Other Poems*, McClelland & Stewart, Toronto, 1949; *Poems,* edited by Germaine Warkentin, New Press, Toronto, 1972; and *Selected Longer Poems*, Press Porcepic, Victoria, B.C., 1976. "Orders" from *A.M. Klein: Complete Poems, Part 1*, edited by Zailig Pollock, is reprinted by permission of University of Toronto Press. Lines from "Ookpik" by Dennis Lee from *Nicholas Knock and Other People*, published by Macmillan of Canada, © 1974 Dennis Lee, "A bump on your Thumb" by Dennis Lee from *Alligator Pie*, published by Macmillan of Canada, © 1974 Dennis Lee, and "Three Tickles" by Dennis Lee from *Jelly Belly*, published by Macmillan of Canada, © 1983 Dennis Lee, are reprinted by permission of McKnight, Gosewich Associates.

Elizabeth Cleaver's illustration "Z" from *ABC* by Elizabeth Cleaver, and her design for "Lake St. Clair" by James Reaney, from *The Wind Has Wings*, are both reproduced by permission of Mr. Frank Mrazik. Illustration by Laszlo Gal from *The Little Mermaid* by Margaret Maloney is reproduced by permission of Stoddart Publishing Company. Marie-Louise Gay's illustration from her book *Moonbeam on a Cat's Ear* is reproduced by permission of Stoddart Publishing Company. Illustration by Robin Baird Lewis from *Red is Best* by Kathy Stinson is reproduced by permission of Annick Press. Illustration from *A Salmon for Simon*, text copyright © 1978 by Betty Blades, illustrations © 1978 by Ann Blades, a Douglas & McIntyre Book, is reproduced by permission of Groundwood/Douglas & McIntyre Children's Books. William Kurelek's "Snowball Weather" taken from *A Prairie Boy's Winter* © 1973 William Kurelek published by Tundra Books, Canada, is reproduced by permission of Tundra Books and Houghton Mifflin. Ian Wallace's illustration from his *Chin Chiang and the Dragon's Dance* is reproduced by permission of Groundwood/Douglas & McIntyre Children's Books. Illustration by Vlasta Van Kampen from *Great Canadian Animal Stories*, edited by Muriel Whitaker, is reproduced by permission of Hurtig Publishers. Illustration by Stéphane Poulin taken from *Can You Catch Josephine?* © 1987 Stéphane Poulin published by Tundra Books, Canada, is reproduced by permission of Tundra Books.

Chronology

1534 Jacques Cartier establishes French possessions in North America.

1621 Scottish Sir William Alexander given title to lands in Nova Scotia.

1654 Prince Edward Island (Ile St. Jean) granted to Englishman Nicolas Denys.

1670 Hudson Bay lands granted to Hudson's Bay Company for fur trade.

1751 First press established in Halifax.

1759 Wolfe's victory at Quebec seals British rule.

1775 American Loyalists begin crossing the border to settle in Upper Canada (Ontario) and the Maritime provinces.

1777 First French publication, in Quebec: Amable Bonnefons's *Le Petit livre de vie*.

1778 James Cook takes possession of Vancouver Island, British Columbia.

1780 *A Mohawk Song and Dance* published for a Quebec child in English.

1788 First English publication, in Halifax: *An Hymn . . . for Sunday Schools*

1824 Julia Hart's *St. Ursula's Convent* places gothic romance in Canada.

1825 "A Lady"'s *A Peep at the Esquimaux* and "Uncle Richard"'s *Northern Regions* reflect interest in Northwest Passage trips.

1836 Diana Bayley's *Henry; or, The Juvenile Traveller* uses Quebec settings.

1844 Frederick Marryat's *The Canadian Settlers* reflects his brief visit.

1847 *The Snow Drop*, juvenile magazine, founded in Montreal.

1852 Catharine Traill's *Canadian Crusoes* is first major novel by a Canadian immigrant.

1856 Ballantyne uses his Hudson Bay experience in *The Young Fur Traders*.

1867 Confederation of British provinces in North America into Dominion of Canada; Manitoba enters Confederation in 1870, British Columbia in 1871, Saskatchewan in 1905, and Alberta in 1906. (Newfoundland completes the present provincial roll in 1949.)

1869 James De Mille's *The "B.O.W.C."* series sites boys' adventures in the east.

1894 Marshall Saunders's *Beautiful Joe* is world's best-selling pet story.

1896 Charles G. D. Roberts's *Earth's Enigmas* begins realistic animal stories.

1898 E. T. Seton's *Wild Animals I Have Known* adds naturalist's delicacy.

1906 Norman Duncan's *Adventures of Billy Topsail* introduces Newfoundland.

1908 L. M. Montgomery's *Anne of Green Gables* and Nellie McClung's *Sowing Seeds in Danny* provide humor, sentiment, and local color for family reading.

1914 Canadian forces join Allies in World War I.

1917 L. M. Montgomery switches from her American publisher to McClelland & Stewart of Toronto.

1911 Pauline Johnson's *Legends of Vancouver* popularizes Indian material.

1922 Postwar interest in fairy tales: Cyrus Macmillan collects and publishes *Canadian Fairy Tales.*

1927 The "Hardy Boys" series by Leslie McFarlane catches boy readers.

1931 British Statute of Westminster recognizes Canada as self-governing.

1939 Canada declares war against Germany as World War II begins.

1943 Roderick Haig-Brown's *Starbuck Valley Winter* begins new initiation stories.

1948 Morley Callaghan's *Luke Baldwin's Vow* adds a moral dimension.

1950 Catherine A. Clark's *Golden Pine Cone* fuses fantasy and Indian lore.

1957 Farley Mowat's *The Dog Who Wouldn't Be* adds family comedy to animal stories.

1958 Michael Hornyansky's *The Golden Phoenix,* retelling stories collected by Marius Barbeau, popularizes French legends.

1961 Jean Little publishes *Mine for Keeps,* her first work on children coping with handicaps.

1965 James Reaney adds irony and fantasy to history in *The Boy with an R in His Hand.*

1967 First serious critical work on Canadian children's literature is published by Sheila Egoff in *The Republic of Childhood;* major children's publisher, Tundra, founded in Montreal. Centennial of Confederation celebrated.

1968 Major poetry anthology *The Wind Has Wings,* edited by Downie and Robertson, appears, with first illustrations by Elizabeth Cleaver.

1969 Edith Fowke collects Canadian children's games and songs in *Sally Go Round the Sun;* Ruth Nichols's epic fantasy *A Walk out of the World.*

1971 Ann Blades begins work as author-illustrator with *Mary of Mile 18*.

1974 Dennis Lee's *Alligator Pie* nourishes love of poetry.

1975 *Canadian Children's Literature (CCL)* founded in Guelph; Canadian Book Centre established in Toronto; Mordecai Richler publishes comic fantasy *Jacob Two-Two Meets the Hooded Fang*.

1976 *Owl Magazine* founded in Toronto; William Kurelek's *A Northern Nativity* portrays humanity and devotion; Myra Paperny's *The Wooden People* records multicultural stress in prairie family.

1977 William Toye and Elizabeth Cleaver collaborate on *The Loon's Necklace*.

1978 Brian Doyle, Gordon Korman, and Kevin Major all produce tough-minded boys' novels; Margaret Atwood writes *Up in the Tree* for first readers.

1979 Margaret Laurence produces *The Olden Days Coat*, a gentle fantasy.

1980 Robert Munsch emerges as major storyteller with *The Paper Bag Princess*.

1982 Suzanne Martel's *Jeanne, fille du roy* is translated as *The King's Daughter*, a feminist historical romance.

1983 Tim Wynne-Jones and Ken Nutt glorify an adventurous pet in *Zoom at Sea*.

1986 Warabé Aska's *Who Hides in the Park?* brings oriental style to the West.

1987 Welwyn Katz's *False Face* highlights the occult; Donn Kushner's *A Book Dragon* plays with the past; Stéphane Poulin's *Have You Seen Josephine?* watches an inner-city cat; Marie-Louise Gay's *Moonbeam on a Cat's Ear* suggests the color of dreams.

1990 Judith Saltman updates *The Republic of Childhood*.

1

"Our Own Space"
Canada's Literary Universe

Geographical Space

Canada is a physical area, a place on the map with natural and political boundaries. Each of its physical features has had intellectual and literary consequences. Canadian stories, poetry, and drama for children over the past 200 years have reflected both the richness and the rigor of this physical environment. Children's books have also reflected the political evolution of Canada since presettlement days.

To the west, north, and east, oceans present cold barriers. The original continental isolation resulted in a native life-style and mind-set unaffected by and often unrelated to the cultures of Europe, Africa, and Asia. Old, unwritten songs and legends retaining the culture of Indians and Inuit (or "Eskimo" as the Indians taught the white man to call these Arctic people) linger in oral tradition and have often been retold in contemporary children's books.

When Europeans first arrived, Canada's nearly impenetrable coastline forced them to settle on islands or in riverbank and seashore areas, isolated from each other, with pockets of diverse settlements unassimilated in religion and language. French Roman Catholics, Irish or Gaelic Catholics or Scots Presbyterians, English Anglicans, Methodists, and Baptists, all brought their nursery rhymes, folktales, prayers, and hymns with them. Canadian literature in the sense of a written record began when printers and publishers appeared in each settlement and preserved this variety. From Quebec presses established soon after the British conquest of 1763 came Roman Catholic homilies in French such as Amable Bonnefons's *Le Petit livre de vie* (1777; *The Little Book of Life*). In Nova Scotia, a Halifax press established in 1751 by immigrant printers from Boston produced *An Hymn to be Sung in St. Paul's Church . . . When a Sermon will be Preached for the Benefit of the Sunday schools, and of the Poor in Halifax* (1788). These works, the earliest for children in Canada, represent the unassimilated cultures of the two colonizing nations, Great Britain and France. The Act of Union of Upper and Lower Canada in 1840 ratified the idea of a bilingual colony under British monarchic rule. The persistence of two official cultures led to a heightened awareness of the process of learning language, and in particular to early and continuing experiments with beginners' picture books, where vivid images augment minimal text.

To the south of the Canadian colonies in the mid-nineteenth century, the natural border of the Great Lakes was extended by an artificial line, visually imperceptible but politically and economically strong. This border line struck eastward through the St. Lawrence Valley of Quebec and into New Brunswick and westward through the prairies to the west coast, where it demarcated British Columbia from America's emerging western states. The border drawn against the United States of America marked an early resistance to American republican ideals. Many children's books in the mid-nineteenth century focused on British immigrants in Canada. Catharine Strickland Traill's *Lady Mary and her Nurse; or, A Peep into Canadian Forests* (1856) typifies the elitist tone in many of these early stories. Others, such as Elizabeth Walshe's *Cedar Creek: From the Shanty to the Settlement* (1863), emphasized democracy. In 1867, one year after the American Civil War ended, British North American colonies formed through Confederation the Dominion of Canada. The fact of the political border between Canada and the United States created a complex of friendliness and antagonism between the weaker country and the stronger one. Canadian books for children came to reflect a sense of national identity, often defined in terms of subtle differences between the British and French colonizers and the powerful American neighbor. A sense of living in a borderland has enhanced Canadian sympathy for all marginalized life: minorities, women, hunted animals, and victimized groups.

From the far north, icy winds blew reminders of nature's power. On the central Laurentian shield, the intensity of colors and shapes stirred awe, while the bitter cold and scorching heat of central Canadian seasons made it impossible to relax and assume nature's benignity. In the western ranges, rocky peaks terrified and challenged explorers and settlers. Adventure stories of the late nineteenth century reflected the rugged terrain and intemperate climate and dramatized the northern struggle to survive. Boys' books such as R. M. Ballantyne's *The Young Fur Traders* (1856) and W. F. Butler's *Red Cloud* (1882) focused on hostile confrontations between man and nature, man and man. The tough tone of many contemporary Canadian books for boys still reflects the northern harshness.

The great interior plains, once known only to fur traders, proved gloriously fertile to late-nineteenth-century settlement. Between the time when the transcontinental Canadian Pacific Railway was completed in 1888 and the end of World War I in 1918, this land of promise attracted a tide of settlers from many countries. But the promise turned sour when prairie lands were overcropped and desolate years of drought resulted. A prairie literature emerged for children as well as for adults. Western life was reduced to a bare-bones essence then fleshed out by ironic humor in stories by prairie writers such as Nellie McClung, whose *Sowing Seeds in Danny* (1908) gave children a glimpse of hard times and warm hearts in early Manitoba.

Bracketing the continental spread, Prince Edward Island and Vancouver Island added a gentler frame. These islands fostered quiet isolation and individualism. L. M. Montgomery's *Anne of Green Gables* (1908), set on Prince Edward Island, illuminated the narrow religious and social mores that can grow in an insular society. Such an island society reflects Canada's insularity in the twentieth century, as Canada quietly develops into moderate nationhood and complacency. But the fictional Anne Shirley uses idealism, imagination, humor, and independent thought to tame society's emphasis on unremitting work, social propriety, and religious conformity. On Vancouver Island, the real-life artist Emily Carr fought similar battles in the same early twentieth–century period. She painted powerful images of west coast island skies and forests and villages and told equally powerful stories of her tilts against social and artistic conformity in *Klee Wyck* (1941) and other books. More recently, Kevin Major has written about life in modern Newfoundland, another island off the east coast of mainland Canada. His young heroes war against new reductive pressures: joblessness, addiction, and the erosion of religious beliefs. But these characters are armed with the same weapons as the fictional Anne Shirley and the real Emily Carr: humor, intense feelings, the will to survive, honesty, and essential kindness. Canadians believe these qualities represent national values.

So varied a terrain, so vast an expanse of continental space, has led to a Canadian focus on travel, in literature and in life. In *Owls in the Family* (1957), by Farley Mowat, for instance, the owls move out from their loose cage in Saskatoon to skim over the sloughs, explore the bluffs, and hunt over the gopher prairies. They typify the motifs of voyage and quest that dominate both realistic stories and fantasy in Canada.

This country is no longer easy to skim over mentally. Canada is no longer simply a place of gophers and gardens, north winds and lonely expanses, fisherfolk and traditional biculturalism. Over a third of Canadians now live in the three multicultural metropolises of Montreal, Toronto, and Vancouver. In 1971 the government proclaimed Canada officially multicultural. Pierre Trudeau, the prime minister at the time, announced a commitment to "a policy of multiculturalism within a bicultural frame work,"[1] that would guard human rights, and encourage diversification. The dark side of this ethnic openness is the fact that the pieces in the Canadian social mosaic have not fitted easily together. Hence there has been an upsurge in "problem novels." In *From Anna* (1972), by Jean Little, the half-blind, totally unhappy German-born child who comes into an alien environment offers a correlative for every young reader who feels handicapped and lonely.

How can any child meet such challenges of society and also cope with the problems of immense space and unrolling time? The answer lies in the power of human creative imagination. Writers of books for children, responding to particular Canadian places and times, have shaped these responses into stories, poems, or plays; children reading these books use them to gain understanding of their own new-found lands of space and complexity.

The poet Dennis Lee in *Nicholas Knock and Other People* (1974) prays to an ancient God of the Canadian north:

> Ookpik,
> Ookpik,
> By your
> Grace
> Help us
> Live in
> Our own space.[2]

"Our own space," for Canadian writers and for the children everywhere who read their books, consists in the real world in time, the continental northern spread of a contemporary nation, and also in the inner world of ideas and emotions, fears, and desires. Both worlds are captured in children's literature.

Literary Space

From the position of cultural historian, children's books can be regarded as products of time and place. The *Literary History of Canada* (1965; rev. ed. 1975), includes a chapter on Canadian children's literature by Marjorie McDowell; the revised edition (1975) includes a very different account by Sheila Egoff. Both critics survey the sequence of literature for young people as part of the cultural record of the country. Neither author, however, does

justice to the wealth of early material to be found in collections
such as the Children's Library Services at the National Library
of Canada in Ottawa, the Canadiana collection held in conjunc-
tion with the Osborne Collection at the Boys and Girls House of
the Toronto Metropolitan Library, and the holdings in the libraries and archives of many Canadian universities. Greater knowledge of the early works found in these collections will augment
understanding of cultural history by adding "uncanonized" works
to the books traditionally dignified by critical attention.

A writer roots his or her own work not only in a specific country
and century but also in a literary universe. Most authors read and
echo the work of writers from other times and places, and literary
works are sited internationally and cross-temporally. Canadian
books for children display their authors' responses to *Alice's Adventures in Wonderland, The Wizard of Oz, Winnie-the-Pooh, The
Cat in the Hat, Pippi Longstocking,* and *The Story of Babar.* Lillian Smith, Canadian author of *The Unreluctant Years: A Critical
Approach to Children's Literature* (1953), is accepted internationally as a critic who showed the way children's authors bypass national boundaries in their work.

Each work in the universe of children's books is governed by
conventional considerations: accepted ideas about what belongs
in a poem, a play, a fantasy, a romantic novel, a case history, a
joke, a fairy tale. In *The Republic of Childhood: A Critical Guide
to Canadian Children's Literature in English*[3] Sheila Egoff cate-
gorizes books by genre: historical fiction, the realistic animal
story, mystery-adventure stories, folktales and fairy tales, and
so on.

Literary conventions do, indeed, bind artists. A poet follows or
noticeably rejects poetic traditions. The "Ookpik" fragment reminds us of the graces of rhyme, rhythm, echoing sound, and the
placement of the poem on the page. It also suggests the innovations that were shifting poetic conventions in the 1970s. Canadian poetry for children, by Dennis Lee and others, has been
studied in articles by Perry Nodelman, Gerald Noonan, Sarah El-
lis, and other Canadian critics, in journal articles in *Canadian
Children's Literature,*[4] the international *Children's Literature Association Quarterly,* and the *Horn Book.* Writers of poetry for chil-

dren renew awareness of the fresh excitement words once held for all of us, and stories for little children are like minipoems, each memorable word carefully chosen and placed.

The writer who tells a story plugs into another primary capability of the human mind: the ability to hold events in memory, to recount them, shaping them into structured narrative. The narrative urge works itself out in many types of stories—epic, fantasy, case study, joke—and each type has its own conventions. Because children's stories are relatively simple and straightforward, they reveal narrative urge and narrative skill sharply. Similarly in children's theater and informative nonfiction, the conventions of each genre become clearer when seen in specimens designed for a young audience. Judith Saltman extends and updates Egoff's generic approach in *Modern Canadian Children's Books* (1987), specifying three major genres—fiction, the oral tradition, and poetry—and assessing work in these genres since 1975; she puts extra emphasis on a fourth genre: the picture book. The ministories in children's picture books are indeed part of another genre that is governed by different conventions. Saltman adds to the genre approach the special insight of a writer who has herself produced a good picture storybook for children, *Goldie by the Sea* (1987).

Every literary work is a matrix catching the individual artist's dreams, reveries, experiences actual and vicarious, aspirations, and beliefs. Sigmund Freud pointed out the similarity between an author's work and the play of a child: "Every child at play behaves like a creative writer, in that he creates a world of his own, or, rather, rearranges the things of his own world in a new way which pleases him."[5] Noting the rearrangements made in a single work and relating that work to the artist's oeuvre is another way of moving into literary space. Several major Canadian authors have written books for children, and these should surely be placed within the artist's total creation. For example, Margaret Laurence's fine time-shift fantasy *The Olden Days Coat* and her quiet story of family reality *Six Darn Cows* should be related to the vision that produced adult novels such as *The Stone Angel* and *The Diviners*. Similarly, James Reaney's plays for children such as *Names and Nicknames* and his historical novel *The Boy with an R in His Hand* should be fitted into a full study of his achievements. Like *Profiles* (1982), Irma McDonough's compilation of interviews with Canadian authors and illustrators, *Canadian Books for Children: A Guide to Authors and Illustrators* (1988), by Jon Stott and Raymond Jones, focuses on individual artists. Stott and Jones add analytic depth in their brief biocritical studies. They mention all the work for children written by each author and provide a comprehensive view that is impossible in critical studies that emphasize genres and historical development. Their book clears the way for further studies about writers not only like Reaney and Laurence but also like Ruth Nichols and James Houston, whose principal audience has consisted of young adults.

Finally, each literary work is itself a space, a stage to which the reader brings experience and imagination. The reader, responding to the artist's construct, embodies the characters with features drawn from experiences with people, fills out lacunae of plot with imagined gestures, and voices the dialogue in a native rhythm and dialect. The reader decodes the book, working out some of its puzzles, bypassing others, adding private connotations to names and settings. The reader also concretizes the story, adding to the author's primary creation.[6]

In *Michele Landsberg's Guide to Children's Books* (1985) the author bases her choices and comments on the responses of children to books designed for them. She organizes her study around the developing tastes of children and reflects on her own remembered childhood reactions and the comments of her children and their friends. This generous guide sweeps over all English-language books and organizes its materials by themes. The emphasis on reader response can be applied more locally to Canadian children's books and can be tied more specifically to theories of child development.

Children in Time

In *Narratology* critic Gerald Prince laughingly lists the kinds of readers who have been considered by reader-response critics:

"Ideal readers, virtual readers, implied readers, informed readers, competent readers, experienced readers, super-readers, archreaders, average readers, and plain old readers."[7] The child reader, who may be any or none of the above, should be added to this list. But child psychologists and educators note that different powers of reading develop at successive stages. There is no such thing as "the child reader": there are child readers capable of certain responses and incapable of others at each successive stage of development. A child who cannot put a series of things in order and who has limited understanding of time and of the relationship of past to present cannot "read" a complex narrative, even if physically able to decipher all the words arranged on the page. A young person capable of thinking abstractly about cause and effect relationships will no longer relish decoding "A is for Archer." To discuss the response of child readers, it is necessary to recognize the chronology of child development.

Developmental psychologist Jean Piaget delineates what cognitive processes a child is capable of at each successive stage and what responses are impossible. Piaget postulates the development of every child through the same phases: sensory-motor, preoperational, intuitive, concrete operational, and formal operational. These phases are sequential and interdependent, though neither linear nor age bound.[8] Piaget has been criticized for his methods, and some of his findings have been superseded, but the Piagetian schema still underpins current educational practice. Similarly, curricula are built around Erik Erikson's theory of psychosocial development. Erikson believes that trust, autonomy, initiative, industry, and identity are perceptible stages, each ongoing and each an outgrowth of a previous one.[9]

Teachers believe that the children in preschools, elementary, and secondary schools manifest clearly these intellectual and psychosocial phases. Educators further note that critical stages of language development and concomitant competence in reading coincide with these phases. As each new kind of reading pleasure becomes possible, a new kind of book catches the child's attention. Critic Jack Zipes alerts us to other factors that condition the child's potential response. Noting gender-based and class-based differences as well as age levels, Zipes asks, "What does a king mean to a five-year-old, to an eight-year-old, to a girl or boy, to girls and boys of different races and backgrounds?"[10] In this study I have adhered to Piaget's scheme because, as one critic puts it, Piaget "encouraged us to seek the child in the child and to use this inquiry as a basis for understanding how adult mentality comes about and what it consists of."[11]

The Appeal of Canadian Children's Literature

The first book-length publication of the Children's Literature Association urged attention to how and why certain books appeal to children.[12] The answer to the first question—how certain books appeal—must be worked out by close critical reading of specific texts to see how they meet literary standards established by critics of all literature. The answer to the second question—why certain books hold child readers—seems to me to be threefold.

The first reason is psychosocial usefulness. When young children begin to read, they are led by nursery rhymes and folktales into the real world of family life and play group, friendship and rivalry, conflict and achievement. Schoolchildren learn to cope with their antisocial selves by reading animal fables, their escapist tendencies by indulging in books about imaginary voyages, and their personal tensions by identifying with children in problem novels. Older girls and boys, reading tales of adventure, fantasies of romance, histories and science fiction, again move imperceptibly forward into the grown-up world of citizenship, courtship, and careers. At each stage, children's literature previews and prepares the child for the next stage of the life journey. For example, the Canadian novel *Anne of Green Gables* has served well for generations of girls as a gentle lead into experiences of building self-esteem, handling friction, learning culturally acceptable ways of asserting themselves, and responding to the onset of love and the inevitability of death.

Feminists speak of certain books as "empowering" female readers—endowing them with strength to pull repressed dreams and fears out of the depths to which patriarchy assigns them. In the same way, good children's books can empower children and free them to accept growth and the limits of growth. A good book helps a child recognize a new self as it emerges in the sequence of development. Even a book for very little children, such as Margaret Atwood's *Up in the Tree,* can help the reader grow toward environmental sensitivity, sexual fairness, and innovative adjustment to change.

But children enjoy books not for guidance in solving problems, finding peace of mind, or living happily ever after; *Anne of Green Gables* and all other good books bring sheer immediate joy, the rapture of a secret life dazzling and transporting children as they read. *Anne of Green Gables* may indeed be praised for its psychological function as imaginative preparation for the next stage of growth, but it is also for hundreds of thousands of readers an unabating pleasure, an immediately accessible source of tears and laughter. Sometimes books that seem trivial or mediocre to adults may offer this joy to younger readers. Therefore these books deserve another look. Maybe recognizing the source of their appeal will contribute further to understanding the mechanisms of response.

There is a third reason for the appeal of certain books. Children's books offer national acculturation and international illumination. For the Canadian child, books by Canadian authors, set in Canadian scenes and dealing with Canadian facts, problems, and achievements enhance a national sense of identity. For the young reader in another land—the United States, Europe, South America, Asia, Africa, or Australia—Canadian books document another way of life, similar in basic human desires and fears but different in details, rhythm, and tone. Canadian children's books fix an image of the country that will endure and that may well affect international relations in the future. The true image of Canada is a composite of savagery and sweetness—like literature, like childhood.

2

Nursery Fare

The miraculous control over life gained by a child in the process of developing language has been studied by Laurie Ricou in *Everyday Magic: Child Languages in Canadian Literature*. Ricou asserts that like creative writers, children "struggle every day with the mysteries of the language and the frustrating possibilities of verbal expression."[1] To facilitate the everyday magic of language, babies need books. From wordless board books through alphabets, Mother Goose nursery rhymes, and nonsense poems, children move from a prelingual stage toward a plane of thought marked by readiness for reading. The mechanisms of language acquisition have been hotly debated by linguists such as Noam Chomsky and child psychologists such as Jean Piaget. More pragmatically, language development has been studied and facilitated by parents and educators, past and present.

From earliest times, special attention has been paid in Canada to the business of learning to read and also to the early joy of encountering books. Jesuit and Recollet missionaries in New France produced Algonquin alphabet books that were among the first volumes printed in Quebec. To other early Canadian colonies, Lowland Scots brought the doctrine of John Knox: "A school in every village, a college in every town," and a dream of universal literacy. In the 1770s, loyalists from the American states brought to the Maritime provinces and to Upper Canada a wealth of Tory books and printing presses. English half-pay officers who emigrated after the Napoleonic Wars imported a British pride in the literary heritage of Shakespeare, Bunyan, and Defoe, and their wives contributed to the early-nineteenth-century wealth of little stories and verses for children.

As bilingualism was legislated into national policy after the 1867 confederation of the Canadian colonies into a single dominion, a Canadian focus on the bases of language increased. The neuropsychological research initiated in Montreal by Dr. Wilder Penfield in the 1940s added to interest in the processes of language acquisition.[2] In the 1960s the Royal Commission on Bilingualism and Biculturalism reinforced this focus on language learning. Simultaneously in Montreal and Quebec city innovative European linguistic, semiotic, and structuralist ideas, first published in France, permeated Francophone colleges. Such studies have spilled over into experiments among writers and artists in creating books for beginning readers. Even in areas where interest in official bilingualism is minimal, Canadian children benefit from its intellectual and aesthetic consequences in books that reflect experiments in language, second-language teaching, and prelingual graphics.

Books without Words

Picture books tilt the baby toward the joy of reading. Books without words, presenting graphic images of familiar objects, hasten the child's language development, which is an essential tool for all learning. Sharing these books also enhances the parent-child relationship, which will form the foundation for later relationships.[3] Such sharing used to begin with cloth books of the kind one can now see in museums, with "pages" of material sewn together and decorated with stitchery outlining simple shapes: a ball, a block, a boat. The Dominion Games Company of Toronto mass-produced comparable simple cloth books in the early part of the twentieth century.

Board books, sturdy little productions without text but with vivid pictures of familiar things, have replaced those rag books. Dayal Kaur Khalsa, a gifted young Montreal artist, produced in the 1980s a set of widely accepted baby books that perform the important function of helping babies perceive two-dimensional symbols as related to three-dimensional objects. Through the stylized representation of baby, towel, cup, bathtub, and other objects in Khalsa's Baabee series the child is stimulated to perceive contours. Focus on shape is emphasized by the bright colors, strange to an adult eye: one baby is bright blue, another is rose-pink; water in a tub may be green, or yellow, or white. Babies react with delight to the shapes in Khalsa's images and seem undeterred by the color shifts. Presumably they find a correspondence to the mental image that psychologists postulate as forming in a prelingual stage.[4] Baby language begins with single metonyms, names of persons, objects, food, animals, and words that demand action, such as "up," "look." Such is the vocabulary implied in these wordless books.

Language complexities in bilingual Quebec have led many Francophones to invent wordless books, and a vigorous creative milieu has produced a galaxy of graphic artists. Philippe Béha's *The Tree (L'Arbre)* and *The Sea (La Mer)* both open up like an accordion to show fascinating denizens. In similar format, Stéphane Anastasiu's *My House (Chez moi)*, Marie-Josée Coté's *My Street (Ma rue)*, Marie-Louis Gay's *The Garden (Le Potager)*, and Mireille Lévert's *The Train (Le Train)* are wordless books fully filled with images of people and things. Pierre Pratt's *The Fridge (Le Frigo)* seems like a parody: it too opens to a picture almost a yard long showing all the dwellers in this habitat. The title *Le Frigo* suggests a second concern of these picture book artists in Quebec: they not only counter the influence of the English language by presenting books that can be "read" in French, but they also provide alternatives to the children's books from France that do not depict a North American life-style: this fridge is filled with delights unknown in Europe.

Designed for children just past the "baabee" stage, these board books are more complicated than rag books and less likely to be chewed. They still offer tactile and other sensory pleasures: pulling apart the velcro closing, standing the panorama on end, spreading it out full-length. They also begin the association of "book" with "story."

Alphabet and Counting Books

More literally literature, books in which pictures are accompanied by simple single words follow the wordless board books. The adult draws the child's attention to the print, creating awareness of the relation between black marks and the sound of words as well as the relation of words to pictures. From word-and-picture books, babies learn how language arises from the page. The child also gradually develops a sense of the connections between the signs (words and pictures) and the objects signified. Both the objects named and pictured and the predictions about those objects must be relevant to the child if the response to books is to be meaningful; this implies that at least some of the picture books presented should have regional or national coloration.

The earliest alphabet and counting books in Canada—for instance, those books published from around 1770 (and now held in the National Library of Canada at Ottawa, in the Lawrence Lande Collection at McGill University, Montreal, and in the Osborne and Canadiana collections in the Toronto Public Library system)—show no special difference from British ones. "N: Nurse; Q: Queen; U: Union Jack" is part of the standard nineteenth-century list. "A was an archer and shot at a frog" runs the opening of *An Illustrated Comic Alphabet*, produced by Amelia Howard-Gibbon in 1859 for her little pupils in Sarnia, Ontario, (where there were few sporty archers, though many frogs).[5] But the alphabet in Palmer Cox's *The Brownies' Primer* of 1901, like all his "Brownies" books, shows a mocking response to the British neighbors of Cox's Canadian childhood. One funny Brownie wears kilts; another appears in spats and a monocle. Like all alphabet makers, Cox releases to the child a selected view of the world and its people, its flowers and objects and animals. Palmer Cox became an American citizen, but his alphabet encapsulates some essential Canadian elements.

In the early twentieth century some Canadian business firms hired hacks to adapt alphabets for sales purposes. The London Life Company for instance, published an *ABC of Good Conduct* in 1932, preaching

> C is for Canada
> Land of the free;
> We'll all stand for Canada
> In the years to be.[6]

These products add further to our sense of how childhood was perceived and what national values young Canadians were expected to absorb. Woodcuts of blossoms and fairies by "Janet" illustrate one of many airier alphabets. In Dorothy Allison's *A Fairy's Garland of B.C. Flowers* (1947) fairies recite verses such as "X is for Xanthium, the cockle-burr. / It tears our wings so gossamer."[7] A late example of the doctrinaire alphabets from the Dominion Department of Resources and Development (1950) includes "J is for Jack, the Lumberjack bold," and "K is for Keen, Which children should be / In guarding the land of the green Maple Tree."[8]

Nowadays most preschool children build up a sense of the alphabet from television. Even with the quick-paced devices of Sesame Street, however, television learning cannot replace ABC books that can be slowly savoured, reexamined at an individual pace, and shared with an adult rather than a machine.

Some alphabet books appropriate both to childhood and to modern Canadian consciousness have appeared in bilingual form. Barbara Wilson and Gisèle Daigle in *ABC and/et 1 2 3* (1980) select words shared in the two languages, such as "D: Dragon; 1: Unicorne," and produce a lexicon of exotic beasts with polysyllabic names. In a book that presents a real-life setting, Stéphane Poulin offers two versions of his pictorial alphabet in *Ah, belle cité!* and *A Beautiful City* (1985). Here an Anglophone child can find "flowers" and a Francophone can find *"fleurs"* in the quaint

1. "... brilliant simplicity." Elizabeth Cleaver, *ABC* (1984).

pictures of Montreal's botanical gardens that appear in both versions.

A different kind of bilingualism joins naïve drawings in the English-Chipewyan counting book *Byron and His Balloon* by the children of La Loche, with editor David May. More sophisticated images of a wild natural environment combine with rhythmic verbal play in Ted Harrison's *A Northern Alphabet*. Neither bilingual nor particularly Canadian in content, Elizabeth Cleaver's *ABC* nevertheless has the universal appeal of brilliant simplicity. Preschoolers need the experience of such a book as they start along the path to not only literacy but also a love of reading.

Mother Goose

That love, however, really begins not with one-word books but with nursery rhymes, recited by heart by the lucky parents who remember their own Mother Goose days, or read from a book by those whose link with the Mother Goose tradition is thin or non-existent. Like babies all over the world, Canadian infants first learn the joy of patterned language through nursery rhymes. Traditional Mother Goose verses help babies laugh, clap hands, go to sleep as Iona and Peter Opie remind us in that indispensable book *The Oxford Nursery Rhyme Book*.[9] Dandling rhymes, tickles, taunts, and nonsense singsongs lift the child into self-awareness and into the delights of rhythm and rhyme. These poems also perform the social function of preserving cultural continuity. Canadian babies join an English-speaking world when they bounce to the rhythm of "ride-a-cock horse." But for a high-rise child who has never seen and never will see a stile or a castle, or for the supermarket kid who will never be served pease porridge or a Christmas pie, the old rhymes baffle as much as they tickle. Modern Canadian parents, mostly urban in life-style, may worry about the archaism, pastoralism, sexual stereotyping, and alien allusions in candlestick maker and baker's man, curds and whey and sewing a fine seam, London Bridge, and Yankee Doodle.

So, as in every part of the English-speaking world, Canadians have supplemented the tried and true old rhymes and baby books, alphabet and counting books. Canadian writers such as Dennis Lee have naturalized Mother Goose for Canadian goslings.

We will never know what rhymes the first settlers added orally to the traditional jingles they had brought with them from the old countries. The first real record of Canadianized nursery rhymes appeared when oral tradition was caught in published form. In 1888, for instance, the Warne Company of London published *Young Canada's Nursery Rhymes*. The editor deleted 21 items contained in the British edition and changed "In the month of February / When green leaves begin to spring" to "In the merry month of May, / When green leaves [more appropriately] begin to spring."[10] In 1900, in a bilingual book titled *Mother Goose's Bicycle*

Tours by "Mary Susan Goose," the answer to "Pussy cat, pussy cat, what did you do?" is *"J'ai mangé la souris tout à coup!"* (I've eaten the mouse, all of a sudden!).

David Boyle, in *Uncle Jim's Canadian Nursery Rhymes* (1908), localized not by deletion or bilingualism but by creation. His dandling rhyme begins "'I'm going to see Toronto Fair' / said little John Jumper," and a counting rhyme begins "Five little boys from Halifax."[12] Larks give way to loons, and the Grand old Duke of York is replaced by the Governor-General. Where a traditional finger-play rhyme says, "This is a church; this is a steeple," Boyle adds a humbler local twist: "This is the roof of the shanty" (Boyle, 9). Bits of folklore about Ontario counties condense into aphorisms: "Dundas for men of dare and do / Stormont for women fair and true; / But Glengarry's best for both of the two" (Boyle, 59). The appearance of this interesting and handsomely produced nursery rhyme book coincides with the appearance of illustrator C. W. Jefferys (1869–1951), who would play a major role in the first stage of Canadian-based writing and publishing for children.

Another Canadian-born artist, Elmer Boyd-Smith, produced a world-renowned *Mother Goose* in 1919. A long period of uninspired productions followed, broken only by work in a cognate area. Folklorist Edith Fowke published children's game songs in *Sally Go Round the Sun* (1969), a collection that reminded Canadian scholars and parents that Canadian variants of traditional jingles were plentiful, colorful, and treasured by children in their play. The magic of these incantations is invoked by Margaret Laurence in *A Jest of God* (1966), an adult novel in which children's skipping songs provide metaphors for a troubled teacher's longing to escape.

Most Canadian versions of Mother Goose issued recently have experimented with evoking local elements through illustration rather than with naturalizing the verses themselves. Barbara Reid's *Sing a Song of Mother Goose* (1987), decorated with plasticine (modelling wax) illustrations of Canadian farm and home life, is the most successful of these.

When Dennis Lee, Toronto poet, essayist, editor, and publisher, already popular as a creator of verse for children, turned to nursery rhymes with *Jelly Belly* (1983), he produced a full original range of tickles and taunts, dandling rhymes and lullabies, ministories and charms and riddles, all contemporary, kinetic, and Canadian. Here is one of the rhymes:

> Pizza, pickle,
> Pumpernickel,
> My little guy
> Shall have a tickle:
> One for his nose,
> And one for his toes,
> And one for his tummy
> Where the hot dog goes.[13]

Easy to memorize, hard to resist, many of the new songs contain refractions of archaic patterns. Miss Muffet's rhythm as well as her spider are remembered in "Little Miss Dimble," who "met a mosquito / And called him 'My sweet-O' / And married him under the moon" (*JB*, 9). Intertextuality gives a grown-up reader pleasure in "Lazy lousy Liza Briggs / Wouldn't get up to feed the pigs" which revamps "Elsie Marley," or in "Hugh, Hugh / What'll you do?," which echoes "Do, do, / What Shall I do?," or in "Mr. Lister lost his dog / and Mrs. Lister found him," which recalls Lucy Locket and her pocket (*JB*, 8, 10, 34). In "The Tiny Perfect Mayor," Canadian facts melt into nonsense in the true nursery rhyme way, and the rhyme remains caught in child memory long after the adult world has forgotten that David Crombie, short in stature but high in respect, was thus tagged by cartoonists when he presided over Toronto politics in the 1970s. This adult response to the *Jelly Belly* version of Mother Goose rhymes can never be matched by the 1990s child; but the grown-up reader's delight in the whimsical, sly, satirical elements communicates the rich responsive pleasure of reading. The listening child shares at least one level of that pleasure: the joy of subtle rhythm and carefully manipulated rhyme.

As was true of board books, Mother Goose has an extraliterary dimension. The classic pictures of nursery rhyme children and places, whether rendered by Boyd-Smith or Kate Greenaway or

Walter Crane, have taken on the quality of icons. Adults measure a new Mother Goose against older memories. Canadian adults, reacting to a new version that is palpably national in its variants may feel doubly bothered by the *Jelly Belly* illustrations. The illustrator, Juan Wijngaard, happens to work in England. Too many of his details are English: baby buggy, bathroom geyser, tidy front gardens with little wire fences. The look of the pictures just does not go with the content of "Chicoutimi Town" or that "Bundle-Buggy Boogie" roll call: "Athabasca, Abitibi, Bona Vista, Malaspina, Bella Bella, Bella Coola, Batchawana, Baie Comeau!" (*JB*, 18).

Children, untroubled by the national discrepancies, and without iconic memories of other versions of Mother Goose, perceive the book differently. They respond as they do to English books by the Ahlbergs or Anthony Browne—they search for hidden tiny details that link picture with picture. Thus Tyrannosaurus Rex, ferocious in "The Dinosaur Diner," is reduced to a bedtime toy in "Bundle-Buggy Boogie," and enormous Jelly Belly, menacing on the front cover, is reduced to a Christmas tree ornament inside. The small delicate details of Wijngaard's paintings tone down the rowdy qualities in Dennis Lee's verse.

Poetry for Children

Children's poetry other than Mother Goose rhymes has traditionally been more gentle and whimsical. Many poems by nineteenth-century Canadians, familiar because they have been included in school readers, have inculcated pleasure in rhyme and rhythm, wordplay and metaphor, cadence and nonsense—pleasures that parents have passed on by reading or reciting memorized pieces. The best and most beautiful collection of Canadian poems for children is *The Wind Has Wings,* edited by Mary Alice Downie and Barbara Robertson and illustrated by Elizabeth Cleaver. It contains poems by Pauline Johnson, Isabella Valancy Crawford, Charles G. D. Roberts, poems lilting, haunting, vivid in regional details such as W. W. Campbell's smoky hills and sumacs, and Robert Service's icy Arctic trails. These poets all blend Canadian

22

IV
Lake St Clair

I once knew a bear
Who swam in Lake St Clair
And after the experience
Said, "Hoity Toit
I don't like the way Detroit
Pollutes the air there."
Then after a while
He added with a smile,
"And I don't like the way Windsor
Does, either."

51

2. ". . . vivid regional details." Elizabeth Cleaver, design for James Reaney's poem "Lake St. Clair", in *The Wind Has Wings* (1968).

topics with echoes of the lyricism of late nineteenth-century British poets. Bliss Carman in particular reflects the rhythms and poetic stance of Robert Louis Stevenson, the Scottish poet whose book *A Child's Garden of Verses* (1885) had become a major source of pleasure for Canadian families.

In the first quarter of the twentieth century, Canadian parents and children learned to treasure the delicate and dreamy poetry published by the Englishman Walter de la Mare in volumes such as *The Listeners* (1912) and the arch whimsy of A. A. Milne as found in *When We Were Very Young* (1924) and *Now We Are Six* (1927). Canadian poets learned to adapt these British tones to nursery poems rooted in Canadian life. The best of the many Canadian books of preschool poetry carrying echoes of the "Christopher Robin" school is *Saucy and All* by Helen Shackleton (1929). Shackleton's verse shows the skill, the versatility, the simplified syntax, and the fresh and often comical logic of Milne. Saucy and the other toys belonging to Geraldine and Patricia, the garden, trips, and "our winter clothes, / our blue blanket coats / with the sashes tied in bows, / And our red tuques and mitts / And the red stockings too,"[14]) offer evidence of the way childhood was perceived, what language children were assumed to use, and what conventions and taboos pressed on the poet in the 1920s. Desmond Pacey in *The Cat, the Cow and the Kangaroo* (1968) was still reworking A. A. Milne's kind of material in a conservative reminder of the period just prior to the activism and nationalism of the 1970s.

Other poets between the 1920s and the 1970s have written poems with a sharper appeal—poetry not intended for children but nevertheless accessible to them. *The Wind Has Wings* added many newer poets—Raymond Souster, James Reaney, Milton Acorn, and Irving Layton, among others—to the older names that appear in the collection. "Orders," the poem by A. M. Klein chosen to open the volume, epitomizes its intensities:

> Muffle the wind;
> Silence the clock;
> Muzzle the mice;
> Curb the small talk;
> Cure the hinge-squeak;
> Banish the thunder.
> Let me sit silent,
> Let me wonder.[15]

This is sophisticated verse but it uses a syntax much like that of a child in a mood of imperious egocentricity. The clipped clauses are like the telegraphic speech that children use when they move beyond one word or two word utterances. The wordplay—"muzzle" / "muffle," "curb" / "cure"—is like a child's, and so is the sound play—"hinge-squeak"—like first onomatopoeic imitative soundings. The adult poet's play of thought (framing things that can be silenced—clock, mice, talk, squeak—with things that cannot be controlled—wind, thunder) parallels the animistic child's blurring of categories in the world outside the self.

The incantatory power of verse makes pleasurable listening for a very small child. Klein's poem is just one example of many in *The Wind Has Wings* and other Canadian anthologies.[16] Through later experiences of reading and learning "by heart," poetry retains its singing strength.

Dennis Lee was not included among the poets of *The Wind Has Wings*. He had established a reputation as a meditative political poet for adults with *Civil Elegies* in 1968, but did not begin publishing verse for children until 1970 with *Wiggle to the Laundromat; Alligator Pie* and *Nicholas Knock* both appeared in 1974. In all his volumes, Lee's rambunctious rhymes catch the beat of an epoch of social activism, national ebullience, and educational iconoclasm.

Dennis Lee's literary model was William Blake. His impish nonsense songs also show a debt to Edward Lear and A. A. Milne. This last influence is directly acknowledged in the subtitle of "The Hockey Game": "With thanks to A. A. Milne." Another poem, "Friends," takes us along the same tame path: "When Egg and I sit down to tea / He never eats as much as me."[17]

But in *Alligator Pie*, Lee also includes a modernist, nationalistic manifesto entitled "Hockey Sticks and High-Rise," which announces rebellion (*AP*, 63). To the polite childishness of the A. A. Milne mode Lee adds verses that are reductive and antiauthoritarian: "On Tuesdays I polish my uncle" (*AP*, 32). Some of these songs of experience are brash and greedy: "I can stare in the eyes of a toffee surprise / And polish it off with a slurp" (*AP*, 53). Some are deeply frightening: "A monster ran off with my mum / My mum" (*AP*, 18). And all are delightful to children. As incantations, they release egocentric energy:

> Alligator pie, alligator pie
> If I don't get some I think I'm gonna die;
> Give away the green grass, give away the sky
> But don't give away my alligator pie! (*AP*, 8)

Some critics—Michele Landsberg, for one—object to the "bad-little-kid" quality in Lee's poems.[18] But many a Mother Goose rhyme adds the shock of violence to its other appeals, including "Goosey Goosey Gander," who finds an Old Man, "takes him by the hind leg / and throws him down the stairs!" (Opies, 26). There is no denying the swinging appeal of Dennis Lee's subsocial language in the tickle song: "With a bump on your thumb, / And a thump on your bum / And a tickle my tum in Toronto" (*AP*, 33). Laurie Ricou in a laudatory chapter in *Everyday Magic* notes the relation between the "range of articulation" in that "intricate, self-enclosed, nonsense monologue" "The Sitter and the Butter and the Better Batter Fritter" and the realities of child language (Ricou, 117–26). Lee himself comments, "I don't romanticize children, in spite of the fact—or maybe because of the fact—that I go on being children myself,"[19] and the experience of preschool educators is that the disgorging of terror in "A dragon has eaten my dad. . . . A monster ran off with my mum" (*AP*, 18) serves to discharge disturbing emotions. As an adult craftsman, Lee believes his carefully contrived poems contribute pace and decorum to the language and attitudes of the child.

Dennis Lee toured Canada in the 1970s and early 1980s, reading his poetry to audiences that were so enchanted, so voracious for more that the poet eventually groaned to adult listeners,

> "Alligator rhyme, Alligator rhyme;
> Once you get the habit you won't be worth a dime.
> First you'll turn to jelly, then you'll turn to crime,
> But you'll never get away from Alligator rhyme!"[20]

Characteristic wordplay and rhythm remain even in his lament. In the original poem, Lee impishly pairs the merry tripping sound of "alligator"—exotic beast to the Canadian child—with the homely thud of familiar nourishing "soup" and "stew" and "pie." The images are violently yoked together, as Blakeian Lee, perhaps under the influence of his mentor Northrop Frye, uses his art to mock the mechanistic rhythms of urban life and the rationalism of a materialistic world.

Perry Nodelman suggests in an article in *Canadian Children's Literature* that in the title poem of *Nicholas Knock and Other People* (1974) Lee presents his "most subtle analysis of a child's relationship to his own childishness."[21] This volume also presents the most wide ranging use of the subtleties of language by a very accomplished poet.

Dennis Lee has published other books of verse to be read to children: *Garbage Delight* (1977), *The Ordinary Bath* (1979), and *Lizzie's Lion* (1984). In the denouement of *Lizzie's Lion* (wittily illustrated by Marie-Louise Gay), the child pulls her lion away from his grizzly lunch by calling out his name, that is, by exercising the mysterious power of words. The children who love listening to Lizzie's story have moved beyond the baby stage of simple metonymy, the naming of things present to the senses and have reached the stage of metaphor, the use of words to associate things held in the mind. *Lizzie's Lion* gives them a metaphor for the power that is released and controlled by the everyday magic of language.

Contemporary Canadian poets continue to turn that mysterious power to the production of poetry for children. Bp Nichol, for instance, in *Once, a Lullaby* (1983), takes time to repeat a simple verse pattern over and over again, with incremental changes. Anita Lobel's homey pictures add to Nichol's incantation. Gilles Vigneault, a major Quebecois poet whose song *"Mon pays, ce n'est pas un pays, c'est l'hiver"* (My country is not a nation, it's a wintertime) fed the Quebec liberation movement of the 1970s, has produced verse and stories for children that have not yet been translated or published in English. Some have a haunting sadness of tone:

Fais ton somme
Petit homme,
Plonge, plonge,
Dans ton songe

(Slip into sleep,
little man, little man;
drop down deep
into your dream).[22]

Like Dennis Lee's poetry, and like many of the traditional nursery rhymes, Vigneault's verse reconnects the very young child to an irrational, antisocial self.

We trust the poets to keep the affirmative, imaginative spirit of the 1970s alive. When Dennis Lee released the children from the Anglo-Saxon stodginess of pease porridge, he turned them on not to maple sugar, but to the nonsensical excitement of alligator pie. The openness and flexible energy of writers like Lee can help children position themselves not only in a single, sensible universe of place, time, metonymous language, and self-containment, but also in a richer, more affirmative personal and social universe of metaphor and association.

3

Traditional Stories

Before children can read, they encounter a rewarding and important literature—oral literature, the traditional folktales and fairy tales once a part of tribal and village experience but now largely the domain of the child who says, "Tell me a story." Canadian children have access to several streams of traditional tales. Indian and Inuit legends have been preserved partly by the system of native reservations, where the elders resisting change treasure the old stories. The modern Canadian mosaic of ethnic groups also preserves variant and contradictory folk traditions: Chinese, Ukrainian, Caribbean, and a world of other legends as well as fairy tales in English and ghost stories in French. In outposts and isolated settlements, old folks still relay tales untouched by modern media; in urban childcare centers trained storytellers keep the old art alive for its pleasure giving and social value.

The craft of storytelling is recorded on tape and in films. Canadian publishers have also made available many retellings of the traditional tales for adults to read out loud, embroidering as they go, asking questions, raising suspense, involving listening children in some of the hermeneutic pleasures that will develop later when they explore the world of silent reading. Traditional tales, retold to four-year-olds in Canada, in that period when children begin to connect their lives with the outside world, relay temporal and national coloration and feed into children's sense of place and time.

The question of adapting traditional stories, modernizing them, modifying them for children, and explaining the exotic and strange values in them raises controversy. In Canada, this argument rages particularly strongly in reference to adaptations of stories of the native peoples. Two special issues of *Canadian Children's Literature* (31 /32, 1983), edited by Jon Stott, and 62 (1991), present a wide range of articles on the topic of "white versions of Indian stories."

A more general controversy on the uses of folktales also waxes strong between American critics such as Bruno Bettelheim, who suggests that children find deep psychological restorative powers in the folktale archetypes of princess and dragon, stepmother and forest, and Jack Zipes, who directs attention back to the facts of folklore origins and suggests that a child picks up from them attitudes toward the work conditions, sexual codes, labor and class structures that they encapsulate.[1] Canadian critic Constance Hieatt insists that traditional stories work when writers "call up spirits from the vasty deep . . . not . . . in the name of therapy, social reform, politics, progress, or even patriotism," but in the name of the storyteller's instinct.[2]

For folktales are in their essence story, and through hearing them a small child begins to savour the pleasure of narrative. Their emphasis is on story line, not on form or texture. In lyric poetry such as "Muffle the Wind" not a syllable can be changed. But in a story, each retelling will bring little improvisatory touches of humor or horror. The listening child expects some formulaic phrase for opening ("Once upon a time" or "One time, in the old days"), but from that point on the words dissolve and the imagination finds its own place, time, group of people, and set of actions, marked in their sequence and consequence: "and then," "and then," "and so."

Indian Legends

Although the first bit of Canadian folklore preserved in published form was Henry Caldwell's *A Mohawk Song and Dance . . . A Tune to an Indian Drum, Printed for Little Master Caldwell* (1780),[3] the folklore of the indigenous Indian and Inuit people barely impinged on the imagination of settlers in the early days. But Indian folklore existed, in full and rich form.

Native peoples, Indian and Inuit, treasured a heritage of stories and legends, tales of such heroes as Raven and Nanabhozo, and fables that explained how natural things came to be: how the birch tree got her stripes or why the beaver has a broad tail. These tales differ in detail from region to region, from east to west, from lake land to Arctic. Nevertheless, some common patterns and motifs marked the unique native response to the realities of this northern half of the continent.

Indian and Inuit legends encode a different way of viewing time, animals, material possessions, and male/female responsibilities. Native people believe they live in a world shared with all other natural and supernatural beings, in a land that belongs to everyone, not to any one in particular. Powerful spirits reside in men and women, in animals, and in all other natural forms; animals, even when pursued and hunted are to be respected. Native storytellers refer to Raven and Coyote the trickster god indiscriminately as "he" or "she"; without being gender-specific, stories of the gods allow "both boys and girls to identify with wit, courage, intelligence, and humour."[4] Narrative form in traditional tales reflects a native sense of time as circular and flowing; stories take a traditional form and include the use of archaic words and phrases not understood in ordinary conversation.[5]

Early explorers, missionaries, settlers, and traders rejected and distrusted these native views and the art forms that preserved them. The past two hundred years have seen the emerging recognition that these values and art forms are well attuned to nature. Over the past two centuries, non–native Canadian writers have absorbed the native folklore while also retaining and adapting stories from their own traditions. In the last 20 years there has been an outburst of Indian legends retold for children. Recently, native storytellers have updated formulaic stories and have begun publishing as well as recounting the tales orally.

The American poet Henry Wadsworth Longfellow had poeticized the legends of the Canadian Mohawk Indians in *Hiawatha* (1858). *The Hiawatha Primer,* by Frances Holbrook (1898), containing some of the best early work of Elmer Boyd-Smith, carried parts of the Hiawatha story to little children. In 1904 Howard Kennedy's *The New World Fairy Book* proved how effectively Indian stories could be woven with other traditional materials into a strong Canadian frame story. In this well-told story about storytelling, a little boy and his Hudson's Bay Company family swap Scottish stories for Indian ones. A curious extension of native legends into a full-length novel, *The Red Feathers* (1907) by Theodore Goodridge Roberts, was designed to give older readers a romantic sense of the native blurring of physical and spiritual realities.

These non–native versions of the legends may have influenced, and certainly encouraged, Pauline Johnson (Tekahionwake). A gifted, theatrical woman, Pauline Johnson besides composing poems of contemporary Indian life that gripped generations of children also collected in *The Shagganappi* (1912) and *The Mocassin-Maker* (1913) some of the traditional tales of her father's people. She collected *Legends of Vancouver* (1911), which recounts Squamish tales, not from her own community but from the west coast Chief Joe Capilano. Reading *Legends of Vancouver* is still one of the best ways to convey to little children the tang of native style as well as the strength of Indian modes of thought and action.

Just before the outbreak of the First World War, Cyrus Macmillan, assuming a role like that of the Grimm brothers in Germany, set out to hear and record the stories of native people. The war broke out, and Macmillan, overseas with the McGill University battalion, found himself correcting the proofs for his *Canadian Wonder Tales* while crouched in a dugout near Vimy Ridge. The volume, published in Toronto by Gundy and in London by Lane in 1918, is a collection of animal legends, transformation stories, charms, and answers to conundrums such as "Why Frog Croaks." There are Blackfeet stories such as "Star-Boy and the Sun Dance," Glooskap stories from the Maritime Micmac people, all seriously told. There are also some romances about beautiful princesses and handsome young braves, and it is these that set the tone for the illustrations. George Sheringham, the illustrator, paints beige-skinned beauties in robes that look like Aubrey Beardsley creations, with buckled shoes and art nouveau hairstyles. Paradoxically, the beauty of the production undercuts the force of Macmillan's work.

A plainer book by Muriel Burkholder appeared in 1923. *Before the White Man Came,* illustrated by C. M. Manly, prefaces each legend with a note about its geographic setting. The introduction clarifies points about the widespread legends of "Gloscap" (Glooscap), "Nanna Bijou" (Nanabush, Nanobhozo, We-sa-ka-chak or Whiskeyjack, or Coyote) and "Michabo." Finely tuned for young listeners, stories in this book explain the northern lights, Indian summer, the coloration of autumn leaves, and other Canadian phenomena, and add tales of Moon Woman and other goddesses that show interesting links with European myths. A wide range of "Totem Tales" also came from American publishers in the 1920s. One might speculate that the wartime experience in Europe had left many writers on this continent eager to explore the mythical roots of their own world.

Many fine retellings of Indian legends for younger children by Canadians from other ethnic backgrounds reflect the continuing popularity of these stories after the Second World War. Frances Frazer's *The Bear Who Stole the Chinook* (1959) tells a trickster story from Blackfoot lore in a tone appealing to young listeners. Christie Harris's *Once upon a Totem* (1963) is credited by Sheila Egoff as having most fully realized "the potential for children's literature inherent in the Indian legends" (Egoff, 21). Harris's realizations, however, involve diluting some of the mysteries of Indian storytelling. Greater praise might be accorded to Ronald Melzack for *The Day Tuk Became a Hunter & Other Eskimo Stories* (1967), a retelling of tales from the far north that keeps the swing of oral tradition. *How the Chipmunk Got Its Stripes*

(1975), an Algonquin legend retold by Nancy Cleaver and illustrated by Laszlo Gal, is simple, funny, and authentic in tone. William Toye and Elizabeth Cleaver acted as a writer-artist team to create *How Summer Came to Canada* (1978), a Micmac legend, and *The Loon's Necklace* (1977), a Tsimshian legend. *The Loon's Necklace* is the most popular of all these books because its fragile collages, although far removed from the conventions of native art, aptly evoke the skimming flight of the bird over a twilight wilderness lake.

Non-Indian children, not only very little ones but also school-aged and young adult readers, have found great pleasure and illumination in these "white" retellings of the stories of the native peoples.

For Indian and Inuit children, the question of preserving Indian stories has a different force. Teachers in native schools and parents in native communities face problems when their children encounter European legends. An interesting pair of articles in *Canadian Children's Literature* dramatized the difficulties. Perry Nodelman recounted the inability of his University of Winnipeg students to create a locally meaningful version of "Little Red Riding Hood": they all added details from Disneyland to augment the traditional Perrault story designed to protect little girls from ravening males.[6] Agnes Grant responded with the story of problems faced by her students, native teachers in training at Brandon University, Manitoba, when they were asked to recount "Little Red Riding Hood."[6] In their version of the story the wolf, brother to man, posed no threat to Red Riding Hood except that he wanted her basket of goodies. The little girl took food to her grandmother as a regular duty—the "goodies" were emphasized and described in detail—and the story ended with feasting. The emphasis was on the wolf's trickery in getting the food. The young teachers amended European views of family structure, property, sexual propriety, food sharing, and animal life. Their variants of the Red Riding Hood story reflected the disparity between native and European cultures.[7]

One consequence of this native sense of the inappropriateness of imported legends has been the publication of folktales by native people. As early as 1967, George Clutesi set a model for accurate replication of tone and values in *Son of Raven, Son of Deer: Fables of the Tse-Shaht People.* Fourteen stories from precontact days (the days before the Indians had encountered the white race), collected by Alex Grisdale and compiled by Nan Shipley in *Wild Drums: Tales and Legends of the Plains Indians* (1974), include several tales in which women appear as heroes. The teller of *Why the Beaver Has a Broad Tail* (1974) was Mary Lou Fox, an Ojibwa elder from Manitoulin Island. From elders of the Rama Ojibwa Band, Emerson and David Coatsworth compiled *The Adventures of Nanabush: Ojibway Indian Stories* (1979), with notable illustrations by native artist Francis Kagige; and Ojibwa historian Basil Johnston joined Cree artist Shirley Cheechoo to re-create *Tales the Elders Told* (1981). Murdo Scribe's *Murdo's Story: A Legend from Northern Manitoba* recounts a traditional tale of the seasons and the northern lights.

Views significantly different from European conceptions of authority and property appear in Anne Cameron's retelling of "Raven" and other stories, such as *How Raven Freed the Moon* (1985) and *How the Loon Lost Her Voice* (1985). Cameron emphasizes the androgyny of Indian gods. Out of the matriarchy of nomadic life, she says, comes the mythology of the Bear Princess and other spirits. Anne Cameron's stories, interesting to students of feminism, are also entertaining for children and valuable in offering a schema that counters European assumptions about male/female hierarchy.

The most effective use of native materials, however, was made by Maria Campbell in *Little Badger and the Fire Spirit* (1977). Campbell, a Métis from Saskatchewan, offers Little Badger, a hero much more appropriate for all Canadians than the solo epic figures such as Prometheus, Beowulf, or Jack-the-Giant-Killer. Little Badger is young and blind, and he needs all the help he can get from his fellow creatures as he searches for fire. Campbell frames the legend with a scene in a contemporary Indian home, where a small girl asks her grandparents for a story. According to the legend, the traditional figure of Grey Coyote appears as a helper, and older members of the tribe help the blind boy find the home of the Fire Spirit. The story culminates when the Fire Spirit, more in harmony with the needs of the world's inhabitants than are the fates or gods of European tales, recognizes Little Badger's need for warmth and adds to his gift of fire the gift of sight. The people act collectively, unlike the rival siblings in many European traditional tales. The blind child subdues menacing beasts not by force but by gentleness, and the Fire Spirit is not a jealous or selfish god. For Indian children, such a story reinforces traditional beliefs. For other Canadian children, it offers a useful and appropriate myth about life in a harsh, wintry land.

New ecological consciousness makes us see native stories as a valuable way to transmit to children a sense that humans need not be antagonists or victims of nature. For modern children, Indian folktales offer a welcome alternative to the traditional tales brought to Canada from Europe.

French Folklore

European legends, fairy tales, and myths came to Canada with the first settlers. They did not always serve their traditional function of communicating accepted views of natural phenomena, family life, or political regime. Stories such as "The Three Bears," "Little Red Riding Hood," and "The Twelve Dancing Princesses," for instance, did not transplant easily to a country where bears were not comical, the forest contained no paths and no welcoming grandmother, and courtly and aristocratic manners had to be modified by the exigencies of life and the influx of republican principles from the neighbor to the south. Nevertheless traditional tales were imported and treasured in their original forms as links to the old homelands.

The majority of first settlers in Canada were French. Folklore from Normandy and Brittany was augmented by oral tales based on Quebec experiences and attitudes: tales about *le loup-garou* (the werewolf), *la chasse-galerie* (the canoe that soars over the mountains and villages), *Ti-Jean* (little Jack) and *Bon-Jean* (good John—perhaps Bon-Jean is the original tall-tale hero Bunyan;

stories of a giant lumberjack are still being told in the Ottawa Valley). Authentic versions of these stories were collected by Marius Barbeau and published in stylish retellings by Michael Hornyansky as *The Golden Phoenix* (1958, reprinted 1980). Marius Barbeau's afterword, "About the Stories," clarifies their sources and explains how they have been carried from one region to another and adapted to new settings. Many nineteenth-century novelists, French and English, including Phillippe Aubert de Gaspé and Gilbert Parker, have incorporated these materials in adult novels.

For children, many of the French-Canadian legends have been presented in attractive form in English publications including Paul Wallace's *Baptiste Laroque* (1923), which includes mostly Ti-Jean stories drawn from a French-Canadian *conteur* (teller) and recounted in phonetic dialect; Natalie Carlson's *The Talking Cat and Other Stories from French Canada* (1952), which includes a comic *loup-garou* (werewolf) tale; Frank Newfeld's handsomely illustrated version of *The Princess of Tomboso* (1960); and Claude Aubry's *The Magic Fiddler and Other Legends of French Canada* (1968), which most successfully captures the flavor of Quebecois customs and speech. Claude Aubry also used legendary sources to create an original fable in *The Christmas Wolf* (1965). He imagines a miracle of wintry conversion to faith, setting his story in a Quebec village and recounting it in the dignified French fable style of Jean de La Fontaine.

Mary Alice Downie's *The Witch of the North: Folk Tales of French Canada* (1975) was illustrated by Elizabeth Cleaver, an artist who was born in Hungary but settled in Quebec, where she developed a poetic sense of the land and the folklore. Downie's more recent *How the Devil Got His Cat* (1988) is more humorously decorated by Jillian Hulme-Gilliland with witty silhouettes that sharply delineate the cat, the villagers, the nuns, and the devil. In a note to *How the Devil Got His Cat* acknowledging her immediate source, *Baptiste Laroque: Legends of French-Canada* as retold by Paul Wallace, Mary Alice Downie points out that another version of the same tale was retold by James Joyce in a letter to his grandson in 1936. This literary footnote recognizes the universal spread of traditional tales, across times, languages, and continents and also points to the value of such tales as sources for adult creators and as gifts for small listeners.

Fairy Tales

Immigration to Canada between the conquest in 1763 and the Confederation in 1867 was dominated by Scots and Irish farmers and laborers. Both Gaelic groups enjoyed stories of giant warrior-heroes and tales of little people: brownies, leprechauns, and elves.

Many folklorists blur the distinction between folktale and fairy tale. For example, in his excellent studies such as *Fairy Tales and the Art of Subversion* Jack Zipes applies the term "fairy tale" to stories in which no "fairies" appear–fables about talking animals and humans such as "Little Red Riding Hood." Such a blurring of terms is inappropriate in Canada, where pure fairy stories featuring tiny beings, elves, gnomes, fairies, and brownies pre-ponderate. Canada owes this cloud of fairy folk to her Celtic in-heritance. In Scotland "fey" people were recognized as being able to see "ghoulies and ghosties and long-nebbit-beasties." Nine-teenth-century Scottish writers such as Andrew Lang and George Macdonald (author of *The Princess and the Goblin*) capitalized on their native fairy lore, and in Canada people of Celtic descent have carried on the fairy tale tradition.

Isabella Valancy Crawford, a fine post-Confederation poet best remembered for her use of Indian symbolism, made her living by supplying fairy stories to the popular press in the 1880s. Bridget Kavanaugh's *The Pearl Fountain* (1872) and Jessie Saxby's *Snow Dreams* (1882) are drawn from Celtic roots and are original Ca-nadian fairy tales for children. And when Palmer Cox published his books about the "Brownies" in the 1880s and 1890s, he always added a little sign on the frontispiece noting that they came from "old Scotch tradition."

Slightly later, another writer of Scottish descent made an interesting effort to locate fairies, dragons, and talking animals in Canada. James Miller Grant ["Grant Balfour"] in *The Fairy School of Castle Frank* sets his story in Toronto but places the action in the distant past, "a hundred years ago"—ancient times for a Canadian child. In this setting little Robin first keeps school for the squirrels; then he moves alone into the forest to encounter fairies and other strange beings—a serpent, a bear—in a plot that is a curious mix of reality and magic.

As the forests disappeared and the primitive life gave way to more sophisticated societies, some of the power of fairy stories disappeared. But the taste for gauzy little beings was renewed in the years before the First World War by the enormous popularity of *Peter Pan* (1904), written by yet another Scot, James M. Barrie. Barrie's Tinker Bell pleaded, "Clap if you believe in fairies."[8] In answer, an outburst of rather flimsy fairy tales showed that the taste for these little beings was undiminished; Canadian writers were in the forefront of those demonstrating their willingness to pass along a belief in fairies to little readers. Virna Sheard's pretty book *The Golden Apple Tree* (1920) is interesting because of the feminist twist and the verbal wit at play in stories such as "A Rose Enchanted" and "The King's Opal." A full-length magic story, equally witty and equally attractive in its silhouette decorations, is Thomas Marquis's *The King's Wish* (1924). Most fairy stories of the 1920s, however, emphasize the fragility and pathos of fairyland. A touching example is Caroline Fortier ["Maxine"]'s "The Fairy of Birdieland," "The Lame Dwarf," and "The Lonely Princess," published in *Unknown Fairies of Canada* (1926).

Other Scots Canadians were interested in presenting more traditional fairy stories to children. In his preface to *Canadian Fairy Tales,* Cyrus Macmillan professed to have collected stories from fishermen, lumbermen, sailors, and spinning women. Macmillan, a scholar born in 1880 in Prince Edward Island and raised there, presented fairy stories similar to those which *Anne of Green Gables* author L. M. Montgomery remembered hearing in the 1880s from her grandfather, a great teller of traditional Scottish stories.

Macmillan's volume, beautifully illustrated by Marcia Lane Foster, is also an important respository of Indian folktales.

Classical Legends

Many of the earliest Canadian publications in English and in French reflected not the interest of the folk but that of a ruling class trained in classics, and these books consisted of simple retellings of the myths of Greece and Rome: stories of Midas and Prometheus, the lost Atlantis and Troy, Persephone and the Amazons. Oral versions of classical myths that would haunt the imagination of later generations of literate adults continued to be passed along to impressionable children.

Northrop Frye's conclusion that classical myths along with the Bible stories are the keys to the kingdom of imagination led to an attempt to revive these legends in the 1970s. School curricular requirements at this time included *The Four Ages of Man,* Jay Macpherson's fine compilation of classical myths.

The medieval legends, another part of European traditional materials, also remained part of Canadian traditional lore. Besides listening to stories of King Arthur, many little children have enjoyed medieval tales in a less elitist form, the comic strip. In the 1950s Hal Foster's King Arthur comics, including his stories of Prince Valiant, had a wide following. The comic book format offers an excellent mixed media means of initiating a child into the conventions of dialogue as part of narrative: the child can "read" the pictures while the adult decodes the ballooned speeches. The comic book format remains very popular with Quebec artists, who follow perhaps the lead of the French classic comic *Asterix* in using this medium to purvey stories of classic times.

Medieval legends have also been retold effectively by Canadian writers such as Constance Hieatt, whose *The Sword and the Grail* (1972) is one of a series of vigorous retellings of parts of the Arthurian cycle. Muriel Whitaker's *Pernilla in the Perilous Forest*

(1979), elegantly embellished with illuminated designs by Jetska Ironside, catches the mysterious tone of the quest stories. This beast fable moderates the traditional doctrine of the seven deadly sins and leads Pernilla through fabulous but unfrightening adventures. Seven beasts in succession refuse the little girl's request for companionship before she finds the ideal friend, a unicorn. The style of the story, matched by clever illustration, blends medieval alliteration with the snap of modern colloquialism:

> A west wind whirled willow leaves down the path and the wild red strawberries at her feet gleamed like drops of blood.
> And there stood a wolf . . . .
> The wolf gnashed his teeth so that flecks of foam fell like feathers on the flowers.
> "Get out of here. Get out of here before I eat you!" he shouted angrily.[9]

Few adults could resist rendering such a story with dramatic force. A child, identifying with Pernilla, will be led into a long-ago world of romance and morality by the precise, suggestive artwork.

Multicultural Tales

Non-British immigrant artists and writers have enriched traditional children's literature with varied gifts. Artists have created fresh versions of Hans Christian Andersen stories, as in Laszlo Gal's *The Little Mermaid,* and new versions of animal fables, as in *Fox Mykyta,* a Ukrainian story retold by Bohdan Melnyk and illustrated by William Kurelek.

William Kurelek has also offered through the luminous intensity of his paintings a restoration of central stories of the Christian tradition. His situating the Christmas story in a modern Inuit community in *A Northern Nativity* is a wonderful way to

3. ". . . polished paintings, beautifully designed." Laszlo Gal, from *The Little Mermaid* by Margaret Maloney (1983).

hand a child a naturalized version of the sacred story; a comparable gift is offered in Margaret Laurence's *The Christmas Birthday Story,* illustrated in a more impressionistic modern style by Helen Lucas.

Laszlo Gal, who came to Canada during the Hungarian Revolution of 1956, has illustrated five recent adaptations of folktales with polished paintings, beautifully designed and richly colored. Of these books, the most elegant and the most accessible to children are *The Twelve Dancing Princesses* (1979) and *The Little Mermaid* (1983). The text of the latter, significantly, was written by Margaret Maloney, curator of the Osborne and Lillian H. Smith Collections at Boys and Girls House, Toronto Public Library. Maloney's scholarly interest in folklore is joined with her awareness of the unique magic power in the original Andersen story. In 1984, Gal added evocative designs to a gathering of tales from many nations that are retold by Eva Martin as *Canadian Fairy Tales.*

In *The Violin Maker's Gift* author Donn Kushner re-creates the world of European legends, rather than retelling a single traditional tale. Like Ti-Jean and Tête-Jaune in the French-Canadian tales, Kushner's Gaspard is an ordinary, well-meaning fellow. The marvellous bird that he rescues and cherishes arouses the cupidity of another villager, the tollkeeper Matthias. Kushner works out the story with the fabulist's acceptance of good and bad, altruism and avarice, and he enjoys the traditional plot twists of sudden reversal, trickery, and inventiveness, whether in the hero or the villain. For a small child, this tale has the feel of a folktale; Kushner's chuckling addition of a bonus of insights, wordplay, and philosophical resignation to the ups and downs of fortune gives extra pleasure to the adult reader who shares this book with a small reader.

Folklore reworked for young Canadians has mostly come from Europe, but there is a growing interest in publishing materials from other sources. Borrowing an Oriental style, Laszlo Gal has illustrated eastern legends, such as *The Enchanted Tapestry* (1987), which are brought to Canada by non-European immigrants from more ancient civilizations. A talented poet, Gwendolyn MacEwen, who had interested herself in Egyptian and other North African antiquities, created *The Honey Drum: Seven Tales from Arab Lands* in 1983. Joining these non–oriental purveyors of tales from the Far East, Chinese Canadians have written out the legends persisting in oral form in their own communities. Shiu Kong and Elizabeth Wong have translated *Fables and Legends from Ancient China* (1985) followed by *The Magic Pears* (1986), and Wong Ying added intriguing oriental illustrations. In a final reversal, a Japanese-Canadian artist has reworked native Indian and European-Canadian legends. Warabé Aska's beautiful trilingual book, written in Japanese, French, and English, *Who Hides in the Park?* (1986) pictures Stanley Park in Vancouver as haunted by legends of all the peoples who have moved around or within it. This book indeed subsumes rather than retells the traditional tales.

Tall Tales

A final group of people who have contributed in a major way of Canadian folklore are the storytellers who work in childcare centers, preschools, and libraries. They satisfy the demand for familiar repetitive narrative. Their work is also efficacious in suggesting to parents and other caregivers how stories should be told for best effect.[10] There are storytelling schools, and storytellers are included in the membership of the Canadian Society of Children's Authors, Illustrators, and Publishers (CANSCAIP).

One of the most popular of the new storytellers is also the author of wonderful little books of tall tales for little children. Robert Munsch came from the United States in the 1970s, when a particularly strong stream of idealistic, rebellious, antiauthoritarian Americans moved northward. American folklorists have always delighted in the tall tale and have always fostered irreverence and lèse-majesté of the Mark Twain variety—the sort of rollicking irreverence that appears in stories told by Robert Munsch.

A child needs to be steeped in folklore to get the most out of Munsch's *The Paper Bag Princess* (1980). Traditionally, the hero of a folktale slays a dragon, marries a princess, and ascends to a position of power. Most children know that story. But they respond happily to modern battle stories suggesting that war gets us nowhere, to tales about courtship updated to accommodate antichauvinism, and to epics about power adapted to democratic egalitarianism. Little children respond to Munsch's upbeat formulaic repetitions all the more joyously if they remember the old repetitive refrains in old-time fairy tales.

In the opening moments of *The Paper Bag Princess* a disastrous dragon is casually introduced. This dragon will be tamed not by the prince but by a cheerful, ingenious, and in the end nonviolent heroine. (She exhausts the dragon rather than spearing him.) Like Cinderella or the Little Mermaid, her home is in ashes, but she makes do with a paper bag for a dress, rather than asking someone else to provide a ball gown. And rather than waiting for the prince to find her, she rescues him. Ungrateful him—he sees only her messy appearance and shoos her away. The princess, however, has the last word: there will be no marrying and living happily ever afterwards for this heroine. She jumps off into the sunshine, a powerful person who is also a rumpled, rambunctious child.

It would be perverse to say that a child needs to be steeped in traditional lore only so as to be able to appreciate the fun of a parody. Folklore in Canada—Indian and Inuit, French, Scots-Irish, British and American, European, African, and Asian—offers its own values. Many new examples of the tall tale are presented with wit and finesse, although with no modification of traditional attitudes to legendary marvels. Examples include Robin Muller's jaunty *Tatterhood* and Carole Spray's *The Mare's Egg*, handsomely illustrated by Kim LaFave. Many of these works are produced by smaller presses, not in the great urban centers. From the small fishing villages in Newfoundland where traditional tales linger comes *Borrowed Black* (1979), a tall tale reinforced with the visual drama of Jan Mogensen's watercolors, of "a boat that was built in the back of a whale." The story ends as a good "*pourquoi*" story should:

> To this very night on the Labrador
> When you stand and watch from the tall, dark shore
> You can see the cracks in the moon round and high
> And the silver it left on its way to the sky.
> And fishermen say if you follow the trail
> You'll come to the boat in back of the whale.[11]

These tall tales, like all the other traditional legends, follow a narrative pattern that is appropriate for unsophisticated listeners. There are no gaps in the narrative, no flashbacks, and no disrupted time flow. Following such sequential stories helps a preschool child develop logical powers. Emotionally, the nonjudgmental nature of the fables fosters the openness that is essential for the child who is moving towards experiences that take place away from home base. Listening, the child connects with the past and prepares for sequential change.

4

Easy-to-Read

Whether the words say "We live in a tree, Way UP in a tree," or "Dick sees Jane," or "An ox can pull a cart," the first time a child finds meaning in a sequence of printed words marks an ascent to a new plane. A child of five, more than "just alive," has already lived through a period of fabulous perceptual and cognitive growth. Multimodal clues picked up in preschool days have led to expectations about print and an assumption that meanings and pleasures will open when letters begin to "make sense." Soon comes a crucial period and a proud pronouncement, "I can read."

Books at this stage must fit children's capabilities and their interests. With the onset of symbolic functioning, children between four and seven have just become able to recognize the semantic function of words. Their language is repetitive and tends to monologue, and they have become deeply engrossed in symbolic play and in the rules that bind their actions in games. Reading is for them a kind of rule bound game, a play of mind, eye, and inner ear.[1]

The mystery of the first encounter with printed language has recently absorbed several of Canada's major writers. Because gifted writers such as Margaret Laurence and Margaret Atwood happen to be fascinated by this mystery, they have produced some fine books for beginning readers. Their work in this form can be viewed not only as a private artistic achievement but also as an accomplishment of national importance. Their publications appeared after a significant and unfortunate gap in the production of Canadian books for little children.

Early Canadian primers, the schoolbooks designed to teach children to read, had reflected the aspirations, moral bias, and sociocultural context of adult life in this country. Then, after a century of developing an independent way of looking at books as well as politics, religion, economics, and taste, Canadian publishers floundered in the problems of producing a national product that would be viable in a small market and a big cost system. Recently, however, new small presses in Canada have joined reviving big ones in focusing on books for children. A child-oriented generation buying more books in a time of general affluence, a shift in educational theory to a "whole language" approach emphasizing variety in reading experiences,[2] and a continuing sense of a crisis in national identity together have led to this revival.

Creating a book for a beginning reader is always a political act. Assumptions regarding sex, race, and class drop into place, as do notions about the proper balance between reality and imagination. Aesthetic assumptions also arise, involving decisions about how important it is that the child associate the job of reading with the joy of reading.

Primers

In early colonial days, schoolmasters imported and used English primers.[3] Then local publishers got to work, and in 1841, the year of the union of Upper and Lower Canada, children began their life of reading with William Corry's *Spelling Book,* published in St. John. They moved in a single first lesson from alphabet to word, early educators finding no difficulty in what we now see as the complex perception of words as units. In 1841 six-year-old boys and girls were expected to move swiftly to a first experience in reading meaningful sentences such as these:

All sin. I sin. You sin.
Sin is bad.

Do not sin at all. Sin is not hid.
God can see it.[4]

Monosyllabic grimness in the first days at school presumably
placed little Canadian readers in a theological and social scheme
of rigidity, human evil, and accountability. During about the same
period Canadian children learning to read from *The Small Preceptor,* though presented with a sunnier theology, still absorbed,
in monosyllables, the idea of a God-centered life: "God is by me
all the day. My joy is in God."[5]

An alternative set of values and an emphasis on more material
aspects of reality inhere in slightly later primers. Again, each
word chosen reveals the bias of the Canadian educators. Vocabu-
laries appropriate to a rough farm background run from "axe" to
"ox," and the child learning from *A First Book of Lessons* in 1859
fits reading into a work-oriented scheme: "Is it an ox? An ox can
pull a cart."[6] In the *First Book of Reading Lessons* published in
1867, the year of confederation, the child learns to push the work
ethic even on tired pets: "Get up, old fat cat, and get the rat."[7]

Primer texts are not literature. Yet a look at early Canadian
examples reminds us that aesthetic qualities can be part of first
reading. Indeed, modern educators tell us that pleasure must
come first if cognitive results are to follow. Even primer sentences
can have a pleasant flow of rhythm. "Get up, old fat cat" rolls
more pleasurably off the tongue and in the mind than the sledge-
hammer emphasis of "God sees sin." Soon after confederation
united British North America in a single dominion, the Canada
First Movement developed, dedicated to resisting the culture and
politics of the "gilded age" in the United States. Canada First sen-
timents stirred the development of a post-Confederation school of
literature, and this is in turn encouraged Canadian publishers.

In Toronto, Bryce, Briggs, and Musson publishing houses
brought out many gift books for children while Morang became
the major producer of school texts. Morang's *Modern Phonic
Primer* of 1901 centers on local activities: lesson 1 is on rolling a
snowball; lesson 3 is on sap "buck-ets" and "ma-ple sy-rup." *From
Far and Near,* from the same publishing house, is a school text
for first grade containing such little rhymes as "The Swing," "A

Pony," "Laura and a Poor Girl," and "Warming a Snow Ball"—nice touches of pathos, humor, and play. Grace Duffie Boylan's *Our Little Canadian Kiddies* came from a New York publisher in 1901, but it has the same jolly affirmative quality regarding winter sports: "Take the toboggan" says one poem, "and we'll all have a ride."[8]

Primers in the twentieth century reflect the growing influence of American theories of learning, Dewey's in the first decades, Gesell's in the 1920s. The Little Folks Canadian Stories Series, published in 1926, fits in with the vogue for "silent reading." Stories about Teddy's train ride are followed by practical questions and suggestions for nonliterary activities. Muriel Lancaster's *Jingles for Juniors* (1929) neatly enhanced by black-and-white cutouts, presents a range of topics representative of the many books for use in first grades in Canadian schools: colors, vegetables, and seasons, including a heavy cargo of winter poems. British influences also persist, however. In her *Cargo of Stories for Children* (1929) Toronto kindergarten teacher Emma Lorne Duff quotes "Mr. Barrie's Tinker Bell" and adds, "Fairies are God's messengers."[9] She adds Canadian materials, including schoolyard taunts such as "Tell tale tit, / Your tongue shall be slit" and notes that she learned from Canadian poet and teacher Alexander Muir, author of "The Maple Leaf Forever," her version of "Chicken Licken" with its wry independent ending: "I saw it with my eyes, I heard it with my ears, and part of it fell on my head" (Duff, 137).

In the late 1920s, handsome American books and their solid, heavy paper British equivalents established standards against which it was hard for Canadian publications to compete. Writing for small children became increasingly unrewarding work in Canada. The title of a 1929 book of verse by H. I. J. Coleman, *A Rhyme for a Penny*, is telling. Between the late 1930s and the 1960s, that is, from the Great Depression through the cold war, Canadian children lost the chance to begin reading in school with anything distinct from the American "Dick and Jane" primers. There was no more ox or cart or rat, no more God or sin; primers now brought schoolchildren into the world of books with little sentences about suburban family life. Gender-based role differentiation was established as Jane learned to keep house and play with dolls. Other choices of words and sentences about pets, food, and clothes all reflected white, middle-class material comforts. Children adopted from such books attitudes and ideals not appropriate to many parts of Canada.

Emergent Readers

Outside school, parents can enrich children's first reading experiences with little books in large print by helping them to decipher some unfamiliar words and concepts. Following a coherent story involves working within all the semantic codes twisted in the text: denotations, connotations, symbolic suggestions. Parents who help children with their reading facilitate the development of social values. Studying the big print books of stories and verse that Canadian parents have bought for little children over the last hundred years, we can trace drifts in Canadian interests and attitudes. Noting the publishing history of these books for emergent readers, we can also see how these interests have been constrained by economic factors.[10]

Most books for emergent readers by Canadian authors combine instruction and delight. Mary Campbell's *Sundays in Yoho,* published in Montreal in 1884, tailored a wide range of tales about people in places all over the world—Egypt, Greece, Ireland, India, Polynesia, Scandinavia—to the pleasure of Canadian children spending quiet Sundays in "cottage country" reading as part of a pious leisurely life. Similarly, Annie Howells Fréchette wrote *On Grandfather's Farm* (1897) about the pleasures of freedom during holiday time, joyful, outgoing, though lovingly protected. She wrote about little animals and the possibility of creating imaginary friends such as elves and brownies. But this book about holiday time was published in Philadelphia by the American Baptist Society, and in it Annie Howells Fréchette (sister of William Dean Howells) preserved her own sense of American roots: the story is set in Virginia.

Easy-to-read stories about the distinctive society in Quebec in the early twentieth century also began to show the influence of American rather than Canadian attitudes. *Little Stories of Que-*

bec by J. E. Rossignol (1908) was published in Toronto by Briggs. Later, however, big print books about Quebec came from American publishers. For example, Houghton Mifflin of Boston published Ethel Phillips's *Gay Madelon* in 1931 and Lee Kingman's *Pierre Pidgeon* in 1943. *Gay Madelon,* handsomely illustrated with strong woodcuts, presents Madelon—as she travels to Tadoussac, dances at the Quebec Chateau, and chats with her friend Jou-Jou—in a light, fresh way but in the slightly patronizing tone that is so often a part of non-Canadian stories about the quaintness of Quebec.

Many of the easy readers from the period around World War I were about winter life in the northern regions. One "shaped book" called *The Angora Twinnies* was cut to fit the bundled-up shapes of the babies who lived in "a place called Newfoundland."[11] This charming though sentimental effort to evoke children's sympathy for an isolated region was published in the United States.

In the 1920s and 1930s many books of all kinds, early readers, volumes of verse, and stories for listening, were self-published— a testimony to the difficulty of finding a publisher rather than to the thinness of talent. One lively example of home production is *Sarah Jane's Bedtime Stories,* published in Hanna, Alberta, in 1936 by the author, Grace McArthur. As the slump in public demand for Canadian work continued into the 1940s, many writers could find a public only through the pages of homely agricultural journals such as *The Family Herald and Weekly Star.*

Watson Kirkconnell, a Canadian poet working in the 1930s and 1940s, found very few outlets for his verse. He published his books for adults himself or with obscure presses such as the Polish Press of Winnipeg or Ariston Publishers of Ottawa. He created a good book of verse for children with the nicely chiasmic title *Titus the Toad* (1934). In *Titus's* flexible, well-handled verse a little boy learns through effective puns about cow punchers, the dust bowl, and the honking of Canada geese. For the little people who love to giggle even when they do not quite get the joke, *Titus* came as a climax to a long string of cheerful books in large print format that were aimed just over the head of the beginning reader. There is a taste of hermeneutic pleasure in such books, the joy of being teased and puzzled. *Titus the Toad* is a pleasant sequel to nonsense verse, for its jokes have a base in reality, and the reality is clearly Canadian. *Titus* stands alone in marking the end of the Canada First Movement in children's literature.

A new obstruction that slowed the publication of good books for beginning readers was posed in the 1940s by the very popular story hours that aired on the radio. "Just Mary" (Mary Grannan) for instance, provided story values without demanding the effort of reading. When the early days of television followed, Mary Grannan went on to create the "Maggie Muggins" show. Her favorite stories also appeared in print (*Just Mary* in 1941, *Maggie Muggins* in 1944), but like the program "The Friendly Giant" in the 1950s, Mary Grannan inadvertently diverted the taste of young readers to the easier medium.

The educational theory of that era, which tended to be permissive, offered no resistance to the shift. Furthermore, theorists in the 1930s and 1940s such as Dr. Blotz of the influential early education center in Toronto encouraged children to create their own stories rather than depend for entertainment on the published work of adults.

A few Canadian editors at the big presses in Toronto, such as Hugh Gray of Macmillan, William Toye of Oxford, and Jack McClelland of McClelland & Stewart, continued to encourage the production of children's books reflecting specifically Canadian values, landscape, and history. But their productions mostly consisted of retellings of native legends or tales of adventure for older children—nothing to compete with Dr. Seuss as fare for beginning readers. In the 1960s American parents, tired of "Dick and Jane," had delighted in the appearance of Dr. Seuss's irreverent books for beginning readers. Canadians, too, welcomed books like *The Cat in the Hat*, with its rhythms and humor that counter the stodginess of Puff and Spot. But even nonsense has a national coloration, and Dr. Seuss's energetic verses reflect American values just as strongly as Winnie-the-Pooh reflects British values.

In the 1970s new small-scale publishing houses sprang up in Canada. Many of these were founded as part of the antiestablishment spirit of the times (a spirit fostered in part by the presence of Americans who had crossed the border because they disapproved of American policy in Vietnam). Some of these new small regional presses swung into experimental production of children's books. Big presses, too, became fired by a nationalist feeling that the formation of literary taste should begin with homegrown products. A virtual explosion of books for children ensued, including some very interesting productions for beginning readers.

New Beginnings

In Margaret Atwood's *Up in the Tree,* published by the big Toronto firm of McClelland & Stewart in 1978, language, illustrations, and story line are all simple. The delight of the two little people (unisex in clothes and haircuts) who live in an apple tree bubbles up even when real beginners read the poet's rhythmic monosyllabic phrases:

> We like our old tree,
> Our home in the tree;
> We swing in the spring
> and we crawl in the fall
> and we dance in the branches
> way up in the tree.[12]

Internal rhyme intensifies the anapestic, chiasmic rhythm, catching the free swing of the branches and encouraging the children to adapt their movements to the rhythms of nature.

A dramatic monologue emerges as the simple words are sounded out. The use of colored letters and the placement of clauses on the page helps the reader break the syntagmatic code, but Atwood poses other puzzles as she sets up patterns of ideas. A sequential line is suggested in the spring-fall movement of seasons and the dance-crawl movements of the children. The sequence teases us to ask, "What trouble will come in this world without adults?" We are shocked but delighted with surprise by the answer: two beavers chew away at the ladder by which the children have climbed to their happy height. The rhythm changes: "Oh moan! oh groan! There's no telephone!" (Atwood, unpaginated). (Atwood has not submitted to the convention that beginners can only read words of one syllable; she knows that smart kids can figure out words such as "telephone," "umbrella," "forever," and "horrible" just by following the hints in the rhymes and rhythm—another bit of hermeneutic sport.)

The kids in the story solve *their* problem first by accepting the friendly help of a strong-winged bird and later by tacking stairs to the tree so that they can stay at their chosen height after the sun goes down and the moon comes up. Since this is Atwood, I bet it is a mythic moon, the moon of a five-year-old's creativity. A child might not be able to decode this traditional connotation, but even the youngest child knows there is something mysterious and fancy breeding about the moon. Maybe there is also a nationalist fable in the idea of beavers chewing away at a borrowed access to the world of the tree, thus forcing people to climb up the tree itself. That would not be surprising in the work of a nationalist author such as Atwood.

In Marie-Louise Gay's fantasies, as in *Up in the Tree,* adults are either absent or unaware of the wild adventures of their children. In Gay's best book, *Moonbeam on a Cat's Ear,* the swift movement of the text parallels the cinematic succession of pictures. First there is the cat's ear, lit by moonlight; then the cat and the mouse that is nearby, in the cat's dream; then the small girl's bed on which the cat and the mouse sleep. Enter, in the moonlight, Toby Toby "with the bright red hair" (who has a bright green frog on his shoulder).[13] Toby Toby pulls girl, cat, mouse, and frog outside to the apple tree, climbs it, and catches the moon. An exciting, frightening trip (the frog falls off into the water) ends with a return to the bedroom. Was it a dream? The last picture shows the cat and the mouse still cradled on the moon; the frog is nowhere to be seen. Everything about the story and the pictures invites the child into the adventure of dreaming.

In a small book by the poet bpNichol, illustrator Shirley Day helps a beginning reader savour a less dramatic trip taken by father and daughter *To the End of the Block.* At each corner,

4. ". . . cinematic succession." Marie-Louise Gay, *Moonbeam on a Cat's Ear* (1986).

Sarah asks in monosyllabic rhyme, "Can we walk one more block?" and the pictures take us past the swings (Sarah swings), past an ice cream cart (both have a cone), past kids playing hopscotch (Pop takes a turn), past the flower store, and back to the beginning of the block. This story makes minimal use of words but gets maximum involvement from the watchful reader.[14]

Pictures and text form an equally friendly match in *Red Is Best*. Kathy Stinson wrote the text and Robin Baird Lewis did the artwork for this 1982 award-winning production from Annick Press. Their spunky heroine, Kelly, knows red is best, no matter what her mom says about matching socks to dresses or not wearing the same mitts day after day. As in *Up in the Tree* and *Moonbeam on a Cat's Ear*, the mother makes no direct appearance in the book. She is just an authority figure to be reasonably convinced that she knows less than a child about the power of color. The pages

But my red boots take bigger steps.

I like my red boots the best.

5. "... the power of color." Robin Baird Lewis, from *Red is Best* by Kathy Stinson (1983).

are filled with Kelly's simple energy: "My red mitts make better snowballs," the little girl says as she flings a snowball against a blue toque.[15] Kelly's arguments are illogical, but increasingly imaginative: "Red barrettes make my hair laugh. . . . Red paint puts singing in my head" (Stinson, unpaginated). Most of the "big words" such as "pyjamas" and "barrettes" are repeated, both for ease of mastery and for the sheer joy of repetition for the small child. Kelly is an artist in rhythms too; the perfect match of rhythm to sense comes in her sturdy insistence on each syllable: "I like red, because red is best" (Stinson, unpaginated). How can we read this declaration except with a child's unwavering emphasis on each and every word? In sense and in sound it is a perfect sentence for a beginning reader.

In Blair Drawson's *I Like Hats* another lively little girl gets help from a dragon as she embarks on adventures. Repetitions of simple words and details in the author's illustrations make this book appealing to readers just beginning to work through books on their own. A better match for *Red Is Best,* however, is Dayal Khalsa's *I Want a Dog.* Here no dragon is needed to satisfy the child's desire: a determined use of imagination and a roller skate on a leash create a special kind of dog. Khalsa's bold, witty style of illustration matches the simple vocabulary, and both celebrate ingenuity and persistence.

Not from suburbia but from the northern wilderness came two other stories on the *I want a dog* theme. As if in response to the blandness of Puff and Spot, Meguido Zola wrote *My Kind of Pup* about an Indian boy's dream. Ann Blades emerged as a major writer for children with *Mary of Mile 18,* the story of another child's desire for a pet.

Many of the first readers are small dramatic monologues, each page consisting of an utterance that is tied to the next page by sound or repeated words, or by logical development rather than narrative drive. The Canadian content in many of the books mentioned so far, including *Up in the Tree* and *Red Is Best,* consists of elusive qualities of attitude, the iconographic use of natural elements such as snow or apple trees, and the suggestive use of color in text or in pictures. In a longer story like *Mary of Mile 18* the Canadian elements inhere in regional details of speech or work habits or family rituals.

Ann Blades, a teacher in Northern British Columbia, wrote and illustrated *Mary of Mile 18* for and about the Mennonite children who were her pupils. Tundra Press of Montreal published this complex study of the need to balance emotion and practicality, individual desires and the good of the whole group. Mary's endurance and self-sacrifice cannot convince her hard-pressed father that she should keep a wolf-dog pup that has come out of nowhere and has followed her home from school. But when the dog's fierce barking alerts the family to a marauding coyote in the chicken yard, the father yields. The pup has proved itself useful, and the family can delight in Mary's joy at keeping her pet.

Although this is a winter story, the pictures of Mary are the opposite of the bundled-up cuteness of the "Angora Twinnies" in the Newfoundland poem of the 1920s. *Mary of Mile 18* reflects the old work ethic, the pride and ingenuity and steady efforts of the father, mother, and children. Stimulated by the bare-bones story of the hard life in an outlying settlement and by the visual contrasts of northern lights and kitchen stove fire, even a young child will sense the joy of both privacy and family solidarity.

Anna's Pet (1980), by Margaret Atwood, adds a different angle to the stories of child, pet, and family. Anna's grandpa and grandma teach her about the animals she wants to bring into the house—the worm, the toad, the snake—and provide at the end of the story a promising tadpole and a lesson on releasing what we treasure. There is a subtext, a second lesson, in this story about loving and letting go: although Ann Blades's illustrations depict the beloved grandparents as childlike figures in their unisex sweaters and slacks outfits, they are obviously elderly.

Another story about accepting change is Heather McKend's first-person narrative *Moving Gives Me a Stomach Ache.* "I still don't like moving. It's hard on a guy," says the child caught in a family change, when there is no room in the packing boxes for the things that really matter—a tree outside the window, a best friend next door.[16] But like so many Canadian stories, this one ends with acceptance and adjustment. There is a tree at the new house, "not so good as my old tree but it would do until I had enough money for bus fare," and a kid next door, good enough to be a second best friend (McKend, unpaginated).

In *Six Darn Cows,* a short, simple story by Margaret Laurence, the family is a responsible, hard-working farm force. Margaret Laurence, who was orphaned and later raised her own children as a single parent, presents broken or incomplete family groups in her books for adults, but in this book for children she reflects the vision enunciated in "Upon a Midnight Clear": "the sense of God's grace, the sense of our own family and extended family, the sense of human community."[17] This major Canadian novelist illustrates the dictum proffered by British critic Fred Inglis in *The Promise of Happiness:* "The best prose is itself evidence of human goodness and a way of learning how to be virtuous."[18]

Laurence uses words of one syllable to tell a story about two good kids and one big black farm dog. Together they track six straying cows through the marsh and the mud, into "the deep woods, the dark woods," where they hear "soft wings—an owl," and where little readers catch the tension of the dark. There is "[a] flick of light," and Mum comes to find them. The story ends with praise for the children, in the colloquial language of real speech: "I think you are brave kids."[19] Children reading *Six Darn Cows* gain access to the value system of a recent Canadian past. The effect, to quote Chinua Achebe, an African novelist much admired by Laurence, is the "restorying" of the family and the community.[20]

Whole Language Reading

The easy-to-read books of the 1970s and 1980s, though widely accepted, were not officially installed as primers or basal readers to be used nationally or provincially as class sets. "Whole language theory," increasingly powerful in Canadian schools in the 1980s, virtually banished basal readers. The theory that children should learn to read by reading from the full range of an exciting language environment encouraged diversification in publishing. Presses large and small found they could place Canadian books not through mass sales of class sets but through smaller runs that were guaranteed a place in the greatly enlarged classroom and school libraries. Emphasis on the language environment relevant to local children encouraged regional and special interest presses. The theory that books contribute to moral and aesthetic growth changed the constraints on vocabulary and content. Writers of informative nonfiction texts as well as novelists and poets took part in increasing the sophistication and aesthetic appeal of all reading materials.

On the west coast, the Vancouver firm of Douglas & McIntyre broke new ground with Betty Waterton's *A Salmon for Simon,* illustrated by Ann Blades. This 1978 production told children about an Indian boy, not seen as a legendary Hiawatha figure but as a small person going about an ordinary enterprise. Simon, a Salish child, is presented visually from two perspectives: his position when he is fishing, and the eagle eye view of him when the eagle, also fishing for salmon, flies strongly contoured overhead. The graphic technique infers that perspective may change our response to the Indian boy and his task. There is symbolic suggestion in the ending also. Simon releases the salmon that like him has been trapped by a fluke of environment. Such images of entrapment and release as applied to both wildlife and native people suggest the cultural attitudes of author and illustrator, and of many other Canadians. Does the reading child understand the message? The artists and the publisher hope that at the emotional level the book will disturb the stereotypes established by Dick and Jane and their successors in books, television, and movies.

The modern life of native peoples generated a very different publication, Bernelda Wheeler's *I Can't Have Bannock but the Beaver Has a Dam.* This book came from Pemmican Publications of Winnipeg, Manitoba, as part of the move to put into the schools books relevant to particular groups of children. This big print book is a modern version of a cumulative tale such as "Pig, Pig, Get over the Stile." To the boy who asks a recurrent "Why?," his mom provides a growing list of reasons that refer back to the first cause: because the beaver chewed the tree the power line fell, the power was cut, the stove would not get hot, so the bannock could not be made. "Bannock" is among the words representing special local vocabulary, to be expected and accepted in a whole reading program. Big soft pencil drawings lead this story to a happy ending and a final picture of the beaver meditatively digesting his own copy of the book.

In another beginners' book Selwyn Dewdney uses powerful first-person narration and blends history with drama to commu-

6. ". . . strongly contoured." Ann Blades, from *A Salmon for Simon* by Betty Waterton (1978).

nicate facts about life in older days among the Mississauga Indians. *The Hungry Time* is illustrated by Olena Kassian, an artist who specializes in paintings of wildlife; in every picture, appropriately, the artist catches details of deer or bears with a fidelity equal to that directed at the human characters.

Bruce Kidd, a Canadian sports hero, wrote for the Lorimer Company's Easy-to-Read Series a story about hockey that satisfies "whole language" ideals while introducing a topic of great interest to young Canadians. *Hockey Showdown* fits Ken Dryden, a real hockey hero of the generation just before Wayne Gretzky, into a story about city kids playing their favorite game under difficult circumstances. Leoung O'Young's soft, realistic paintings match the tone of the book, which gently promotes cooperation and adjustment between the interests of different generations. In a happy final moment the mean older neighbor who has complained about the hockey players joins Bill the cop, little Domingos the hockey addict, and the great and kind Ken Dryden in "the best game Domingos ever had."[21]

In the name of pluralism, Roch Carrier's funny *The Hockey Sweater,* illustrated with pungent primitive designs by Sheldon Cohen, should come into the school as a challenging companion piece to the sports fan approach of Kidd. Young Roch goes through a Quebecois-style hell when his mother mistakenly orders a Toronto Maple Leaf sweater for him instead of the glorious Montreal Canadien one. Once again, there is the phenomenon of a major author working in the genre of children's stories. Carrier brings to this story the combination of farce, emotional intensity, and biting realism that characterize his distinguished adult novels.

Other beginners' stories from Quebec include translations of the bubbling stories by Ginette Anfousse about Jojo and her toy pet Pichou, including the story *Hide and Seek,* about a game milder than hockey but as widely enjoyed.

The mix of story topics signals the readiness of teachers and parents to stimulate creative freedom by welcoming nonconformity. *Bonnie McSmithers, You're Driving Me Dithers* is a funny story about the frenetic life in a modern family. In Fiona Garrick's stylized illustrations, the modern mum looks like a child of the 1970s with her long flowered dress and free-swinging hair. Sue Alderson, the author of three Bonnie McSmithers stories, came to Vancouver after growing up in New York and pursuing graduate studies in California. Her rollicking stories about an uninhibited trouble-prone child have become popular with the two generations that share the emergent reading experience.

Rhyme gets added charm when exasperation creates a neologism: "dithers" is a hard word to read but a hard one to forget, once an adult has helped the neophyte decode it. Both child and adult can enjoy the wordplay as part of the fun of topsy-turvy reversal. Bonnie McSmithers teaches her mother that even language can be turned upside down in a blithery blathery world of new family structures. Most of Alderson's work has been published by Tree Frog Press of Edmonton, Alberta. A small press does not need to bow to the educational panels working with controlled vocabulary lists in the hope of cutting down on beginning readers' bafflement. Bafflement is beautiful, they imply; it offers the same joy as blindman's buff or the give-and-take of open family life in the McSmithers style.

In Robert Munsch's stories, adult authority figures fall into surprising dilemmas in which the children continue to assert their comic, demonic wills. Witness *Thomas' Snowsuit* in which a firm-minded Thomas finally drives the teacher "dithers" and sends the school principal to a rest-cure in the snowless south. In *David's Father,* Munsch implicitly preaches tolerance of overscaled, out-of-the-ordinary beings. Little Julie is shocked to learn that her new neighbor has a father who uses a spoon as big as a shovel and a knife as big as a flagpole. Eventually Julie can say, "Well, David, you really do have a very nice father after all, but he is still kind of scary." To which David replies, "You think he is scary? . . . Wait till you meet my grandmother."[22] And in the final picture an enormous black hairy leg rises from a boat-sized, high-heeled red shoe.

Fun to read and to look at, the spectrum of new books for young children makes reading a joy. Both big and small presses are now producing books for an enlarging market, as Yuppie parents buy readily and schools enrich their holdings of books with Canadian coloration, both in the daylight world of hockey and bannock and also in the dream world of moonlight and owls and apple trees.

5

Imaginary Voyages

Every child setting out for school is a brave voyager. A second world, with different values, is being added to the first world of home; reconciling the role played at home with the new role at school means developing openness and ambivalence, accepting strangeness, hiding fear and uncertainty under the cloak of the intrepid traveller. At the same time a new kind of literary voyaging begins. Full-length books open up, offering in chapter after chapter new worlds of joy and terror, suspense and confusion and radiant return. It is no small wonder that boys and girls, leaping ahead in reading skill around grades 2 or 3, particularly enjoy stories of fantastic voyages such as the American *Wizard of Oz* and *Where the Wild Things Are* or the British *Alice's Adventures in Wonderland* and *Tom's Midnight Garden*.

Some of Canada's major authors have catered to this taste, taking the youngest readers to imaginary worlds like and yet unlike the worlds of Oz and Wonderland and transporting the slightly older readers, lovers of "Narnia," into deeper and stranger dream worlds. In *The Cool Web*,[1] a collection of essays, Mordecai Richler contributes a sardonic reminder that many of the fantasy heroes of comic books, including Superman, were created by Canadians. In *Jacob Two-Two Meets the Hooded Fang*, Richler himself created a smaller hero and transported him to another world both comic and frightening.

The titles of other Canadian fantasies encapsulate formulas used within the genre. Some titles name the talisman by which the voyagers gain access to the fantasy world (e.g., *The Golden Pine Cone*); others name the object of the quest (e.g., *The Marrow of the World*); still others emphasize the essential duality of the adventures (e.g., *The Double Spell*). In all such stories, children sally forth, then transcend the normal expected structures of life, imperceptibly entering a Never Land. The fantasy starts and ends in reality; the imagined traveler and the reading child both undergo subtle change in the process of the story. *Moonbeam on a Cat's Ear* is a miniature imaginary voyage for beginning readers running to 14 pages of big print; for the 7- to 11-year-olds, publishers produce fully developed fantasies in books one hundred to two hundred pages long, usually illustrated in black and white and printed in a typeface slightly larger than that used in books for adults and with extra space between the lines.

Children between 7 and 11 are developing powers in two modes of thought, the rational and the intuitive. During this concrete operational phase there is a strong development of logical skills: children are learning to classify, to place in hierarchic order, to perceive binary divisions, and to form closures.[2] It is the second mode of thought, intuitive, mystical, magical, complex, imaginative, that fantasy feeds. In turn, the enigmas in imaginary worlds incite the young reader to seek logical resolution and understanding. In other words, both modes of thought are engaged while the child unravels "the magic code," to use the phrase that forms the title of a book on fantasy by Maria Nikolajeva of Sweden.[3]

Canadian fantasies naturally reflect Canadian realities as well as Canadian dreams and fears, both in the "real" world from which the fictional characters move and in the "dream" world— the dream within the artist's dream—into which they penetrate. Fantasy is an irrational combining of real elements, and the real places, people, situations, and relationships that fantasy transforms come from home territory.

Early Fantasy

Inevitably, stories of movements through space, real or imaginary, hold special charm in a dominion where travel over long distances is essential to national awareness. The first Canadian book written for children was a realistic travelogue, with the long title: *Henry; or, The Juvenile Traveller, a Faithful Delineation of a Voyage across the Atlantic* (1836). Diana Bayley, Little Henry's creator, conveyed a quintessential sense of the amazing experiences of travel through a landscape suggestive of the strange and shaggy forms of dream. Diana Bayley's successors in the world of children's literature have taken little travelers on stranger voyages as fantasists have developed new points of access, new means of transport, new beings to encounter, new actualizations of the possible.

Fantasy did not develop early in Canada as a favored genre for child readers, in spite of the popularity of Lewis Carroll and George Macdonald in the nineteenth century. Perhaps the thin rocky soil and the cold climate did not encourage writers to dream of moving down a rabbit hole or flying at the back of the North Wind. But in 1903, soon after the American author L. Frank Baum whisked a little girl away from the equally cold farmland and grey poverty of Kansas into a richly colored world in *The Wizard of Oz*, Stewart Edward White transposed the Oz plot pattern into a Canadian setting in *The Magic Forest*. The author lifts his little character Jimmy from a train journeying through the ragged land north of Lake Superior into a dream life with a trapping, hunting, dancing, storytelling Indian band. Months later, when the wanderings of the nomadic band bring them back near Chapleau, Jimmy sleepwalks again and wakes up back in the railway Pullman. We are left to decide whether this is a dream-voyage story or whether Jimmy's shift from modernity into primitivism has really happened. For the reading child, the effect is the same. One world shifts illogically into another, and the traveler, like Dorothy in Oz, slips away from adult mentors, encounters good and evil forces in the other world, and makes his own moral choices there. Although written some years before Freud's ideas had spread, this fantasy is curiously Freudian in its emphasis on the child's resistance to adult pressure to conform and his decisiveness, flexibility, and cooperative actions once he has left his mother and the train they were on.

In this 1903 fantasy we also see a local Canadian element in the strong use of wild northern settings and the extraction of adventure from Indian life. The next Canadian fantasists, however, drew back from such energy into the whimsical world of J. M. Barrie's Never Land. In Helen Sandwell's charming and fully developed 1924 novel, *The Valley of Color-Days,* a friendly owl joins the fairies Burr and Shimmerwings to carry children left alone by their parents to a "once in a blue moon" world. Carol Cassidy Cole wrote several paler books in which a little girl wanders into a forest where small talking animals mingle with fairy-tale people. In *Little Big-Ears and the Princess* (1926), a talking rabbit leads Princess Rosalie into a Canadian forest world of orioles, beetles, turtles, and meadow mice. Rosalie's engaging adventures end when she meets a little boy, inevitably named Peter, who engineers a return to the castle. Donalda Dickie's more convincing character Bill, in *Sent to Coventry* (1929), enters his fantasy world by settling down in the sleepy quiet of his room—and suddenly he finds himself walking down the road of a toy village. Donalda Dickie plays effective word games of the kind children love: the story involves a last straw, some humble pie, and the p's and q's that Bill has to mind.

All these fantasies of the 1920s, written and illustrated in the pretty pastel English mode, reflect a postwar emphasis on British connections, English publications, and the English educational system. This bias also shows the positive force of British middle-class immigrants coming to take up postwar life in a sympathetic Commonwealth country. In the 1920s and 1930s English families brought well-mannered children into the Canadian public school system, as well as a preference for English books. In fantasy, this meant that parents were ready to lead their polite little children into the Hundred Acre wood of Winnie-the-Pooh or into E. Nesbit's enchanted castle.

One talented British writer, who came to Canada with special status, contributed both directly and indirectly to the course of fantasy. John Buchan, Lord Tweedsmuir, was Governor-General between 1935 and 1940. He had already published one children's book during a very productive career as a writer of adventure and spy stories. His wife, Susan Buchan, had also published some well-received children's stories. In Canada, John Buchan set to work on a story based on Rudyard Kipling's *Puck o' Pook's Hill* (1906), in which modern children magically find access to an earlier world and learn the history of their country from the people they meet there. In Buchan's *Lake of Gold* (1941), Donald, a Canadian boy, learns about his heritage through the magic of a Cree trapper named Negog. But Negog makes a stiff uninteresting guide into the world of the past, and the tales Donald hears there lack variety and personality. Significantly, however, Buchan's work suggested to his very large reading public that the Canadian world could be an exciting point of departure for cross-temporal experience. *Lake of Gold* was also published in England as *The Long Traverse,* with an epilogue by Susan Buchan explaining how Buchan had intended to conclude the story, which was unfinished at his death.

While in Canada Susan Buchan wrote a much more interesting example of the fantasy mode. Her *Mice on Horseback* begins in a shack on Vancouver Island where Johnny and his father eke out a haphazard life. On visits to Victoria, Johnny, with the aid of a Chinese cook, penetrates into a world of magic. Excellent regional detail reinforces a carefully evolved romantic plot. The work of Lord and Lady Tweedsmuir gave a certain cachet to the business of writing, and her work with its surprising grasp of the feeling of life on the west coast island communities may have helped writers from British Columbia develop confidence.

Heroic Voyages

A more important influence on the genre was the appearance of the heroic epic fantasies of the British writer J. R. R. Tolkien. *The*

Hobbit (1937) and Tolkien's other stories recount questing voyages through another world in a tone of high seriousness and in language with the richness and verve of primitive sagas. As part of a worldwide response to Tolkien, Canadian novelists returned to the epic past of their own country—the tribal days of the native peoples—and combined the past with elements of animal magic.

The terror of atavistic evil that confronts Tolkien's Bilbo and the clarity of mission that leads him to wisdom and joy are intensities beyond the range of Catherine Anthony Clark's books. But Clark's *Golden Pine Cone* and the five other books that followed it between 1951 and 1966 use Canadian scenes, peoples, and animals in ways that offer Canadian children an alternative to the intensities and stringencies of Tolkien.

In *The Golden Pine Cone* (1950) a boy and girl are swept into great adventures by the chance finding of a golden pinecone earring that belongs to the great queen of the Indian spirit world. They move through a rapid succession of scenes, like the contrasted kingdoms of Oz, or like the incredibly varied real country of the Kootenays, Kamloops, and the Okanagan Valley. Up mountain footholds, down into moonlit lakes, into a creek-foaming canyon, past "peak after peak glimmering white above dark forest slopes furred with snow" they move, witnessing the awesome ranges of Nasookin the giant hunter, the weeping princess Onamara who has lost her heart, the poisonous hatred of the Ice Witch, and the ceremonial grandeur of the good spirit Tekontha.[4] Yet the imagined world, though harsh in appearance like the ranges of British Columbia, turns out to be full of kindness. The children restore Onamara's heart and return her to Nasookin; they return the magic earring to Tekontha and then return with their wolf-dog Ooshka to their own loving home.

Family Quest, Divided Self, Solo Wanderer

Like the family group of children in the English fantasies of C. S. Lewis's Narnia that had begun to appear in 1952, the children in Pierre Berton's *The Secret World of Og* (1961, reprinted in 1971 and again in 1974) move unsurprised into a nearby unfamiliar world. The five siblings drop down through a trapdoor in their playhouse into a world of small green people. Berton's obvious delight in his own fantasy spills over into funny asides, jokes, and surprises—a stylistic overload that gives children one of the pleasures of Lewis Carroll's Wonderland: a joy of stretching not only to accept the fantasy but also to relish the reality that is being parodied. The confident tone enhances the sense of control that is one of the gifts of fantasy.

The five children form a cheerful, happy family, not a group needing to escape from pressures or responsibilities. In Berton's book, developments experienced in the fantasy world contribute to the children's real growth: the oldest child matures into adulthood, the youngest one begins to walk, and the other three also change and develop. The fantastic Ogs mirror the real children; they, too, with the children's prodding, develop and improve, Just as the children prefer their own world to that of the adults, so, too, the Ogs find the upper world of the children flat and silly.

More subtlety and a tragic tone mark Ann Wilkinson's wrongly neglected *Swann and Daphne* (1960). Two beautiful children, one capped with feathers, the other with leaves instead of hair, drift from happy playtime with their parents to misery at school, where they are made poignantly aware of their strangeness. From this incomprehensible situation there is no return to normalcy. The mysterious, irrational tone in this story foreshadows later occult fantasies. The two protagonists, knit in a relationship closer than that of the brother and sister in *The Golden Pine Cone,* introduce fantasies that offer correlatives of the divided self.

The theme of a disturbed childhood that has led to intense comradeship between children is dominant in Ruth Nichols's *A Walk out of the World* (1969) and *The Marrow of the World* (1972). In the former, a brother and sister walk away from a school situation of minor tyranny into a strange wood at the edge of their town. Named for two Old Testament heroes—Judith, the fierce and beautiful savior of her people, and Tobit, to whom good and evil angels appeared in a time of captivity—the children like their namesakes oppose and withstand a wicked usurper. They find strange kindred in a great hall, suggestive in its medieval beauty of the world imagined by William Morris in *News from Nowhere.* The legendary quality blends effectively with local Canadian pioneer detail in Nichols's description of the hall: "Tapestries, stiff with gold and silver thread, glinted on either side of her: the rafters high above were lost in shadow. . . . Already some of the women were carrying in white cloths for the tables and thick beeswax candles."[5]

Nichols's stories also echo Macdonald's *The Princess and the Goblin,* which is not surprising given that the author shares the Scottish novelist's mysticism. But Judith is older and more individualized than Macdonald's little princess Irene, and Nichols's troubled Tobit, her goblinlike dwarves and kobolds and silver-haired queen mix with a new range of strange beings—forest spirits, water spirits—in a realm that strains mysticism through a Canadian consciousness.

A major aesthetic effect in Nichols's work is the delicate use of repetitions. Phrases, scenes, and the order of entry into a new phase are all repeated with incremental changes that unify the narrative and contribute to the dynamics of reception. In the world of home and school, for example, the children walk beneath "tall pale maple trees with silver bark. . . . In autumn the leaves would not flame out but would turn a myriad of pale, warm colors—rose-red and primrose and ivory and orange; and the wind would carry them rustling into the gutter" (*WOOW,* 10). In the kingdom achieved by the children's quest, the promised change of season has come: "[i]t was late autumn, and [the prince] rode beneath a clouded silver sky. The harvest had been gathered, and the leaves had turned to primrose and ivory and drifted, rustling, to the ground" (*WOOW,* 182). The two linked descriptions emphasize the movement from prelude to harvest, but the actual autumn lacks the orange and "rose-red" of promise. The reiterated "silver" in bark and sky links with Judith's silver eyes, and heightens the mystery of her final confrontation with the evil usurper whose eyes are also "silver, like splintered stars" (WOOW, 174).

The central effect of all imaginary voyages, entry into and return from a second world, is also repeated in *A Walk out of the World*. Judith and Tobit are swept from a central moment of great danger in the Black River back to their home. Then Judith is again mysteriously transported back to a continuation of the desperate voyage through the Winter Forest and the chambers of the dwarves, while Tobit, trying to follow her, manages to return to the Lake House where the whole fantasy adventure started. This particular repetitive device heightens the illusion of a penetrable veil between dream and reality. Canadian critic Maria Bortolussi, adapting the theories of Umberto Eco's *Aesthetics of Indetermination,* suggests that fantasy facilitates an essential change in young readers. Reading fantasy, the child moves from a centripetal, egocentric, repetitive response to a centrifugal mental movement outward from the self, creating transcendent new ideas in the process.[6]

Nichols's haunting stories also depict a simpler pleasure, as in the summer holiday dream of *Swallows and Amazons*. *The Marrow of the World* begins in cottage country and evokes the common Canadian experience of two months of school holidays. Two cousins, a boy and a girl, Philip and Linda, camping out on a northern lake, drop from the warm world of home into another realm. They push through dark woods to the depths of a lake and across weary plains, guided by Herne (whose name recalls Samuel Hearne, a very important early traveler through wilderness Canada). When their quest finally leads them into the bowels of the western mountains, their guide is Horn (recalling William Van Horne, leader of the railway builders through the Rocky Mountains). But although such touches mark the Canadian origins of the story, *The Marrow of the World* is a mystic dark fantasy about the universal struggle of good and evil, crystallized in the struggle of the girl Linda. Linda must meet, nourish, and then dismiss her double, a half-sister Ygerna, the child of an evil power in the spirit world.

The creation of another world in which cold and frightening evil lurks offers the reader a challenge to work toward a moral conclusion. Nichols, a theologian, theorizes about the moral basis of fantasy,[7] and for her, fantasy is not an escape from duty but an encounter with it. In her fantasies, access to the deeper world of moral choice is usually found by way of water—an interesting deviation from the traditional entry from a meadow, a circle of stones, or a room in a house, as in the English models.[8] Another notable innovation in her work is her use of the continental drive from lakeland to mountains and back, which conveys a sense of strenuous journey through the imagined world.

Three other fantasies different in setting and less intense in tone but curiously linked to *The Marrow of the World* also appeared in 1972. Towrie Cutt's *A Message from Arkmae* and *Seven for the Sea* carry the reader to the legendary caves of the Scottish Orkney Islands. There, two Canadian cousins are led to realize that they are linked in blood to the seals. This modern fantasy is particularly relevant because of the preponderance of Orkneymen in the early days of the Hudson's Bay Company. Also the legends of kinship and responsibility link with primitive native attitudes toward wildlife in the north.

The same message of responsibility and respect for wildlife and natural life infuses Christie Harris's *Secret in the Stlalakum Wild,* also published in 1972. Harris returns to the interior lakes and mountains and the Indian legends of British Columbia so ably evoked in Catherine Clark's *Golden Pine Cone.* Unlike Clark, Wilkinson, Nichols, and Cutt, however, Christie Harris does not focus on an intense relationship between two lonely children and does not imbue the western world with a sense of mysterious significance. In her story, a recalcitrant child within a big family forays alone into the wild. The "secret" discovered there is not very exciting, and the imaginary beings who convey it also pale in comparison to Nichols's evil Ygerna or Cutt's legendary Finmen.

Harris's story suggests a return from the misty significance of Tolkien to the family fantasy of the C. S. Lewis story and a comic mode. In 1975 Mordecai Richler used his sense of family drama and his memories of a fantasy life based on comics and horror movies to create the brilliant parodic fantasy *Jacob Two-Two Meets the Hooded Fang.* The hero is a six-year-old, fifth in his family, too small to go out by himself, too young to play with his older brother and sister, the "Child Power" superkids, and too small to attract attention unless he repeats everything twice. In his fantasy trip to court, to jail, to Slimer's Isle, to the lair of the Hooded Fang, Jacob is ultimately helped by his siblings, the Intrepid Shapiro and the Fearless O'Toole, by a supersonic beeper, a mysterious chocolate bar, and a child's best weapons—sunshine, flowers, ignorance, honesty, and laughter.

Jacob is a solo voyager. Not a twin, not travelling with his family, not aiming to find a kindred spirit, Jacob is just ready to grow a bit as a single, separate person.

Richler set his fantasy in London, England, where he was living when he wrote it for his children. Yet Richler shows none of the nostalgia for a pastoral world that characterizes many English fantasies. Jacob's adventures take the reader to a world like Richler's own remembered Montreal of the late depression, a comic-book city of petty criminals and corrupt officials. These memories are bathed in laughter however; evil dissolves, and it turns out that even the Hooded Fang has just pretended to be cruel. Enjoy him and you will come back from your journey of terror, says Richler, back to a family that is delighted to see you and to produce a special T-shirt emblazoned (two times) with the superkids' "Child Power" emblem.

Like the famous spider in E. B. White's *Charlotte's Web,* Richler is a good friend and a good writer. He is an amused and sympathetic observer of children and an ingenious craftsman whose narrative bravura brings his fantasy to a cheerful double conclusion, in dream and reality.

Another Canadian writer who, like Richler, lived in England during an important creative period is Margaret Laurence. In a more pastoral mood, she offers children a time-shift fantasy in *The Olden Days Coat* (1979), which carries young readers back to a gentler time in the author's homeland. As in so many imaginary voyages, a child unhappy in her present family situation gains access to another world through a special talisman. In this case a modern little girl, Sal, in jeans and a down-filled jacket comes across a set of winter clothes that many older Canadians may still remember: a Red River outfit of navy blue and scarlet, like that worn by voyageurs in the old northwest. The dreaming child takes a trip less dramatic than that of the old coureur de bois. She travels to a world filled with ordinary life and movement. She rides along a country road in a jaunty cutter, with sleigh bells on the harness and a buffalo robe for comfort in the brightness of a clear cold Canadian Christmas day. Sal makes a friend named Sarah in that dream world and accepts her gift, a box with a butterfly on it. She comes back to present reality ready for a new relationship with her grandmother, who turns out to be the Sarah who once wore that Red River coat and who now offers a butterfly gift. For children, the imaginary trip to the past may spark sensitivity toward the older generation. For adults, the fantasy has a richer suggestiveness in its play with time.

The Olden Days Coat is the kind of fantasy that is near the edge of realism. The child's trip can be rationally explained as a dream, and the voyage has led to no arcane revelations of mysteries. Yet mystery remains, appropriate and delicate, in the gift of a butterfly from the olden-days Sarah to the modern-day Sal.

Into the Occult

Other and more disturbing stories of imaginary voyages do not end with a quiet return to the daylight world, nor are the struggles in the secondary world dismissed as mere fantasy. Gaston Bachelard wrote that children have a terror of being overwhelmed by the phantom world.[9] Given the limited experience of reality of a 10- or 11-year-old, they are susceptible to a perilous quality in fantasies that affirm occult powers. Welwyn Katz's The Prophecy of Tau Ridoo (1982) begins with the same device that Berton used in Og: toys disappear from their normal place and a family of children (including a set of twins) set out to recover them. The choice of this device suggests Freud's theory of play, his interest in the way children rearrange and manipulate the things in their world as an expression of a form of control. The toys in this story become, as in a game of make-believe, larger, animated, and inexplicably propelled. But Katz's children trace the toys not to a funny world of grumpy green people but to a dark universe of warring forces. The comic realism of the children's dialogue heightens the real terrors of imprisonment, broken bones, fire, thirst, and dark tunnels. The expectation that the twins will fulfill a mysterious prophecy proves unjustified; it is Jamie, like Jacob Two-Two, the youngest in the family, who brings the downfall of darkness. Magic stones, brought back from Tau Ridoo, remain in the ordinary world to prove "It was real, all right." Welwyn Katz later and more appropriately used her power to create frightening suggestions of witchcraft in books for older children and young adults; in *Tau Riddoo,* written for and about little children, the confusion between fantasy and reality can be disturbing.

Time-shift fantasy often creates a mood of hallucination and occultism. The "other" world can be situated in a real past, a past that has left its traces in physical antiquities. The widely admired British fantasy *Tom's Midnight Garden* uses an old clock as the herald of a slip into a past time, and a pair of skates is proof of the reality of Tom's expeditions there. Similarly, in Janet Lunn's *Double Spell* (1983, published as *Twin Spell* in the United States) an antique doll gives 12-year-old twin girls access to the past. As present-day Toronto fades and scenes of a hundred years ago flood the girls' consciousness, the intrusion of past into present is made more terrifying as each twin realizes that her dreams are invading her sister's dreams. This, too, is an extension of a device used in *Tom's Midnight Garden,* where Tom learns that an old woman has been mysteriously pulling him into her dreams of the past. In *Double Spell* the strange interlacing of the twins' thoughts and dreams threatens to unsettle the girls' reason. A series of time-travels helps the twins work out some of the mysteries of the past and outface the evil that haunts their house, but there is no easy explanation for the strange effect of the antique doll. The author plays with the edges of schizophrenia in this novel, as the differences between past and present, waking and sleeping, individual and twin all blur.

The Comic Ordinary

Probably more appropriate for younger readers are fantasies that ask for no frightening suspension of disbelief: comic adventures developed in a spirit of fun by extensions of ordinary life. The ebullience of books by Robert Munsch, Dennis Lee, Tim Wynne-Jones, and others, shows the impact of Maurice Sendak's *In the Night Kitchen* and other fantasies, where imagination runs unleashed. In Robert Munsch's *Jonathan Cleaned Up. Then He Heard a Sound* a child discovers that his Toronto home has suddenly become a busy subway station. The title *The Tooth Paste Genie* tells all: in Frances Duncan's story (1981) Amanda's wish is granted by a purple genie released by rubbing a new kind of magic vessel. Out of a bathtub tap come a host of creatures in Dennis Lee's *The Ordinary Bath* (1979). Conversely, an imaginary voyage begins when a child is pulled down the bathtub drain in Stan Dragland's *Simon Jesse's Journey* (1983).

A small cat is the traveller in Tim Wynne-Jones's *Zoom at Sea* (1983). To satisfy the cat Zoom's yearning, friendly Maria twists an enormous wheel in the wall of her house, and the sea rushes in to carry him away on a tumultuous voyage. When the voyage is over, Zoom asks for and is promised another trip. Zoom's joyous, repeatable adventure parallels the voyaging that is possible for every young reader who picks up a book.

In *The Act of Reading* Wolfgang Iser describes two selves, one enacting "the role offered by the text," the other maintaining "the reader's own disposition . . . [and] the one can never be fully taken over by the other."[10] But when a young child reads, that takeover can almost come to pass. Donn Kushner's *A Book Dragon* (1987) both plays with this potential and undercuts it. This intricate, comic story involves the reader in the travels of a brave, funny dragon named Nonesuch, who can be (like Alice in Wonderland, and like every young reader) huge or tiny, depending on how others view him. The reader journeys with Nonesuch from the days when everyone believed in dragons to the present time. The treasure that Nonesuch guards is itself a book, a manuscript in which his image had been delicately inscribed in the Middle Ages.

Through time, Nonesuch has shrunk to the size of a dragonfly, but he can still battle to defend his treasure and the people who respect it. The adventures are exciting, but so, too, are the little devices that restore the reader's sense of the book as book—on one page, for instance, a tiny archer has shot the page number off the upper left-hand corner.

All literary fantasy facilitates travel like that of Nonesuch. The fluent reader moves from a center of home, self, and known experience, through widening gyres of space and time, into an apparently unlimited universe.

On Stage

Going to the theater involves a double trip: to the stage world of greasepaint and illusion and thence to an imagined world through which the actors move. That second world, in the hands of a poet such as James Reaney, may carry child theater-goers only as far as Ontario reality, in *Apple Butter,* or to the universe of children's games, in *Names and Nicknames,* or across the continent, in *The Geography Match.* The trip may lift readers into the skies for a comic, heroic battle in Len Peterson's *Billy Bishop and the Red Baron,* or it may take them back into Indian and Inuit legends, as in Eric Nicol's *The Clam Made a Face* or Henry Beissel's *Inook and the Sun.* In very many Canadian plays, children are asked to participate. There is also a noticeable innovative use of puppets and marionettes—a use of triple illusion. Yet even at the height of the fantasy, many Canadian dramatists use their art to draw children more deeply not into dream but into involvement with real social and environmental problems.[11]

6

Problems and Solutions

Many books for young children focus on social and moral problems and suggest possible solutions through plot development or direct preaching. Such books are designed to sow seeds of positive social action.

There is a proper time for sowing such seeds. Child psychologists suggest that around the age of 9 or 10 children emerge from self-absorption into an awareness of the physical, social, and religious peculiarities that differentiate people. At this stage they begin to absorb social biases and to observe, to suffer from, or to inflict social and religious discrimination.[1] By 11 or 12, they will enter a period in which complex attachments are formed and relative independence is achieved. In this transitional period books can help young people's moral and social growth.[2] The books must, however, satisfy a developing mental capacity for symbolic thinking. Metaphor and simile can now clarify beliefs and motives. Children around 11 years old "burn through" books, to quote Louise Rosenblatt, live through them, enthralled and absorbed, deeply affected by the symbolic substructure. Their reading, says Rosenblatt, besides being "aesthetic" (i.e., they respond to beauty and form) is also "efferent" (i.e., they carry away ideas on ways of coping with moral and social complexities).[3]

Yet modern critics condemn "preachy books." Since the late nineteenth-century cry of "art for art's sake," the use of literature

for moral instruction has been suspect. Sheila Egoff dismisses the
books that suggest ways to solve social and psychological problems as "bibliotherapy" (Egoff, 186); and Michele Landsberg
warns, "Children do not 'catch' morals, good or bad, from books,
and it would be a shame if parents began to pop books down their
children's throats like pills" (Landsberg, 96).

Arguments about the didactic element and the instructional
function of literature for young people loom large in Canada, perhaps because so much of Canadian literature is and has been
driven by extraliterary intentions. Early writers produced tract-
like tales purveying theological and moral lessons on salvation,
temperance, and mission work. Later, writers proffered sociolog-
ical lessons: how to view and treat native peoples, new immigrants, and the handicapped. Canadians pride themselves on the
openness of their mosaic society and its stated ideal of being free
from class, racial, and religious prejudice, and government funds
have been used to help writers, publishers, and distributors
spread information about the problems posed by the ethnic and
geographic diversity of the country. Most recently, authors have
used books for children as a way to teach them how to cope with
increasingly common personal problems: family breakup, rootlessness, or the loss of parents or grandparents by separation or
death.

Native Virtue

The earliest children's books about Canadian life, designed
for English readers, focused on Indians and Inuit. *A Peep at
the Esquimaux* (1825) by "A Lady" and *Northern Regions* by
"Uncle Richard" (1825) informed child readers of the historic
voyages of Parry and Franklin in search of the Northwest Passage and also preached tolerance and sympathy for the alien
ways of the "people of the ice." The story *Bellegarde, the
Adopted Indian Boy, a Canadian Tale* (1833), published anonymously, used fiction to explain missionary efforts to Christianize
native peoples.

When Catharine Parr Strickland Traill, the first major writer of Canadian children's books, published *The Young Emigrants; or, Pictures of Canada, Calculated to Amuse and Instruct the Minds of Youth* (1826), she brought it out anonymously, as "By the author of 'Prejudice Reproved.'" (The "prejudice" in this little story was directed against blacks in England.) *The Young Emigrants*, a didactic travelogue, written six years before Traill herself emigrated, warns against discontent and repining and envisages an ideal life in Canada for two fictional families, the English Clarences and their protégés, the Scottish Gordons. After moving to the colonies, Traill wrote again about young emigrants. This time, in *The Canadian Crusoes* (1852), she included Canadian Indians among her characters. Hector and Catharine Maxwell, children of a Scottish father and a French mother, and their French-Canadian cousin Louis, lost in the bush, are joined by a Mohawk girl whom they name Indiana. Like Robinson Crusoe, the children are forced to depend on their own strengths and virtues and on the mercy of God. The story moves to a dramatic climax when the white children are rescued from a hostile Ojibwa princess through the skill and courage of Indiana.

Victorian Canadians expected their children to find in books a powerful resource for self-improvement, and in *Canadian Crusoes* Traill effectively obliged by providing lessons for survival in a strange land. With 30 years' experience as an immigrant behind her, she preaches prudence and courage. Traill presents a Darwinian message of change, growth, and adaptation, but she also preaches Christianity: Indiana has been converted by the right-minded white children. Finally, through the characterization of Catharine Maxwell, Traill also emphasizes the Victorian feminine virtues of gentleness, piety, and motherly concern.

Tract Fiction

Literary historian Margaret Cutt in *Ministering Angels: A Study of Nineteenth-century Evangelical Writing for Children* suggests that one reason for the small early production of literature in the colonies was the ready availability of cheap, easy-to-read tract fiction (i.e., stories designed to supplement the messages of evangelical tracts). Tract fiction was available from English publishers such as the Religious Tract Society and the Society for Promotion of Christian Knowledge.[4] These publishers together with the American Tract Society and the American Baptist Publishing Society not only supplied books that established a taste for pious tales, including some Canadian examples, but also eventually encouraged the founding of Canadian presses with a religious base such as Westminster, Briggs and Ryerson.

The London Religious Tract Society published anonymously *Cedar Creek* (1863), a story about a young Irish emigrant, the work he finds in Canada, his piety and his romance. Published as part of the company's list of "adult and juvenile literature," this novel tucks a young boy and a little girl into the story, so that children can enjoy family readings and pick up their share of lessons about Sunday observance, self-sacrificing filial duty, and cheerful kindness to Indians, runaway American slaves, and ragged laborers. With *Willie Burke; or, The Irish Settler in America* (1850), Mary Anne Sadlier began a long career as the producer of the popular "Tales for the Young." Although written in Montreal, Willie's lively story is set in New York, but the details would fit anywhere that Irish Catholics were a disadvantaged but ambitious and inventive group.

Lyntonville, or, The Irish Boy in Canada (1867), published (anonymously again) by the American Tract Society of New York, is more directly intended for children. A pious tract it is, but it contains attractive glimpses of the balsam and blossoms and ferns in a Canadian clearing. Here young boys query an old Indian about early days and learn to respect him. Here, too, a timid Irish lad loses his home by a fire set by a jealous neighbor and consequently loses hope of schooling and a good future. The moral ending restores justice because the boy arsonist repents. A double reward follows when the Irish boy comes into an inheritance "at home" and returns to the old country.

Service and Self-Help

Children's books of the later nineteenth century show increasing confusion between two contrary sets of ideals. The late Victorian optimism about an ameliorating life in this world through ambition and self-help clashed with the evangelical piety that stressed devout self-denying charity as a more appropriate preparation for a better world. An example of this ambiguity is *The Old and the New Home: A Canadian Tale* by "J. E." (published in Toronto in 1870). Irish immigrants Murty and Biddy and the O'Brien family struggle toward prosperity, but a travelling missionary offers different precepts and a holy example of life in the bush.

A comparable blend of worldly and otherworldly values is implied in *How John Norton the Trapper Kept His Christmas* (1890), a Christmas story beautifully presented with handsome typography and decoratively bordered pages, which suggest that opulence and charity can coexist. Yet another novel of life in the bush, Edward Garrett's *A Black Diamond* (1899), offers children a Canadian version of a theme heavily emphasized in tract fiction— the sin of slavery. In his story an American slave has run away from a lynch mob.

All these late Victorian books attempt not only to preach Christian virtues but also to teach little readers about the realities of life in Canada. Best known of the pious regional novelists was Ralph Connor (the Reverend Charles Gordon), and of all of his novels the one best adapted to hold the attention of young readers through gripping, amusing, and sentimental incidents combined with firm messages on moral courage is *Glengarry Schooldays* (1902).

Ralph Connor's hero is winsome Hugh Murray, the minister's son—son also of a sensitive mother whose devout spirit influences the small backwoods community of Scots Canadians. *Glengarry Schooldays* is filled with battle, from the spelling match in the schoolroom where the master governs by love and praise, through a deathly struggle in the forest against a bear, when Hugh has run away from subsequent teachers' misrule, to a final battle on the ice in the game of shinny (an early form of hockey). The latest schoolmaster leads Hugh and his friends to victory in sport and then on to better schooling and a final choice of studies for the ministry. The visible battles make very exciting reading. Symbolically they transmit the deeper theme of inner spiritual battle.

Ralph Connor's work, here and in other novels more obviously directed at a popular adult audience, climaxes the early period of tract fiction. It poses moral questions in vivid regional terms and sites the moral battle at the child's level. The excitement of vigorous life in a primitive Ontario community is matched by the posing of intense problems of sin and conscience in Hugh's heart.

Problems of Poverty

Ralph Connor's contemporaries elsewhere in Canada concentrated on the problems of poverty, especially in outlying regions, where the primary industries such as fishing and logging offered no easy panaceas and the traditional faith in hard work and enterprise were easily eroded. Norman Duncan's *Adventures of Billy Topsail* (1906) drew attention to Newfoundland, reflecting a dialect and a life more melodramatic and rhetorical than Ralph Connor's, but again giving young readers a moral message.

The strong series of didactic works culminates in Nellie McClung's *Sowing Seeds in Danny* (1908), a book of deserved and enduring popularity. McClung, a deft and humorous storyteller and an early women's rights activist, preaches some of the old morality of self-help and piety. Her spunky heroine, Pearl Watson, is a Canadian Crusoe facing a new wilderness of social problems such as drunkenness and economic exploitation of the working class. Pearl is a child of the doubly dispossessed: driven by poverty from the bushland of the Ottawa Valley, her Irish immigrant parents have been forced to uproot a second time to a little Manitoba town. Pearl's mother, the overworked provider for nine children, needs virtues different from those that had bolstered earlier Canadian women.

McClung preaches an evangelical doctrine of Christian charity. Through Pearl she suggests to young readers that a child's practical goodness can change the lives of many in her community. McClung also uses vivid symbols to suggest the talents and values brought to the new west by its pioneers: poppies and hymns remind overworked young people of the beauty and tradition of England; Irish ingenuity turns an abandoned railway boxcar into a warm home for Pearl's family; and Scots-Presbyterian grit helps a nerve-shattered young doctor and a drink-befuddled old one overcome their problems.

McClung still assumes that the proper function of literature is to prepare young readers for moral choice, but her work reflects the change that had occurred in the tone of all novels for young people. Whimsy and nonsense had come in with Kipling and J. M. Barrie, and priggish, affected child characters were being swept away by the downright honesty of E. Nesbit and Frances Hodgson Burnett. So, when in McClung's novel a sentimental lady waxes poetic about the possibility of "sowing seeds" in impressionable Danny, Pearl doggedly scours out his ears as a preventative. Yet McClung, for all her mockery of sentimental didacticism, sows seed of her own: ideas about the problems of the immigrants, about addictions, particularly alcoholism, and about the persecution of the powerless.

For succeeding generations of Canadian writers, these problems, rather than those of survival and salvation, would be predominant. The tone becomes lighter, the didacticism more muffled as twentieth-century novels replaced Victorian tract fiction. Norman Duncan in a charming Christmas gift book titled *The Suitable Child* (1909) mixes wit and sentimentalism as he shows the way a small person can break down the self-centered apathy of wealth. Duncan sets his tale not in the Newfoundland outports or Glengarry or Manitoba but on the Winnipeg westbound express train—a "place" suggesting the swift change to mechanization and material prosperity in the days before the First World War.

A darker tone returns in Dillon Wallace's *Grit a-Plenty,* a novel published in 1918, which recognizes the persistence of personal and social problems in spite of progress. In this tale Doctor Joe, an alcoholic, works out the troubles of addiction in a remote Labrador port. In a climax rather like that in *Sowing Seeds in Danny* he rallies his forces and performs a successful operation.

Very few books for children in the period between the two world wars focused on problems, theological or social. The 1920s and early 1930s saw a flowering of fairy tales and fantasies. Some nonfiction such as the brief biographies in Archer Wallace's *Stories of Grit* (1925) preached directly to young readers. And little church magazines proliferated as platforms for didactic messages about Christianity at home and mission work abroad. Children's books also became the agency for preaching national pride; one such patriotic publication emphasizing the British heritage is *Canada's Past in Pictures* (1934), written and illustrated by C. W. Jefferys. One of the few books published between the wars that sets out to teach the old lesson of sympathy for people outside the WASP establishment is Vilhjalmur Stefansson and Violet Irwin's *Kak the Copper Eskimo* (1924).

Affirmation and Acceptance

The Second World War following the drought and depression of the 1920s and 1930s brought deep doubt about the efficacy of prayer and hard work and exploded the Darwinian corollary that the fittest survive. No one could teach young people any simple way to face the problems of loss and death in nature and in human society. But W. O. Mitchell's *Who Has Seen the Wind* (1947) found wide acceptance among young readers as a powerful confrontation of darkness and an affirmation of light.

The child Brian in *Who Has Seen the Wind* faces a sequence of deaths—a casually observed animal, his dog, his father, and, finally, his grandmother. A second child, the Young Ben, is traumatized by the imprisoning structures of school and the condemnatory stance of the small town. Meanwhile, the good earth erodes, the soil blows away over the ill-treated prairies, and human compassion crumbles in the village institutions, the church, and the school. Mitchell presents a small prairie town, like that of Nellie McClung, and he only slightly enlarges the ethnic mix beyond her Scots-Irish-English base to include a glimpse of the "China Kids," tragically set outside the community's concerns. Mitchell offers no panaceas for any of the pangs felt by a growing child in this world. He does imply that some pain can be accepted and that other pain may begin to be alleviated. He preaches ecology, eternity, and liberty, not directly but by recurrences, by cadence, by humorous indirection, and by lyric description. Like many children's "classics," *Who Has Seen the Wind* was not written for children. But children of 10 or 11 who find it in school or in the library tap into a book that serves deep needs. Such a book does offer bibliotherapy. It heals.

Immigrant Problems

In the next decades a new generation of authors poured out further fictions not whimsical but therapeutic, designed not to evade problems but to reflect them and to guide young readers into ways of solving them. It seemed to the writers of the 1950s and the 1960s that children of that era faced not the savage bushland of *The Canadian Crusoes* but a moral and social wilderness, and that they needed new codes of action and behavior. Many of the social problems were brought about by the coming of waves of "New Canadians" as immigrants who were neither British nor American were called in the 1950s. Mabel Dunham's *Kristli's Trees* (1948) about Mennonites, Ann Macmillan's *Levko* (1950) about Ukrainians, and Lyn Cook's *The Bells on Finland Street* (1950) about Finnish newcomers begin a long array of books treating the troubles of children in new non-WASP immigrant groups. Lyn Cook's *The Little Magic Fiddler* is documentary fiction that traces the success of an actual violinist of Ukrainian extraction. Cook creates a suggestive symbol in the small wooden figurine of a violin player, carved by a neighbor who maintains the old Ukrainian village traditions of music and gives it to the young would-be musician. The wooden figurine, symbol of an inherited ethnic pride and talent, serves as a secret talisman.

In an article entitled "Painful Stories: Narrative Strategies of Immigration," Adrienne Kertzer uses *Levko* as a particular example of the way immigrant stories for children sidestep the pain of immigrant experience and the strain of conflict, guilt, and betrayal by providing a traditional happy ending. Such endings, she says, falsify reality in showing immigrant children as confident, lucky, or adaptable.[5] The British surnames Dunham, Macmillan, and Cook perhaps explain the unrealistic characterization of "New Canadians." Or perhaps these stories reflect the essential optimism in Canada, the confidence that social safety nets such as healthcare, family counselling, psychiatric help, and children's aid will fill the voids left when people cannot count on traditional religious consolations or the comforting warmth of a rooted extended family.

Family problems and problems of identity are, of course, not limited to children of immigrants. Most modern children face the essentially unsolvable problems of torn and disrupted tradition. For the majority of Canadian children, who have not directly experienced physical uprooting and resettlement, these stories of immigrant problems function on two levels: On the surface they increase sympathy for the obviously traumatic life of new Canadians, and on a deeper level they use immigrant experience as a symbol for the trauma of all uprooting, loneliness, and rejection.

Social Problem as Symbol

The best of the stories that combine immigrant problems with other tensions is Jean Little's *From Anna* (1972). Anna and her family come to Canada from Nazi Germany. Anna, whose vision is impaired, is symbolically subtly linked to the country from which she has fled—a country blinded by prejudice. When the family arrive in Canada a third version of the theme of "sight" emerges: to understand each other, the family, the school, and the community need insight. Tied to this play with the idea of sight, blindness, insight, and vision are other themes, subtly worked out in symbols. Music, important to a child whose hearing is better than her sight, runs throughout the story until the culminating song "Silent Night, Holy Night" marks the reintegration of the German heritage into a Canadian Christmas celebration. There is a new epiphany in the familiar phrase, "All is calm, all is bright!" Food, hands, books, snow, and gifts also function symbolically to excellent but not obtrusive effect. Anna herself presents a gift to any troubled child, because she represents the yearning, creative, baffled, awkward part of every self. Jean Little thus preaches to immigrant children, to those who suffer from physical handicaps, and to all other children as well; but she preaches indirectly, through plot manipulation; and she promotes insight by tone, setting, character, and symbolic action. Her messages, like those of most modern teachers, are tentative, sometimes ambivalent. But she nevertheless funnels through her fiction useful messages of instruction.

Little has explored the problems of children in a long series of admirable novels. The problems range from loneliness (*Look through My Window,* 1970) to physical impairment such as cerebral palsy (*Mine for Keeps,* 1961), and from timidity (*Different Dragons,* 1986) to the death of a parent (*Mama's Going to Buy You a Mocking Bird,* 1984). Each of these novels begins with a situation that creates fear. Each moves through a serious and complex confrontation of problems to a surprising conclusion that creates a sense that life and moral codes have been reborn.

Jean Little may derive her urge to present healing messages from the missionary background from which she emerged. She may also have drawn it from her days at Victoria College, University of Toronto. There Northrop Frye, a powerful teacher and critic, insisted that fiction, even in its realistic phase, its low mimetic mode, functions as myth once did. It enables us to realize the universe and clarifies the archetypal patterns underlying details of present life.[6] Jean Little's work demonstrates that she has absorbed Frye's sense of the central revelatory function of fiction.

Problems with Parents

In many children's books, the handicaps of the New Canadian are compounded by other tensions. In William Kurelek's beautifully illustrated autobiography *A Prairie Boy's Winter* (1973) a father's harshness adds to the miseries of immigrant farm life in Manitoba. In a lighter tone, Ian Wallace's funny illustrations for Angela Wood's *The Sandwich* (1975) emphasize the point that good humor is a great defense against ridicule at school; and a Jamaican child in Yvonne Singer's *Little Miss-Yes-Miss* (1976) emphasizes the need for pride and self-possession in the face of the pressures of the inner city.

"Being different" is the central problem of *The Wooden People* (1976). This fine novel by Myra Paperny presents a disturbing picture of the wall set up around the Stein family by the immigrant father's insistence that no friendships be formed, no roots put down—his reaction to memories of suffering from pogroms in the old world. The enforced maintenance of old ways keeps his children "different" and reduces 13-year-old Lisa and 12-year-old Teddy to despair. Lisa loves her sensitive, explosive father; Teddy has turned against him. Together, the children find an escape from their frustrations by constructing and manipulating "wooden people"—marionettes—and this becomes their link with the other children in their new hometown. The Stein children, puppets in their father's hands as he moves them from town to town, learn to manage their own show. The marionettes, which also come from a European tradition, free the children, and, in turn, their success frees their father from his fear of the theatrical and the communal.

Just as Ralph Connor used realistic physical conflicts to symbolize a boy's inner struggles of conscience, so Myra Paperny uses the marionettes as an effective metaphor. Stories such as Pinocchio and the Nutcracker suggest the mysterious attraction of puppetry: Modern psychological studies affirm the value of "wooden people" in therapy, arguing that disturbed children can, indeed, reveal through puppets what they would normally repress or sublimate. Paperny subtly uses these connotations of puppetry.

90

7. "... luminous intensity." William Kurelek, from *A Prairie Boy's Winter* (1973).

Regardless of the special marionette motif, the Steins' feelings of strangeness aptly reflect preteen uncertainties in an expanding world of clubs, teams, work groups, sports, and arts classes. Paperny, like Jean Little, offers suggestions and solace for healing small as well as great distress.

Being Different

Myra Paperny's work marks an extension in point of view beyond the white, Christian, European orientation of the original settlers. Fostering pride in multicultural differences is a part of official Canadian policy: there is now a government department of multiculturalism, and government funding aids the work of writing, publishing, and distributing books for children that reflect Canadian ethnic diversity. Thanks in part to this funding, books about the present-day life of Indian and Inuit people join stories of other Canadians whose traditions are non-Christian. The protagonists range from very young children to adolescents, but the problems are felt with equal intensity at every age. A teenaged girl of Korean origin in *Kap-Sung Ferris* (1977) by Frances Duncan suffers a double loss of identity because she has been adopted by a Vancouver family. Shelley Tanaka's *Michi's New Year* (1980) suggests the real dislocation suffered even by a very small child in the midst of new rituals, new scenes.

In some stories the characters find a source of strength in their own heritage. The boy in Joan Weir's *So, I'm Different* (1981) uses Indian myths to modulate the tensions he feels as the only Indian in his school. In *Chin Chiang and the Dragon's Dance* (1984), written and illustrated by Ian Wallace, a small boy is helped by his grandfather to perform the traditional rituals of his people in a new and perhaps unfriendly setting. Ian Wallace's illustrations for Jan Andrews's *Very Last First Time* (1985) use subtle color symbolism to suggest the mythic dimension beneath the story of Eva Padlyat's brave venture, when she walks on the bottom of the sea beneath the ice, when the tide is out. The spirit world of her people's traditional belief is revealed in patterns of darkness and light, images of fear and assurance. Some books strike a sadder note: Joy Kogawa's *Naomi's Road* (1986) recalls the intense suffering of Japanese Canadians interred during World War II, a suffering intensified rather than mitigated by traditional cultural assumptions.

In the best of these problem stories, details of nature and family life take on symbolic force. Flowers, like the flaming poppies of Nellie McClung's story, serve in Betty Waterton's *Petranella* (1980) to connect the acceptance of death with the affirmation of continuing beauty. Petranella, a frightened child travelling across the prairies, grieves at the loss of the flower seeds entrusted to her by her grandmother. Springtime blossoming proves that Pe-

92

8. "... the mythic dimension." Ian Wallace, from his *Chin Chiang and the Dragon's Dance*, a Groundwood/Douglas & McIntyre Book (1984).

tranella has indeed sown her grandmother's gift in the new soil. Similarly, a doll with something of the empowering force of Paperny's "wooden people" or the "little magic fiddler" appears in Ron Berg's moving illustrations for *Michi's New Year*. Little Michi holds a familiar doll for comfort as she sits like a small Crusoe on unfamiliar steps in the strange Vancouver rain. The doll, like the gift from Jean Little's Anna, is a small thing, but it has been created with fidelity and imagination. Like the words and pictures of a book, created also with careful detail and a deep desire to bring comfort, the doll offers some healing. Through these "problem books" children can be helped to recognize restorative forces: time, family sympathy, unfolding friendships, artistic diversions, and the sober pride of facing problems independently.

7

Animal Studies

Realistic animal stories have generally been considered a Canadian specialty. At the end of the nineteenth century Charles G. D. Roberts and Ernest Thompson Seton caught world attention with their stories of "the kindred of the wild." Since Canada was presumed to consist of forest and barrens, it seemed natural for Canadians to present tales of wild beasts. Comparable anecdotes had long been circulated in the memoirs of British soldiers traveling through Canadian forests and in reports of missionaries, culminating in Joshua Fraser's *Three Months among the Moose* (1881) and Egerton Ryerson Young's *My Dogs in the Northland* (1902).

Writing before Roberts and Seton, Marshall Saunders and other Canadian authors had created pen portraits of animals as pets, as heroes, and as friends. They were contributing to a genre long popular with English-speaking readers, and one that had recently been reenergized.[1] In 1859 Darwin had resituated man in the animal kingdom. In 1865 Alice had moved in Wonderland through a queendom where animals and people talked and jostled and raced on equal terms. *Black Beauty* had used the autobiographical form to heighten sympathy for abused animals in 1877, and the Uncle Remus stories of the 1880s had revived the traditional use of animal fables for teaching and entertainment.

Children's love of animal stories throws light on their social and psychological development. In *Totem and Taboo*, Freud theorizes, "Children show no trace of the arrogance which urges civilized men to draw a hard and fast line between their own nature and that of other animals. Uninhibited as they are in the avowal of their bodily needs, they no doubt feel themselves more akin to animals than to their elders, who may well be a puzzle to them."[2]

For over 120 years Canadian animal stories have both helped and entertained child readers. In a story like Stéphane Poulin's *Can You Catch Josephine?* (1987) very small children in early days of reading and reasoning can find a small instinctual being still enjoying unfettered, unhurried life. Such a story engenders a sense of fun, charms children, and perhaps helps them deal more easily with their own animal selves. For children who are 10 or 11 years old, longer stories about the complex relationships between children and their pets offer other values. In Farley Mowat's *The Dog Who Wouldn't Be* (1957) readers can find imaginary friends that are warmer, more spontaneous, and more faithful than real peers. Through Marshall Saunders's *Beautiful Joe* (1894) they can clarify their sense of adult cruelty and folly. In a serious novel such as Morley Callaghan's *Luke Baldwin's Vow* (1948) preteen readers find correlatives of the dualistic tensions that all human life presents: conflicting pulls of forces animal/spiritual, masculine/feminine, normal/eccentric, and socialized/individual. Reading Roderick Haig-Brown's *Ki-Yu, a Story of Panthers* (1934) the older child returns to the wilderness worlds presented by Charles G. D. Roberts in *Earth's Enigmas* (1896) and Ernest Thompson Seton in *Wild Animals I Have Known* (1898) and faces ecological and moral questions about the coexistence of man and his animal kindred.

Fellow Creatures

English settlers in Canada brought their traditional fondness for pets with them. Catharine Strickland Traill, like her sister Susanna Strickland Moodie, bore her share of "roughing it in the bush," and she revealed the persistence of that sympathy in the stories collected in *Lady Mary and Her Nurse* (1856; reissued in the United States as *Stories of the Canadian Forest,* 1861). In "Nimbletoes and His Sisters, Velvetpaw and Silvernose," for example, Traill communicates her charmed response to the timid gentle fauna of the new world—in this case the deer who come to the edge of the clearing. All of her stories of Canadian animals are told by a Canadian settler who acts as nurse to the little English newcomer to the forest. Traill offers a child reader the gifts that Beatrix Potter would exercise some 60 years later: accurate observation, a serious tone, and the delicate delineation of details of habit and habitat.

Other early Canadian writers followed, adding to Traill's interest in small wild animals of the forest an equally careful detailing of pets. A fine early example is Flora MacLean's *True Anecdotes of Pet Animals* (1882), which includes stories of the lives (and death and burial) of seven kittens, a Skye terrier, and a lamb named Daisy in an Ontario country home. Flora MacLean's Scottish name reminds us of the influence of Robert Burns's love of our "fellow creatures" such as the "wee, sleekit, tim'rous, cowering beastie" in his poem "To a Mouse."

Animal as Victim

But Canadian stories about small animals modulated into more serious didactic uses. Largely under the influence of *Black Beauty,* animal biographies decrying human encroachment on the lives of defenseless creatures appeared before the nineteenth century ended. Marshall Saunders's *Beautiful Joe* (1894) was written to order for a competition mounted by the American Humane Society. It is the "autobiography" of a dog who has been cruelly treated by his first owner, and who witnesses comparable unkindness meted out to other pets and farm animals. Years later Robertson Davies declaimed in one of his "Marchbanks" columns, "What a grisly book it is. Cruelty, drunkenness and meanness abound in it, which accounts for its popularity with the young, who love cheap sensationalism."[4] John Rowe Townsend calls *Beautiful Joe* "a riot of anthropomorphism."[5] But *Beautiful Joe* outfaces its detractors, then and now. Its vigor, humor, pathos, and richness of incident made it a world best-seller, and it remains a powerful story.

Marshall Saunders had had an idyllic childhood in Nova Scotia, in a warm extended family. She found her ambition and creative power were thwarted by the restraints placed on her sex in her time. Sent to finishing school when her brothers went to college, saddled with family responsibility for aging parents, impoverished by publishing practices that exploited and underpaid women writers, Marshall Saunders created in her fiction an archetype of suffering and resistance. She gives her small mutilated animal hero a masculine name, "Joe." In him Marshall Saunders releases her sense of the curtailment of her "masculine" powers; and through him she helps young readers release their own self-pity. But through Beautiful Joe's concern for the sufferings of other animals, Marshall Saunders also achieves, and gives to little readers, a second gift: the ability to transcend self-pity and to move on to a social sense.

With this book, Marshall Saunders launched a writing career that yielded 19 books for children, beginning with titles such as *Charles and His Lamb* (1895), *Nita: The Story of an Irish Setter* (1904), *Princess Sukey, The Story of a Pigeon* (1905), and *Alpatock: The Story of an Eskimo Dog* (1906). Of the whole series, the most memorable is *Beautiful Joe's Paradise* (1902), in which Saunders gently responds to the death of a beloved pet and adds a mix of fantasy and fun to the idea of a paradise for animals. The approach to death is as matter-of-fact as in *Charlotte's Web;* like that American classic, *Beautiful Joe's Paradise* helps children absorb the concept of mortality and vicariously experience and release grief.

Imitators attested to Marshall Saunders's popularity. In A. G. Savigny's *Lion the Mastiff* (1895) a dog tells the story of the troubles of his life in East Toronto, preaching against cruelty and vivisection. Life in *Peter, a Canadian Cat* (1904) by Elizabeth Guelton ends sadly when a neglected pet freezes and starves to death.

Only one novel of the early century stands out in sharp contrast to the sentimental tone of Saunders's stories about pets. Valance Patriarche's *Tag; or, The Chien Boule Dog* (1909) weaves a sprightly little romance around an ugly bulldog and his little French-Canadian owner, who together turn a Canadian train ride into a glorious farce.

Saunders's popularity has waned. But in their day her novels satisfied a huge audience. Like the equally popular *Bedtime Stories* of American writer Thornton Burgess, her work focuses young readers' attention on the wide range of creatures that share our world. As Charles G. D. Roberts wrote in his preface to *Kindred of the Wild,* the animal story frees us "from the mean tenement of self."[6]

Animals in the Wild

Between *Earth's Enigmas* (1896) and *Eyes of the Wilderness* (1933) Charles G. D. Roberts produced 32 books of realistic animal stories, admired by adults and devoured by young readers. The lynx, the bear, the eagle, and the otter are presented not as if they were talking, thinking humans but with a sense of the real mystery of animal instincts, habits, and means of communication. Roberts presents dispassionately the fierce swoop of the hunting eagle, the evasive slink of the fox, the crashing violence of the rutting moose. The frisson of danger and conflict is available for readers, only partly distanced by the animal mask. The child could revel in passages like this one: "Peter caught sight of a rabbit which went bounding off among the fir-trunks. He watched its flight with interest, and was startled to see a small, snaky brown form dart upward in the fugitive's path, snap fangs upon its throat, and pull it down. A short sharp screech from the victim, a convulsive thrashing with its long hind legs, then stillness."[7] Some adults may be concerned about the violence portrayed in Roberts's books, and they may wish to explain to children that people are different from these predators.

Perhaps the sharpness of Roberts's vision shows an Indian influence, an absorption of the native sense of man and animals as fellow habitants of earth whose life cycles are intertwined. Roberts did his best work in *Kindred of the Wild* (1902) and *Watchers of the Trail* (1904). In *Red Fox* (1905, reissued 1972) he focused on a particular animal yet communicated his general belief that all animals are driven by a Darwinian need for survival—survival of the individual and of the species, which manifests itself in the fierce battle to satisfy basic wants for food, rest, mating.[8] Roberts does not soften, but he also does not sensationalize the idea of nature "red in tooth and claw." He adds a poetic response to the wilderness setting, the deep of the woods.

Ernest Thompson Seton, like Roberts, wrote from careful observation of animal life. He developed his knowledge first from boyhood ramblings in the Ontario bushland, later from scientific studies in natural history. From *Wild Animals I Have Known* (1898) to *The Buffalo Wind* (1938) he created 18 volumes of animal stories. Seton asked his readers to identify with some traditionally unsympathetic animals, such as the grizzly bear and the wolf. In *The Lives of the Hunted* (1901) he leads young readers from the excitement of participating in the animals' life on the prowl into the recognition of their vulnerability to aging and predators, including man.

Seton was also a fine graphic artist. His illustrations for *Bird-Wood* (1898) by J. H. Stickney and Ralph Hoffman, for example, are loving in detail. Contemporary animal studies by other artists and writers, such as A. M. Long's *Ways of the Wood Folk* (1899), *Following the Deer* (1901), and *Northern Trails* (1905), which features the leap of salmon in Labrador waters, all illustrated by Canadian artist Charles Copeland, show the influence of Seton's pleasure in detailing the life of air, marine, and forest animals and testify to the consequent wide popularity of nature stories.

Directed at young readers, the stories of Roberts and Seton were admired because they were seen as a means of increasing knowledge of and sympathy for fellow habitants of the earth. When we turn to a book such as Clarence Hawkes's *Shaggycoat, the Biography of a Beaver* (1906), also illustrated by Copeland, we see how easily writers can slip from the purity and accuracy of Seton and Roberts to a sentimental approach. "When Shaggycoat thought of the old days and his family, he could remember warm summer afternoons upon clear sand banks,"[9] imputes inappropriate emotional affiliations and memories to the animal protagonist. Similarly, Agnes Herbert in *The Moose* (1913) sentimentalizes and softens wildlife stories.

Frank modification of actual animal capabilities had proved to be a valid fictional device in W. A. Fraser's *Mooswa* (1900). Told from the perspective of forest animals of the Roberts and Seton ilk, this novel recounts the fondness of moose, wolf, and bear for a frontier boy. It blends excellent Athabaskan wilderness atmosphere with an incredible but entertaining story line. The animals' efforts to save and rescue the trapper's boy when he is marooned in an outpost are ingenious; their story is interspersed with anecdotes about the life of Hudson's Bay Company men, missionaries, and hunters in the far northwest. *Mooswa* is a good early example of stories about the mutual devotion of a boy and his animal friends. With it, we begin to move toward the power of similar stories by Morley Callaghan and Farley Mowat.

Meanwhile, up to and during the First World War, Roberts, Seton, and Saunders continued to please an ever-renewing audience of young readers with annual publications. Together with Robert Service, Stephen Leacock, and L. M. Montgomery, they demonstrated that Canadian authors could find and satisfy world readership in the first quarter of the twentieth century.

Furry Friends

A few little stories of pets or small field animals appeared in the 1920s, some in "shape" books such as a production called *Laddy* (1920) from the Canada Games Company. The same company in the same year also brought out *A Book of Dogs,* consisting of nursery rhymes about animals. Stories about pet dogs also became very popular in the 1920s. Some were not particularly distinguished—Jemima Remington's *Percival, Plain Dog* (1924) represents the arch variety of dog story, Benson Walker's *Scottie: The True Story of a Dog* (1927), the sentimental brand. Hubert Evans, a much more accomplished writer, produced three books about "Derry," an airedale terrier, beginning with *Derry, Airedale of the Frontier* (1928).

In *Velvet Paws and Shiny Eyes* (1922) and *Downy Wings and Sharp Ears* (1923), both by Carol Manchee ("Carol Cassidy Cole"), small birds and animals talk, as do the animals in Kenneth Grahame's *The Wind in the Willows*, or Beatrix Potter's mice and rabbits and squirrels, although unlike those fictional animals they do not wear clothes. Like both English writers, Cole reduces animal life to a cosy domesticity. Another set of little books with a small-scale English tone and a nice light touch was produced by Hugh Heaton and H. E. M. Sellen, beginning with *Professor Porky* (1937).

Realism Restored

Two English immigrants restored the realistic Canadian animal story to new strength in the 1930s. Archie Belaney, who disguised his origins and passed himself off as the Indian Grey Owl or Washa-quon-ashin, published *The Adventures of Sajo and Her Beaver People* in 1935. Drawn from Grey Owl's life as a naturalist trying to foster an environment for endangered species, it is written with simple grace. Stronger and more complex was the work of Roderick Haig-Brown, who came from England to British Columbia first in 1927 at the age of 19, and who worked first as a bounty hunter, a guide, and a fisherman and eventually developed a fine double career as a government administrator and an award-winning writer.

As an immigrant, Haig-Brown, like Grey Owl, had an intense perception of his adopted country and a vision of what he termed "the unity of natural things".[10] His life-cycle stories of fish and animals, concrete and honest in detail, rhythmic in prose style, report the full truth of nature as he saw it. *Ki-Yu: A Story of Panthers* (published in Britain as *Panther,* 1934) directly describes the violence of hunting and killing. It implies that it is normal that man should shoot the panther not for bounty or protection but as an instinctual response to a menacing presence. *Return to the River* (1941) swings with the same clarity to the story of the chinook salmon. Although this is not really a child's book, its straightforward style makes it accessible to young naturalists. Haig-Brown's other fine books intended for children include historical fiction and adventure stories. But *Ki-yu,* powerfully illustrated by Vlasta Van Kampen in Muriel Whitaker's *Great Canadian Animal Stories* (1982), combines the order and force of animal life to demonstrate the undiminished appeal of wilderness stories for children.

Frank Conibear kept that appeal strong in *North Land Footprints* (1936), *The Wise One* (1949, reissued 1980), *The Devil Dog* (1954), and with Kenneth Conibear, *Husky, the Story of Cap* (1940). *The Wise One* patiently and pleasantly details the life of a beaver, emphasizing its steady drive for survival. Conibear's tone of lively sympathy in these simple animal biographies attracts young readers. Another contributor of animal stories for children before the Second World War was Archie McKishnie; the best of his nine books was *Dwellers of the Marsh Realm* (1937). Zoologists say that Mel Thistle's *Peter the Sea Trout* (1954) has an accuracy of detail like Haig-Brown's.

Canadian children still read stories by Haig-Brown, Seton, Roberts, and Grey Owl in school readers designed for grades 4 and 5 and they can learn more about the real life of animals from two magazines, *Owl* for older children, *Chickadee* for the youngest naturalists. But strong stories of wilderness animals, with a few notable exceptions, have diminished. Perhaps, as Alec Lucas said in an important essay in *The Literary History of Canada,* "people [grew] tired of learning that animals and men are alike and learned from two world wars that they are too much alike."[11]

Animal Friends

In one postwar story, however, the much revered novelist Morley Callaghan uses the relation between child and animal to reaffirm his belief in human dignity, loyalty, and power of choice. *Luke*

9. ". . . order and force." Vlasta Van Kampen, from *Great Canadian Animal Stories*, ed. Muriel Whitaker (1983).

Baldwin's Vow (1948) centers on the boy rather than the dog, but the subtle connection between the two becomes the hinge of the plot. Luke's father, a beloved physician, is dead, and Luke lives with the old collie Dan in the sheltering but uninspiring home of his uncle and aunt. Three times Luke rescues the crippled and half-blind dog, once by restoring Dan's personal beauty and grace that have been tangled by neglect, again by beating off the attack of the brutal dog Thor, and the third time by plunging into deep water to resurrect the dog when he is thrown into the river to die.

At this point Callaghan has created several possibilities for a traditional happy ending for Luke and his Dan: they could move away to join the solitary Mr. Kemp and his 12 cows on the nearby farm, or they could separate, Dan to live with Mr. Kemp while Luke stays in the practical world. But Morley Callaghan, having given readers the hermeneutic pleasure of foreseeing such an end to the puzzle, outwits us. Mr. Kemp's strange advice is that both Luke and Dan should move back home to the practical world of the uncle and aunt. There, Luke can buy the dog's freedom from his Uncle Henry by making money and succeeding in the uncle's terms. Callaghan's narrator quietly offers an enigmatic comment on the power of money:

> In the world there were probably millions of people like Uncle Henry who were kind and strong and because of their strength of character and shrewdness, dominated and flattened out the lives of others. Yet . . . if you knew how to handle yourself, there were fascinating ways of demanding respect for the things that gave your life a secret glow. Putting his head down on the dog's neck, he vowed to himself fervently that he would always have some money on hand, no matter what became of him, so that he would be able to protect all that was truly valuable from the practical people in the world.[12]

The compelling story of the boy and the dog rises to a powerful dimension in this strangely pragmatic conclusion. Callaghan's complex vision of the double pull of the world and the spirit finds here a symbolic expression in terms that are appropriate for children.

Boy and dog reappear as central characters in Farley Mowat's *The Dog Who Wouldn't Be* (1957). In all his deeds the dog Mutt gives physical expression to the dream of the small boy who has been carried from one place to another by adult decision and moved from the free life of the prairies to the aridity of the city. The engaging nonconformist dog mocks the male macho sport of hunting, terrorizes cats and cows and women, rides like a goggled aviator in a creaking overloaded old car, puts to sea in a strange red-sailed boat, fishes, climbs, and runs away. Mowat's dog character Mutt represents all that is insouciant, recalcitrant, and eccentric in a child.

Farley Mowat has made something of a personal cult of eccentricity. For children the glorious madness of Mutt makes a salutary inroad into the conformity of most living. Mutt's travels across Canada coalesce into a travelogue of free-spirited charm that conveys to Canadian children Mowat's fierce love of his country. Mutt is exasperating, funny most of the time, and in the end tragic, with the poignance of disruptive innocence turned to dust. In Mowat's story, the dog dies. Unlike Morley Callaghan, Farley Mowat does not proffer any hope of adjustment or compromise between the dream of freedom and the mechanistic, materialistic "real" world. When Mutt dies, his young owner says, "The pact of timelessness between the two of us was ended, and I went from him into the darkening tunnel of the years."[13]

Owls in the Family (1963) developed from a single chapter in *The Dog Who Wouldn't Be* in which two pet owls die, thus foreshadowing Mutt's end. Weeps is strangled in an ineffectual effort to get out of his cage; Wol is killed when he tries to return to the Saskatoon home where he lived in a childlike freedom. The second book, written for younger children, is equally funny. But the sad end of Wol and Weeps casts its shadow. Even in the best of families, the energy of child and animal cannot last, Mowat implies. This lesson for children is different from Callaghan's, but it is conveyed with equal honesty and intensity and is purveyed with equally fine style and craft.

In 1961, sandwiched between Farley Mowat's two books, there appeared another very popular story of domestic pets, very different from his work. The Canadian wilderness recurs as the setting for Sheila Burnford's *The Incredible Journey* (1960). Two dogs and a cat, unheroic pets, make a heroic voyage through northern forests and villages under an inarguable compulsion to rejoin their human family. Treated rather condescendingly by adult critics, this novel still has an unequaled impact on children, who accept Burnford's attributing loyalty and longing and endurance to the pets, and relish the dramatic contrasts in their characters.

Children reading realistic stories of pets recover a dream of spontaneous emotional connections. Animals offer a source of love and relationship, in life and in literature, increasingly valuable in a society that represses and controls emotions. Although they offer readers these values, both Burnford and Mowat strain credulity by moving to the limit of the possible in animal behavior. In the 1970s, many animal stories frankly and deliberately overstepped those limits. Using animal protagonists for their known appeal to little children, many authors wrote stories that show little awareness of the realities of animal life.

More recently, a lively series of stories for young readers has been launched by author-illustrator Stéphane Poulin. Poulin uses a cat named Josephine to probe some of the puzzles and tensions of a modern child of a single parent, a big-school city child who is caged like Weeps in *Owls in the Family,* yet who has an animal friend as dear as the old dog Dan in *Luke Baldwin's Vow.* In *Can You Catch Josephine?* (1987) the cat enjoys some of the pleasures of Mowat's Mutt: free movement, wild climbs, hidden mischief, and intrusions into forbidden places.

The cat's name, Josephine, curiously reverses Margaret Marshall Saunders's choice of the archetypically male name Joe. Josephine, doing for the little boy what Marshall Saunders's *Beautiful Joe* did for her, allows the boy to express a repressed side of his personality. Poulin's little boy takes his female cat to school, where she disrupts classes, goes up the down stairway, and almost leads him into the girls' washroom. This female rambunctiousness contrasts with the proper little boy's persona—the

10. "... puzzles and tensions." Stéphane Poulin, from his *Can You Catch Josephine?* (1987).

polite façade of a child living alone with his dad, going to a school where a woman is principal and the teachers are battleship-shaped women all set to repress him. But the principal turns out to have a cat of her own, which comes to school every day.

In the end of *Can You Catch Josephine?* the demonic cat is seen leading a whole parade of other cats to the school. Poulin's story presumably activates all his readers to bring their own Josephines or Joes into the real world of practical learning.

Could You Stop Josephine? (1988) takes cat and boy into encounters with surprised cows, pigs, and horses out on a farm. Urbanization means most children never know farm animals because city life puts up signs saying "No Pets." Perhaps this very separation has built up beastly pressures in little children and has increased the need for stories of animals like Josephine to reconnect the child with instinctual being.

Valuable offerings in nonfiction for children interested in farm animals include Lindee Climo's *Chester's Barn* (1982) and Janet Foster's *The Wilds of Whip-poor-will Farm* (1982). Joanne Oppenheim and Barbara Reid call young children to fine observation in *Have You Seen Birds?* (1986), in which lilting descriptions of specific birds are accompanied by detailed, accurate pictures modelled in brightly colored wax, suggesting the trim, bright texture of eye, beak, and plumage. Realistic paintings of puffins guarantee a charmed response to Pamela Hall's *On the Edge of the Eastern Ocean* (1982), one of the few children's books written in English and then translated into French.

Animal Parables

As we know from watching children respond to *The Tale of Peter Rabbit, The Wind in the Willows,* and *Charlotte's Web,* stories of small animals are particularly comforting and illuminating to little children when they first feel the constraints of discipline and duty, the fickleness of friendship, and the possibility of accident and death, or the simpler stresses of physical maturing.

In some books animals clearly act as substitutes for people, as they do in the French *Babar* stories. One obviously Canadian series follows Ms. Beaver as she travels across Canada, solving problems with endearing panache. Readers pick up activist, conservationist, and feminist messages from *Ms. Beaver Travels East* (1979) and other stories in Rosemary Allison's series, along with a cartoonist's impression of the beaver's appearance, but nothing of the real beaver's ways. Readers get nothing like the detail of animal behavior they would find in *Sajo and Her Beaver People*—which along with its realism also implicitly conveys the conservationist and libertarian ideas of Grey Owl. Reading about Ms. Beaver is fun, but the story does not exploit the intriguing parallels and differences between the ideologically motivated energy of the human and the instinctual industry of the beaver.

Another series closer to Babar uses an elephant named Douglas as a hero. Several good realistic elephant stories have in fact been published in Canada as a result of the accidental death here of Jumbo the famous circus star of Victorian days. Mark Thurman, however, shows us how Douglas the elephant learns to ride a bike, share his toys, and cope with a cold. The books are charming and are particularly attractive to slow learners, who perhaps identify with Douglas's elephantine clumsiness. In *The Elephant's Cold* (1981), Douglas's enormous "nose" makes a bad cold into a terrible problem. But except for his proboscis and his size, Douglas does not reflect to children any of the real attributes of his species. Similarly, *Franklin in the Dark,* by Paulette Bourgeois (1986), makes whimsical use of the turtle's appearance to provide a comforting story for small children bedevilled by fear. Franklin teaches the timid reader to accept and to use his "shell" of natural gifts. Although the story conveys a good lesson for children that involves an observation on a single aspect of the turtle, its self-transported shelter, the story evades any sense of the other aspects of real turtledom.

In producing comforting animal fables, authors and publishers step back from full-length realistic stories intended for 10- or 11-year-olds to shorter books, brightly illustrated, for children in the earlier grades. But audiences often foil the publishers' intentions—witness the adolescents who make a cult of *Winnie-the-Pooh,* or the adults who feel at home following the adventures of the March Hare, the Dormouse, the Caterpillar, and the Cheshire Cat. Some recent animal fables, housed on the junior shelves, slip into the hearts of more advanced readers because of their miniature charm, their fun, and their restorative force.

Such a book is *The House Mouse* by Dorothy Joan Harris (1973). This little book (five-by-seven inches) comes from Warne of London and New York, the firm that gave the Beatrix Potter stories their perfect format. Barbara Cooney's engaging watercolors for *The House Mouse* also are reminiscent of Potter's. Harris's is a longer and more complex story than Potter's, and although the human hero Jonathan is only four years old, the story of his management of a doll's house and his midnight encounters with the brassy mouse who moves in is attractive to older children. The mouse is demanding and inconsiderate (like four-year-old boys).

Jonathan works at keeping the mouse's house tidy and well supplied with chocolate cookies. As the seasons change, Jonathan grows out of his interest in the mouse and the house, and the mouse moves out to the fields. Simply told, with the surface charm of miniaturized detail, this book also carries an effective subtext about growing up.

Marshall Saunders, the eccentric creator of Canada's most widely read animal stories, lived in a fantastic home. Wild birds could fly into the ravine side windows of her home and then flutter up through the domestic menagerie of monkeys, kittens, parrots, dogs, and caged canaries. Then they could fly out the upper windows to freedom. Marshall Saunders helped children see birds, animals, and themselves. Perhaps her strange house symbolizes the effect of animal stories on children: the liberating excitement of wings of wildness moving through the reader's mind.

8

Girls' Choices

Like all genres of women's literature, Canadian literature for girls presents many paradoxes. Girls' books constitute nothing like the bulk of boys' adventure stories, yet of all Canadian books for children those by Lucy Maud Montgomery remain alone in worldwide popularity and influence. Girls are supposed to enjoy romances; but the canon of Canadian stories for girls presents very little to satisfy those who relish love scenes. Indeed, romantic elements had to be written into *Anne of Green Gables* to satisfy a television audience—in spite of the evidence of millions of girls who have accepted L. M. Montgomery's refusal to focus on the Gilbert motif. The happy ending, supposed to be a female addiction, is notably absent in the books Canadian girls have enjoyed most—unless the survival of the rapacious grandmother in *Jalna* can be considered a happy ending. Furthermore, although a good number of Canadian writers, male and female, suffered a disadvantage as outsiders when it came to finding British or American publishers, many women besides Montgomery and Mazo de la Roche found success and prosperity through their pens.

Today the most esteemed writers in Canada are women such as Margaret Atwood, Margaret Laurence, Alice Munro, and Gabrielle Roy. All these women have achieved a wide, mixed audience partly through books that concentrate on the experience of girls. Consequently, we have the unique opportunity to make a comparison between books designed to give pleasure and guidance to an audience of Canadian girls and fiction for adults describing girls' pleasures and aspirations as perceived by witty and sensitive novelists.

Girls between the ages of 13 and 16 are capable of complex mental processes. Adolescent thought is flexible and powerful, moving into formal logical operations, making hypotheses, abstracting, classifying ideas by logical systems, and focusing on possibilities rather than realities.[1] This power of logic, however, may be more inhibited in teenaged girls than in boys, because of a concurrent crisis in self-definition. Self-conscious and self-aware, adolescents are anxious to integrate all aspects of the self into a single identity,[2] but in girls that integration may be deflected by social confusion. Some girls' books about school life have played a particularly strong part in suggesting that girls accept a self-effacing, subordinate role.[3]

Feminists tell us we need a "herstory" of literature. Certainly in children's literature books by and for the female half of the population have not been accorded extensive critical treatment. Shelves of serious studies extend consideration to *Huckleberry Finn* and *Treasure Island,* but nineteenth-century critics, generally trained in a male-dominated university system, have joined male publishers, editors, reviewers, and bookstore owners and buyers in an unconscious conspiracy that has set women's books and particularly books for girls outside the pale. *Anne of Green Gables* is a case in point: no serious analysis was accorded this novel from the time of its publication in 1908 until the 1970s.

L. M. Montgomery's work followed a century of Canadian books for teenaged girls. Her innovations changed the genre in the century that followed. A review of the generally sweet and innocuous stories that preceded Montgomery's clarifies the international formulas to which they adhered, adds a sense of the Canadian differentials, and suggests the gradual swelling of subthemes and counterplots: the "ironic subtexts" to which a modern feminist critic, Rachel Du Plessis, alerts us in *Writing beyond the Ending.*[4]

Domestic Piety

Many of the earliest Canadian books written for women readers were picked up and enjoyed by girls. Adult books could surely be entrusted to them, since Victorian taboos guaranteed that nothing in family fiction would bring a blush to the maiden cheek. Early books bear titles ominously suggesting the alternatives to the expected "happy ending" of courtship and marriage: Julia Beckwith Hart's *St. Ursula's Convent, or, The Nun of Canada* (1824) and H. M. Bowdler's *Pen Tamar; or, The History of an Old Maid* (1830).[5] When she wrote *St. Ursula's Convent* Julia Beckwith Hart was only 17. This adventurous girl, the daughter of a French Canadian woman and a New Brunswick businessman, had traveled from St. John's to Quebec city by canoe. Her novel presents more conventional excitements, however. It begins with schoolgirl friendships, or "convent attachments" in Quebec, then its sprightly young ladies are wafted to the aristocratic home of Lord Durham in England, and to romances with Lord Dudley and Lord Grenville. Before they return to the "gulph of St. Lawrence," the girls uncover the secrets of their own identity and also unravel the tragedy in the life of Mother St. Catharine. Thanks to them, the good nun is released from her conventual vows and restored to her long-lost husband and children. Wedding ceremonies ensue in England, at which astonished villagers are encouraged to join the gentry in dancing on the lawn, in "our Canadian fashion" (Hart, 207). This naive and charming story, probably written "for the edification of the young,"[6] emphasizes the mutual devotion of the girls and concludes with their happiness at spending their summers together, until growing families redirect their affections.

The title and subtitle of another very early book suggests the ambivalence of girl readers' interests. The title of Mary Bennett's 1838 novel, *The Canadian Girl or the Pirate's Daughter,* suggests high-seas adventures, but the subtitle, *A Story of the Affections,* places conventional emphasis on sentimentality.

Hardship, bravely borne, furnishes the plot of several novels of the mid-Victorian period, such as Margaret Murray Robertson's

Christie Redfern's Troubles (1866) and *Shenac's Work at Home: A Story of Canadian Life* (1868), and Agnes Maule Machar's *Katie Johnstone's Cross* (1870). The subtitle of the latter, "A Canadian Tale," recurs in several other books, indicating perhaps that British readers' interest was extended to the loyal colony, or else that Canadian readers could be lured by fiction set in familiar territory. "L.G."'s title, *Jessie Grey* (1870), does not alert us to Canadian content or to trouble, but the author addresses her readers, "Dear Canadian children . . . trouble is necessary to bring the heart to God."[7] Because Jessie's little sister drowns, her mother dies, and Jessie is sent away to school in Toronto, reading this Canadian tale will presumably prepare young girls "for whatever trouble God sends." ("L. G.," viii). Nowhere in these early stories is there a hint of rebellion against either divine or parental restraints.

Girls in Training

The increasing freedom of girls at the turn of the twentieth century is reflected in stories in which parental power is partially eclipsed by the girls' absence from home or their attending boarding schools. *Grace Morton,* by Henrietta Skelton (1873), is set not in the home but in Madame Gratto's "celebrated boarding school."[8] Here an upright, honest girl, reminiscent of Polly Milton in Louisa May Alcott's American novel *An Old Fashioned Girl* (1870), leads her schoolmates to a better life by preaching "love of my Saviour" and practicing charity; but there is fun en route— sleighing parties in the "glorious Canadian winter," schoolgirl slang "by gosh," and devious plotting to facilitate a teacher's romance. (The three girls, Violet, Maude and Minnie, wind up as bridesmaids.)

Two books that approach the notion of a girl's education in Canada less formally are Agnes Machar's *Marjorie's Canadian Winter* (1892) and Anna Chapin Ray's *Janet: Her Winter in Quebec* (1908). Marjorie's story begins and ends with her devotion to her father. When he sends her to Montreal, she becomes attached to a fatherly McGill University professor and gains from him a sense of the natural beauty of the St. Lawrence and the Saguenay, as well as an awareness of the geologic prehistory, Indian legends, and more recent history of Quebec.

Janet's story is livelier. The young British visitor, Janet, with her brother Day and his two friends—one American, one Canadian—and a pretty American girl form an attractive quintet of well-mannered young people. Their social relations are presented with good local color and a well-designed plot; there is a tentative romance, but Janet's main devotion is to her invalid mother.

Both stories still have a strong appeal to girls just hovering at the edge of maturity. Like L. M. Montgomery's stories, they hold the question of mating at arm's length. Yet in the common fashion of girls' school stories (as summarized in *You're a Brick Angela!*)[9] they emphasize that girls should develop a love of home, a deference to authority, and a suppression of any personal dreams of success and fame. The mixture of sprightliness and sentiment in late-nineteenth-century portraits of girls increasingly reflects the rise of "Kailyard fiction"—novels, mostly Scottish, that idealize family warmth.

Towards the Green World

Four other developments foreshadow the appearance of *Anne of Green Gables* in 1908. First, something of the spirit of adventure that boys' books had popularized as characteristic of life in Canada rubbed off onto girls' books. Bessie Marchant's first books, such as *Athabaska Bill* (1900), featured boy heroes, but she turned in 1905 to *A Daughter of the Ranges* and went on to produce a whole series of lively adventure stories with western Canadian settings and female protagonists. In Merchant's books, girls ride the range, rescue the family fortune, lead a group of young friends in brave adventures, and generally play a role the reverse of the pious, suffering young ladies in earlier novels.

Secondly, American interest in the region popularized in Longfellow's poem "Evangeline" led to several children's books about the Atlantic provinces. *Amy in Acadia* (1905) by Helen Reed is one example, rather patronizing in tone and pompous in style, but characteristic in taking an interest in Atlantic Canada. For adult readers, Charles G. D. Roberts, a Maritimer who published his very popular animal stories with the Page Company of Boston around this time, also created romantic novels such as *A Sister to Evangeline* (1898) and *Barbara Ladd* (1902), which featured high-spirited Maritime girls.

More importantly, Roberts's fine landscape poetry, with its evocations of sandshore and meadows and hills slanting to the sea, had created awareness of the beauty of this Canadian region.[10] Other Canadian poets, Roberts's contemporaries such as Bliss Carman and Archibald Lampman, also began to break away from British poetic diction and landscape conventions and to ring the changes in descriptions of Canadian seasons and colors and skies. This poetry, written in the heady days after Confederation fused the British North American colonies into a single dominion in 1867, was widely published abroad and stirred a taste for descriptions of Canadian scenes in readers in Great Britain and the United States. Disseminated at home through the school readers in Canadian schools, the post-Confederation Canadian landscape poets helped the next generation of writers articulate their response to local scenes.

Finally, a series of stories about orphans appeared. Ambitious orphan boys had already starred in the American rags-to-riches tales of Horatio Alger and in more sentimental stories such as Gene Stratton Porter's *Freckles* (1904). Bright, unconventional orphan girls made best-sellers out of such American novels as Alice Hegan Rice's *Lovey Mary* (1903). In Kate Douglas Wiggin's *Rebecca of Sunnybrook Farm* (1903) Rebecca has a mother but is sent, like an orphan, as a poor dependent to hostile substitute parents. In Canada the presence of orphans had a special twist because great numbers of orphaned children had been "exported" to the Dominion in a scheme to relieve British economic and educational crises. The "Barnardo Boys," sent to hard labor in Canadian farms by philanthropist Dr. Barnardo, were just one example of the orphan phenomenon, which most travellers of that time considered a colorful part of the Canadian scene. Anne Woodruff's *Betty and Bob* (1903) follows two Canadian orphans who are shipped by train from Montreal to a farm in Lincoln County, Ontario. The story ends with a Christmas scene in which the reluctant foster parents finally accept the children as son and daughter.

The Imagined Island

Anne of Green Gables presents an imaginative orphan, intense in her response to beauty, eager for love and admiration, and ingenious in her attempts to find this longed-for acceptance. Anne Shirley, the red-haired girl who comes to an unwelcoming Prince Edward Island home, is blind to social proprieties of the kind that so controlled Robertson's character Christie Redfern; she turns the schoolroom into a battleground for her ambition; and she confuses literature and life in her fine and funny yearning for adventure and romance. Thus she lets girls laugh away their embarrassments, their frustrations.

The first half of Anne's story consists of a series of "scrapes"—dyeing her red hair green, getting her friend Diana drunk by mistaking raspberry liqueur for fruit juice, leaping into bed on top of an old lady, in exuberant glee at being treated as a valued guest. In the later part of the novel, the scrapes diminish as Anne sets herself to becoming a sensible achiever. In the end she gives up her vaunting ambitions in order to help members of the older generation and to serve her community as a teacher. The sad-sweet ending avoids open acceptance of the romance formula. Anne does not accept her suitor Gilbert Blythe and the prospect of living happily ever after as wife and mother. She keeps her eye on the bend in the road and remains, for girls in particular and for generations of later readers in general, the embodiment of the desire for freedom, self-expression, and intense, private responses to life.

Anne's creator offered a further gift—an imagined world complete in regional details, including flaming autumn, sparkling snow, frothing blossom time, and summer ripeness, as well as a human society full and funny. L. M. Montgomery continued to return to this world of beauty and friendly sentiment in further fictions: she wrote 8 more "Anne" books, 3 "Emily" books, 2 about "Pat of Silver Bush," and 12 other books for girls.

Feminine Archetypes

Montgomery's imagined island community of Avonlea dominated the market for girls' books for many years. Nevertheless, the British publishing firm of Blackie kept alive an alternative world, the far western ranges of adventure, by publishing a steady stream of stories by Bessie Merchant, and another British firm, Nelson, chimed in with a pair of action-packed stories by E. E. Cowper. Cowper's *Witch of the Wilds* (1910) and *Girls on the Gold Trail* (1911) both concern a girl called Peter, her Indian girlfriend, and their search for a Skookum or Wise Man. Together Peter and Mikawe follow "the trail of the sun dogs into the trackless glory of the wilderness."[11] Olaf Baker's *Heart o' the West* (1912) flings girl adventurers into a similar world of redskins, canoes, revenge, and the search for gold. The prolific and successful writer May Wynne tells the story of a family's search for gold on a western ranch in *Two Girls in the Wild* (1920). An American publisher followed up on the fashion for Anne with *Our Little Canadian Cousin of the great North-west* (1923).

The best of the portraits of a "girl in the wild" appears in Marshall Saunders's *Bonnie Prince Fetlar* (1920). Superficially, as we would expect from Marshall Saunders, this is (to quote the subtitle) "The Story of a Pony and His Friends." But at the intense center of the book is a fiercely rebellious girl nicknamed "Cassowary" after the self-blinding, wild-running ostrich. Cassowary's real name, Jeanne Mance, is her parents' tribute to a French-Canadian heroine of colonial days who was selflessly devoted to nursing; but Cassowary prefers animals to people. In a frontier Ontario setting in Muskoka, Cassowary lives with an adoptive family whose neighbors include a postwar mix of people—a shell-shocked ex-soldier, another soldier learning to walk with artificial feet, and a Russian called "Bolshy." Cassowary is schooled by social and natural forces to accept her own identity and to control her wildness.

Cassowary's sudden jealous furies reflect a world and a time harsher than the golden days of Anne's idyllic island. The continued demand for more about Anne and her island was better met by stories less adventurous than those wild tales and more suggestive of the roles actually open to girls and women. *Anne of the Island* (1915) is L. M. Montgomery's realistic account of a young girl's foray into higher education. It was followed by stories similarly focused on school girls' intense friendships and their endless discussions of values, beliefs, and themselves. Toronto publishers chose authors who used local detail to interest Canadian readers but followed the British *Girls' Own Paper* in modelling boarding school life. Beatrice Embree's *The Girls of Miss Cleveland's* (1920) and Ethel Hume's *Judy of York Hill* (1923) are good examples of school stories. Marjorie McMurchy (Lady Willison) in *Letty Bye* (1937) brought a more contemporary style and vision to the study of girls in a school setting.

In *Anne of Avonlea* (1909) the protagonist has become a teacher, pursuing one of the few careers open to a girl at that time. Anne concludes a happy year by a decision to go to university to further her education, deflecting the appeal of her quiet suitor, Gilbert Blythe. In a romance different in tone and conclusion though comparable in social realism, Nina Jamieson's 16-year-old heroine in *The Hickory Stick* (1921), like Anne, undertakes teaching in a poor, unresponsive school, this time in the Ontario Bruce Peninsula. Jamieson reduces the force of her reforming heroine by providing marriage as a way out of schoolteaching. In an interesting reversal of *Jane Eyre,* a man crippled in the early part of the novel rises to vigorous health and returns to a position of dominance within the family, thus ensuring a traditional happy ending to the story.

Anne's House of Dreams (1917), the most complex of the Anne series, gave readers what so many of them had been requesting: a story of Anne as bride, young wife, and mother. But *Anne's*

House of Dreams shows little of the pleasures of marriage, whereas the misery of marriage is pictured with dark suggestiveness. Anne's neighbor, a mysterious, passionate young woman, is tied to a good-natured, brainless wreck; Anne's days as a bride move beyond the death of her first baby to the birth of baby Jem. In the remote community where *Anne's House of Dreams* is situated, Anne finds new parent figures: Captain Jim, a storyteller who lives in a lighthouse and idealizes women, and Miss Cornelia, who lives in a house painted obtrusively green and hates men. According to Annis Pratt's analyses in *Archetypal Patterns in Women's Fiction,* the symbolism of the story constitutes a provocative subtext: the green world is liberating, the lighthouse stands for sexuality, and Anne's finding new surrogate parents foreshadows rebirth.[12]

A more traditional story of a girl's home-making is Mary Outram's *The Story of a Log House* (1920). Here a golden-haired heroine named Kitty works alone in the forest with her Indian friends, helping her neighbors find redemption from sin.

In the mid-1920s, L. M. Montgomery created a new heroine, Emily, to whom she assigns yet another role, that of creative writer. Emily is another orphan, and her other names are "Byrd" and "Starr." Of *Emily of New Moon* (1923), Alice Munro writes, "What's central to the story, and may be harder to write about than sex or the confused feelings in families, is the development of a child—and a girl child, at that—into a writer."[13] For the modern novelist, Emily's exultant insistence on developing her own gift, the "flash" of creativity, gives the book validity. L. M. Montgomery adds to the novel four minor characters, with suggestive names, who will reemerge in the later "Emily" books as symbols of her alternate selves: Dean Priest, who is cold, crippled, and domineering; Teddy Kent, a curly-haired youth like Laurie/Teddy in *Little Women,* and with Laurie's storybook charm and openness of affection; Mr. Carpenter, the teacher who helps Emily build her craft as a writer; and Ilse *(ipse?),* the strange child of a dead mother and an embittered father. Because Montgomery knew about Freud's theories and was a troubled self-analyst, the psychological depth and originality she lent to the portrait of Emily produced a book that has served deep needs for generations of girls moving (to use Freudian terms) through identity crisis to a consistent self-definition.

Linking the identity crisis to the yearning for romance, Montgomery created a novel intended for an adult audience in *The Blue Castle* (1926). The heroine is named Valancy—probably after Isabella Valancy Crawford, the gifted poet of the 1880s. Because she is misunderstood and undervalued by her family, she escapes into a secret life with a gruff, unkempt, asocial man, who turns out to have not only a heart of gold but also a millionaire's bank account; he is also the author of Valancy's favorite books. In his Muskoka retreat she reenters the green world of nature. Sexual joy is obliquely suggested, but the real bliss in the story comes from a sense of kinship and from Valancy's discovery of her freedom to reject her patriarchal clan and to choose her own companion and her own way of life.

Margerie Bonner's *Rainbow at Night* (1935), a Nova Scotia idyll, ends more tragically, adding dark shadows to romance in a fashion reminiscent of both *Emily's Quest* (1927) and the earlier *Anne's House of Dreams*.

Survival

Girls in the post-World War I years could enjoy many serious romances written for and about young adults. Martha Trent's *Phoebe Marshal: Somewhere in Canada* (1919), like L. M. Montgomery's *Rilla of Ingleside* (1921), presents a response to the experiences of war, as filtered through the eyes of a young woman.

But the novelist who became addictively popular with girls and women in the 1920s and 1930s was Mazo De la Roche. Her first novel, *Jalna,* which appeared in 1927, was followed by 15 other novels. De la Roche also wrote several unusual books for and about very young children. All her novels created for readers in Canada and abroad a picture of tempestuous family life, an exotic style of living, and complex romantic involvements in an Anglo-Irish-Canadian home. De la Roche's matriarch Adeline Whiteoak heralds the creation of many more indomitable aging female characters by later women writers. Margaret Laurence's Hagar Shipley in *The Stone Angel* is an old Tartar comparable to Adeline Whiteoak. Girls have accepted, hated, and identified with these tough old women as part of a maturing process. De la Roche also provides other archetypes for a female version of the "hero with a thousand faces": Alayne, the cool professional; Finch, the tempestuous rebel; and Meg, the egoist who makes a cult of service. De la Roche's immensely popular books have helped change girls' assumptions about the possibility of achieving an independent career.

Unlike the works of both De la Roche and L. M. Montgomery, which took place in pastoral settings, Dora Olive Thompson's stories depict the sordid scenes of depression era cities. Thompson published with the Religious Tract Society a series comprised of 8 lively, well-plotted novels, among which *That Girl Ginger* (1931) is the best. Despite Ginger's unfeminine name, this red-headed child of the depression accepts a mothering, nurturing role, finding unconventional solutions for the problems of her family and her neighborhood. Ginger has grit; she survives. Realistic in tone and setting, the Thompson novels celebrate the power of a well-intentioned girl to withstand poverty and family breakdown under new urban pressures. Ginger's downright goodness recalls earlier "kailyard" fiction such as Alice Hegan Rice's *Mrs. Wiggs of the Cabbage Patch*. Books written specifically for teenaged girls virtually ceased to appear in Canada during World War II. In the "cold war" years, and in the permissive "flower power" period that followed in the 1960s, adolescent girls swung between the adult stories of Mazo De la Roche (whose last novel, *Morning at Jalna,* appeared in 1960) and their counterparts from the English pens of Daphne Du Maurier, Elizabeth Goudge, Norah Lofts, and Rumer Godden. Only from the pen of the French-Canadian writer Gabrielle Roy did there come stories of women's lives and values that were different from standard romances. Her regional idylls such as *Where Nests the Water Hen* (1950) presented very strong pictures of mothers. A series of autobiographical books offer an enlargement of the Anglo-Saxon Protestant values that were dominant in the immediate postwar years: *Street of Riches* (1957, originally published in French in 1955) portrayed childhood in St.

Boniface, the Francophone city twinned with Winnipeg, and *The Road Past Altamont* (1966) described the circle of Roman Catholic life of a girl, her mother, and grandmother. Roy's books have been much admired and widely read.

Nevertheless, the imaginative life of girls of the post–World War II period seems to have been dominated, as Fred Inglis postulates in *The Promise of Happiness,* by a "passion to be loved if possible, but to be wanted and possessed at all costs, including the cost of freedom" (Inglis, 163). In the 1960s, caught in a confusion of desires and ideals between the confrontational politics of America in the Vietnam years and the cheeky cheery fun of Beatles-dominated Britain, Canadian writers produced no literary manifesto and enunciated no revelatory myth. Yet writers of girls' books suggested that an uneasy resentment of their limited roles was felt by young women in Canada as well as in the rest of the English-speaking world.

Surfacing

In the 1970s several talented Canadian women writers joined Gabrielle Roy in offering readers an account of their own maturation. Girls still in the process of reaching adulthood took these finely-tuned books from the adult shelves and glimpsed the complexity of that process. Margaret Laurence's *A Bird in the House* appeared in 1970. Fictionalizing her memories of growing up in the prairies in the 1930s, Laurence offered a portrait strangely reminiscent of *Anne of Green Gables* in many ways: an imaginative lonely girl, dominated by adult powers, responds with sensitivity to the colors and rhythms of her local setting. Alice Munro's tougher, more disturbing *Lives of Girls and Women* (1971) supplies a new ending to the story of *Anne of Green Gables*. In Munro's novel the girl refuses to accept her Ontario village. She gets out of town, taking her gifts of intensity and articulation with her. Mary Peate of Montreal published a third version of the female bildungsroman, Canadian style, in *The Girl in a Red River Coat* (1970), a wry story of depression days.

Laurence and Munro have both attested to the effect on them of repeated readings of L. M. Montgomery's work. The characters Anne and Emily ratified the authors' sense of vocation, their love of words, and their commitment to imagination; and the knowledge that Montgomery had succeeded in weaving her fables out of Canadian materials was an empowering inspiration to these and other later writers.

In 1972, Margaret Atwood published *Surfacing,* an adult novel set in the lake and cottage country north of the urban strip dominated by Toronto, and *Survival,* a critical enunciation of archetypes of the Canadian imagination. Both books had inestimable effects on successive Canadian writing and both were widely read in Canadian high schools throughout the 1970s.[14]

Out west, other powerful influences were gathering force in adult fiction. In Alberta, Rudy Wiebe added intensity, focus on native myths, and moral complexity to the adult novel. The exuberant post-modernist novelist Robert Kroetsch reordered style. "We insist on staying multiple, and by that strategy we accommodate to our climate, our economic system, and our neighbours," he said.[15] The desire to root story precisely in a particular Canadian place while maintaining an openness of style affected Margaret Laurence and other women writers, including those producing stories for girls. At the same time children's literature came under critical scrutiny in Britain, the United States, and Canada, coincident with the feminist insistence on examining uncanonized genres, particularly those in the female domain. A surge of experiments in openness and depth marked novels for girls in the late 1970s and 1980s, which showed a kind of realism very different from both the brash explicitness of teenage exposé novels in America and the class-conscious dark realism in British novels about maturation.

Lives of Girls

Whether they present protagonists who are 10 years old or 16, recent stories about the lives of girls are suitable for teenaged readers intent on embellishing their memories of their own past. Whether they deal with warm but overcrowded families or families in the bleak process of breakup, they suit girls reassessing their own families. Postmodernist disjunction of style is also aesthetically satisfying for adolescents, capable as they are of holding a constant in memory, correlating alternatives, and sorting out disjointed time sequences. Time-shift fantasy makes appropriate reading for readers who are now firmly grounded in reality yet able to play intellectually with possibilities and to compensate mentally for transformations in appearance. Contemporary books for girls fan out to show that Canadian authors fully realize these potentials in their readers. Modern stories reveal the achievements, traditional and new, and the puzzlements, accustomed and unexpected, in the lives of girls.

Some of the newer books are lighthearted. Marian Engel presents a miniature and comic version of a sister's revolt against male dominance in *My Name Is Not Odessa Yarker* (1977). *Here She is, Ms. Teeny Wonderful!* (1984), by Martyn Godfrey, is a spoof of the beauty contest syndrome, and a celebration of the exuberant energy of a real winner who is a bike-racing and jumping addict. Other new books are tied to fads and follies that have been highlighted by media attention. *I Was a 15-year-old Blimp* (1985) is Patty Stren's sad and funny exposé of the sense of inadequacy that can lead to bulimia. The more penetrating stories, however, are set not in the urban high-rise world of Yuppie competitions but in the communities where Canadian particulars of setting, values, and social mix contribute a unique flavor. Particularly in west coast villages, in the mountains, and in the foothill country of Alberta, serious writers have created fictions that use regional details to clarify the pattern of feminine experience.

Many western novels use the devastating summer storms in which nature overthrows human rational ordering and enterprise to highlight events in the maturing process. Ten-year-old Jessica in *The Lady of the Strawberries* is a sturdy, sensible child, racked by family breakdown but doggedly setting out, like Mary in *The Secret Garden,* to make her own "bit of earth" bear fruit. Calgary country does not foster the growth of scarlet beauty: Jessica's strawberries are flattened by a summer storm, and the comforting "Lady" she has constructed as a scarecrow is swept away too. Helen Chetin, the author of *The Lady of the Strawberries*, is an American writer who spent 13 years in Calgary. Her sturdy, simple style shows the influence of Laura Wilder's prairie fiction, but in this novel Chetin recognizes problems unknown to Laura Wilder. Her small heroine finds parent surrogates who reflect Canadian myths, literary and traditional: Shirley, a red-haired teacher, whose name recalls Montgomery's Anne, and a Stoney Indian, who provides a different vision of earth, animals, and people. But this novel ultimately denies Jessica the power of creating and pretending and sets her back into a traditional relation to her parents and to the little brother who is her charge.

A child very different from straightforward Jessica appears in *Julie* (1985). This book, set in the Saskatchewan prairies, was written by Cora Taylor, who studied fiction writing with W. O. Mitchell and Rudy Wiebe. Like Mitchell's *Who Has Seen the Wind* or Wiebe's *Peace Shall Destroy Many*, *Julie* presents a child's experience with mystic intensity. Julie is troubled by a mysterious power of extrasensory perception. Artifacts and natural elements—an old quilt, cloud formations, a bending tree—give her access to foreseeing the future. When she uses her psychic power to ward off death from her father, the effort costs her the strength of her vision; a storm ensues and the old tree falls and other talismans are broken. In this book, as in Chetin's *The Lady of the Strawberries*, the surging sense of personal vision, which Montgomery's Emily called "the flash," is ultimately reduced and controlled. Yet even though the author dims the power of Julie's vision, this intense story casts an aura of significance and dignity over the girl's inner life and special powers.

Other books focus not on the lonely creativity first recognized in prepuberty but on a later stage of development when girls encounter the troubling onslaught of early sexuality. *Snow Apples* (1984) connects the awakening of passion with concurrent troubles in mother-daughter relations. Using first-person narration, Mary Razzell draws on her memories of 1945, the year the men came home from war, to create a turbulent family drama. A bitter and unbalanced mother, a careless, selfish father, a young lover enforcing the double standards for male and female propriety, all frustrate the efforts of the 16-year-old protagonist to develop her own life. Razzell sets this strong story of teenage sexuality on the western shoreline, using ferry rides to Vancouver, local scenes at home, at school, at community dances, and on the beach for symbolic effects. Abandoned by her lover, mistreated by her father, derided by her mother, and debilitated by the terrifying termination of her pregnancy, Sheila descends into a nadir of despair. Ironically, the older woman, Helga, who helps Sheila through the trauma of abandonment and abortion is a woman half demented by the tragic loss of her own motherhood. The ending of the novel effectively presents a series of false closures. The supportive father turns out to be a liar; the golden world that the mother appears to offer is a delusion. Sheila, who seems to be escaping to Vancouver and a chance to train as a nurse, is last seen with a new boyfriend, watching Doris Day movies.

A more complex exploration of the connections between sexuality and the power of the mothering impulse appears in Gabrielle Roy's *Children of My Heart* (1979, first published in French in 1977). Stories based on her experiences in teaching are fused into a serial sketch form, which like the structure of *Lives of Girls and Women* and *A Bird in the House* breaks the norm of narrative. Roy focuses on the job of teaching with an intensity that recalls Nina Jamieson's *Hickory Stick* and L. M. Montgomery's *Anne of Avonlea*. Each of the appealing, disadvantaged, responsive children of western prairie immigrants appears to the teacher as a potential Anne—a child to be encouraged and humored and inspired. But Roy suggests a strange blurring of the roles of mother and lover in the final section of the book. The boy Mederic, the child of a wealthy farmer and a Metis woman, is handsome and wild, lonely, resentful and tender, a student and a child. He also represents a dark and partly savage male force for the young teacher, "child that I was myself." The symbolic sexuality here is more powerfully suggestive than in the specific reportage in *Snow Apples*—though that in turn is infinitely more stirring than the exploitative blatancy of a Judy Blume novel. Dignity and tragedy inhere in Roy's treatment of undeveloped and inhibited passion.

The trauma of working out a relationship with a young man who is knotted in his own problems may drive girls to dreaming of an imaginary lover safely distanced in the past. Ann Walsh's *Your Time, My Time* (1984) uses the time-shift form to gain access to a wistful romance. More depth in creating both the world of dream and the world of reality and in suggesting the impact of the one on the other appears in Janet Lunn's *Shadow in Hawthorn Bay*.

Alternately, some books for girls counteract the steamy insistence on sex by recognizing the power of adolescents to respond to ideals as well as to people. Complex reasoning and complex attachments challenge and satisfy the stretching social sense of the adolescent reader. One dark but dignified account of adolescent idealism appears in *One Proud Summer* by Marsha Hewitt and Claire Mackay (1981). This novel, based on memories of a strike in Valleyfield, Quebec, recollects a time of class conflict when the rebelliousness of young women was harnessed to significant social action. The troubled girls in this novel offer role models not in romance but in social responsibility. In the same year, 1981, Bernice Thurman Hunter published *That Scatterbrain Booky,* the first novel in a three-part bildungsroman that also emends the overemphasis on romance by tracing the intellectual and imaginative growth of a girl in Toronto during the 1930s.

Finally, *Jasmin,* by Jan Truss (1982), makes full and beautiful use of the archetypes of the feminine quest, while richly reusing many of the details now given intertextual force by readers' familiarity with the Canadian literary tradition. Jasmin's junkyard home, her fat and kindly mother, and her sense of being an outsider at school recall the childhood world of Morag in Margaret Laurence's *The Diviners*. The swarming family life also recalls the full family warmth of the Watsons in Nellie McClung's *Sowing Seeds in Danny,* and Jasmin, like Pearl Watson, has been thrust too early into a surrogate mother's role. Like Margaret Laurence, Jan Truss experiments with a mixed narrative voice: some chapters suggest the amorphous softness of the mother overrunning grammatical forms; others catch the cold calculations of Eglantine, the shadowing egocentric sister; in others the cobwebs of a retarded child's bafflement are traced in illogical syntactical structures; and in the main narrative stream Keatsian poetry runs as a clear current in Jasmin's mind as she tries to shut out the other voices.

Jasmin begins her classic quest when the moon comes out, slipping away in her green jacket and straw hat, carrying her grandmother's quilt and a scarlet gown. She drops into the green world of Rocky Mountain forests and ravines, takes possession of this natural world, finds a cave where she can live as she pleases, and then takes possession of her self and her ability to create. She reproduces natural beauty, force, and cruelty in small clay models. Living like a wild thing she finds company in a small coyote, for she believes, like the Indians, that Coyote, the androgynous trickster god, can help girls as well as boys in the moment of transformation.

Summer storms and floods overtake her. The new "parents," strangers who pull her from her cave and drag her through icy water toward life in their golden home, are named "Jules" (suggesting his value, and also echoing the name of the Metis lover in Margaret Laurence's Manawaka novels), and "Hana" (an appropriate echo of "Anne" in yet another red-haired character, and also a suggestion of the Jungian anima). With their help Jasmin regains self-respect and eventually a sense of responsibility. In a terrifying scene recalling the diving sequence in Atwood's *Surfacing,* she pulls Leroy, her retarded brother, into a kind of rebirth. Through her travail and the power of art in her clay models and in Hana Townsend's paintings, Leroy, the mute boy Jasmin has fostered, achieves a voice. He is enabled to articulate Jasmin's name. The Margaret Laurence echo sounds here again: the denouement recalls the final moment in *The Fire Dwellers* when a voiceless girl child first speaks. A similar moment occurs in L. M. Montgomery's *Rilla of Ingleside.* But in *Jasmin* the emphasis is on the desperate effort a girl must make, in order to ensure such articulation in a broken world.

9

Boys as Heroes

The earliest major Canadian adventure story, Catharine Parr Traill's *The Canadian Crusoes* (1852), used boys *and* girls as protagonists and combined a wilderness survival story with home drama and romance. In most nineteenth-century Canadian writing, however, boys' and girls' books reflect a separation in interests, in games, in jokes, and in vocations. Today a unisex world, in Canada as elsewhere, may be changing both literature and life, but the old separation of spheres, while it lasted, produced a phenomenal array of gender-specific initiation stories.

In adventure stories written for 13- and 14-year-old boys, the youthful hero appears as a figure of power, usually set against a hostile nature as well as a human villain. Moving through woods and waters accompanied by an admiring comrade, he pierces the heart of darkness, undergoes ordeals at the hands of animal and human antagonists, and emerges to begin the upward return to his own kingdom. Travelers' stories about Canada's terrain, its savage animal life, and its population of colorful adventurers suggested to early writers that this country could be the stage for all sorts of excitement involving boys: hunting, fighting, mining, ranching, trapping, and camping. Nineteenth-century writers all over the world exploited these Canadian excitements. Jules Verne and Benedict Revoil in France, William Butler and Mayne Reid in Ireland, Robert Ballantyne in Scotland, and Frederick Marryat and W. G. H. Kingston in England led the way, joined by native-born Canadians such as James De Mille, J. M. Oxley, and E. R. Young. All celebrated the redemptive boy hero, as delineated by Joseph Campbell in *Hero with a Thousand Faces*,[1] who saves the social, political, and economic empires of the adult world. For students of archetypal heroic narrative, this heap of books offers wonderful examples for analysis. For boy readers, each story adds a ratification of the rituals of masculinity.

But another kind of Canadian hero was waiting in the wings. Indian legends had long used Coyote the Trickster-god as a protagonist instead of the noble quester.[2] Perhaps a deeper knowledge of the Canadian world—its dramatically changing seasons, its mirages of space, its surprisingly cunning animals, its mutually masked ethnic groups—led to the emergence of a similar trickster as the hero of later boys' stories. The trickster boy-hero may enjoy lawbreaking and outwitting authority figures. He is glib, deceitful, and suspiciously ingenious. He may indulge in sexual games, wear disguises, or transform himself from evildoer to protective savior and back again. Such a young trickster, like the Indians' shape-shifter god Coyote, is a singularly appropriate hero for a land so variable and unpredictable. In the twentieth century Canadian books for boys have increasingly focused on the trickster hero, although the old pure-hearted lad often emerges as one of the trickster's many selves.

Wilderness Quest

Aptly, the first boys' adventure book written in Canada was a story about twins. In 1847 the anonymous author of *The Canadian Brothers: A Tale of the Western World* traced the opposing fates of 12-year-old boys captured by Indians in the Eastern townships of Quebec. But this double-edged story was preceded by the more idealistic, single-hearted *The Settlers in Canada* (1844), written in England. Its author, Captain Frederick Marryat, was already famous for such boys' books as *Poor Jack* (1840) and *Masterman Ready* (1841). In *The Settlers in Canada* Marryat capitalizes on a brief visit to Canada and tells a rousing tale in which trouble at home sends two brave English boys out to Canada with their family, where they are helped by the colorful old hunter Malachi Bone, Canadian-born Martin, and his Indian woman the Strawberry. The boys kill bear, grapple with wolves, cope with Angry Snake and his Indian band, and finally return triumphantly to an inheritance in England. Their younger brothers grow up in Canada and adopt woodsmen's ways. This is less a boy's book than a family story, but it established a setting, a cast of characters, and a set of ordeals that would dominate the boys' adventure books to come.

The Settlers in Canada is also the first of many Canadian quest stories that follow the classical circular pattern of outward voyage and return. Mayne Reid, an Irishman who eventually settled in the United States, produced *The Young Voyageurs* in 1852, in which three American boys travel to Hudson Bay, learn respect for the animals they have come to hunt there, and return safely home. Canada in these quest books is the testing ground; the hero's success there will permit reentry into a more comfortable (though less exciting) kingdom.

Most influential of these early stories is R. M. Ballantyne's *Snowflakes and Sunbeams; or, The Young Fur Traders* (1856). The subtitle quickly became the name by which this cheery, vigorous tale was known. Drawing on memories of his apprenticeship in the Hudson's Bay Company, Ballantyne created a convincing, energetic, funny narrative, and a story that is historically important as the earliest major boys' book mentioned in most histories of children's literature. *The Young Fur Traders* is an exciting tale of two clerks in the great trading company, one lad raised in the Red River Settlement, the other in Scotland; one is sent west to open up trade beyond the Saskatchewan in the Athabasca territory, and the other is sent north to the older and lonelier Fort York on Hudson Bay, near the frozen sea. Two older friends, Jacques Cadorac the woodsman and Redfeather the Indian guide, carry messages between the boys and teach them wilderness ways: how to paddle through rivers and lakes torn by howling northwest winds, how to make and break camp, how to stalk bear and trap silver fox, how to travel by snowshoe and sledge, and how to eat Indian feasts of dried meat, reindeer tongues, and marrowbones. The only villain in this world of comradeship and jokes is Misconna, but his attacks on the four friends end when an anonymous Indian dashes his tomahawk into Misconna's brain. Ballantyne introduces two idiosyncratic portraits of missionaries, one an Anglican the other a Methodist, and allows his high-spirited boys to slip into religious speculations, melancholy, and homesickness. Eventually the four friends circle back to Winnipeg, to Charley's cantankerous but loving father and to gentle sister Kate. Ballantyne adds a charming account of love at first resighting ("O Kate, . . . you've floored me quite flat!" cries the young trader[3]) and a boisterous climactic wedding dance, western style.

Ungava; or, A Tale of Esquimeaux-land (1857) and other later books by Ballantyne further fixed the Canadian north as a great stage for boys' adventures. Ballantyne's style is brisk and friendly, with occasional chatty directions to "you, reader," and for many generations of boys, his voice offers an honest invitation to a challenging, snowy world.

Another prolific writer, the Englishman W. H. G. Kingston, calling on Ballantyne's territory for his stories, introduced a new phase for the boy hero. In *The Trapper's Son* (1873) a boy disappears from home; when he returns years later it is to display the characteristics of the Indians with whom he has been traveling. "Going Indian" is a familiar phrase in Canadian slang; "going Indian" remains in many Canadian novels, and in the dreams of many boys it is an extension of the heroic quest.

It is a short step from "going Indian" to selecting an Indian as the central figure for a story, as William Butler did in *Red Cloud* (1882). Butler's Irish narrator meets the Sioux Red Cloud soon after crossing from the Winnipeg world of courtroom justice and fenced-in property into a realm of savage vengeance and open land. The Indian is intent on avenging the death of his father, who was betrayed by a dastardly white trader. The vengeful quest, lasting many seasons, leads the Indian and his Irish friend across the great lone land to the Rocky Mountains. Three more Indians, a Cree, an Assiniboine scout, and an Iroquois who is far from home, join the avengers. In the moment of crisis, however, Red Cloud is persuaded by the narrator to leave justice and execution to "the Great Spirit." There is no sister Kate to gentle the end of this novel, which has been womanless since the death of the narrator's mother in the opening chapter. Red Cloud's final gift to his white companion is a cache of gold nuggets, which had been hidden in the mountains by an old Sushwap and is now turned over to the white man who can use such stones in the world he will return to.

Boy readers found in Butler's book not only the fun of identifying with a noble savage but also powerful visual images of an empty land, varied in flora and fauna but stretching always to a beckoning horizon. Butler conveys a sharp sense of the movements of the little troupe across this land. Boxing in a hostile camp, zigzagging to escape an ambush, arrowing away from a burned refuge, the travelers lay down a geometric grid over the amorphous prairie. Maybe Colonel Butler's military training shows here, but the logical angular lines also reflect the white man's imposing order on native nomadic concepts of space.[4] Such logical strategies also reinforce the emphasis on mathematics and physics in boy's education.

Western Conflict

Intentions less ferocious than Red Cloud's carry successive young heroes through westward odysseys in late nineteenth-century books. Gordon Stables's *Wild Adventures Round the Pole* (1888) continues the emphasis on the far-reaching travel motif. In C. R. Kenyon's *The Young Ranchmen* (1891) young Ernest leaves a snug farmhouse on Lake Huron to undertake an adventurous westward trek, which ends happily in California. Ned and his friends go still farther west in Phillips-Wolley's *Gold, Gold in Cariboo!* (1894). The best of the far north stories comes from a man with the most experience, Egerton Ryerson Young. Young's lifetime of missionary observations fuses with an obviously intense reading of William Butler's travel books to produce *Three Boys in the Wild Northland, Summer* (1896) and *Winter Adventures of Three Boys in the Great Lone Land* (1899). C. L. Johnstone in *The Young Emigrants: A Story for Boys* (1898) takes his young heroes only as far as Regina and Medicine Hat. Johnstone's boy readers are advised to pull back from visions of wild adventures and settle into hard work.

The sheer numbers of these books attest to the voracious audience for them. The numbers also constitute a mass that permits significant analysis of variants on the boy-hero theme in the late nineteenth century.

Increasingly the boys' stories emphasize neither the voyage, circular or otherwise, nor the hero, British or Indian, but rather the conflict itself: the testing battles in which the lad pits himself against an enemy. The title *The Bear Hunters of the Rocky Mountains* (1875), by Anne Bowman, suggests the shift of emphasis to the huge and menacing grizzly; other stories highlight a frightening array of human antagonists: Yankees in Henry Frith's *The Opal Mountain* (1889); a Blackfoot, uttering 'the dread cry, 'Waugh O!'" in Eleanor Stedder's Red River story *Lost in the Wilds* (1893)[5]; half-breed Pierre in Argyll Saxby's *Comrades Three* (1900); and "Evil-Eye," a pirate, in Oxley's *The Wreckers of Sable Island* (1891). Evil-Eye carries in his mighty hand "a cutlass whose sheen was already dimmed with suspicious stains."[6] In girls' books antagonists tend to be mean, whereas in boys' books they are strong and well armed.

Nature itself is the enemy in Edward Roper's *Icebound; or The Anticosti Crusoes* (1900). In this "Robinsonade," the young heroes, George and Sid, ingeniously survive isolation, hunger, and cold, thus outfacing nature's challenges. The very readable story of winter shipwreck and abandonment reflects a nightmare that troubled many a traveler when that legend-haunted island in the mouth of the St. Lawrence loomed into sight as the first landfall after a long sea voyage. Notably, the usually all-male dream of being a Crusoe is moderated here by the coming of the angelic Gabrielle.

Boys in the East

Beginning in 1869, James De Mille added a Canadian moderation to the boys' stories. In his series of books about the boys who are Brethren of the White Cross, De Mille portrays boy heroes in the Canadian Maritime provinces who spend part of their time in the free world of adventure, part in the doldrums of school. In *The Boys at Grand Pré School* (1870) Bruce and Bart alternate between classroom tricks on Irish Pat and happy camp adventures with Pat as comrade. *Fire in the Woods* (1871), *Picked up Adrift* (1872), and other Brethren of the White Cross stories make a popular and effective display of Maritime settings and personalities, from the rhetorical teacher who bemoans the "obloquy heaped on the venerable commander" to the salty captain who boasts, "Put me anywhars on old Fundy [Bay], an I'm to hum."[7]

From another major author back east came a story firmly rooted in Canadian life and character, Charles G. D. Roberts's *Reube Dare's Shad Boat* (1895). Roberts, not yet established as a master of animal stories, presents two heroes: one a polished college boy, Will Carter, home from his studies, and the other a Huck Finn type, the sturdy, ungrammatical Reuben. Together they discover and foil a dirty plot by a rival fisherman. The chief attraction in this well-plotted mystery is the realistic detail of marine adventures on the Bay of Fundy and along its cave-riddled shores.

Roberts's joy in free movement and the vigorous life of nature is echoed in Valentine Williams's *Captain of the Club; or, The Canadian Boy* (1899). Here Jack and Billy exercise their young strength in lacrosse matches and snowshoe tramps, but sport, for Jack, is eventually replaced by his devotion to his vocation as an artist. As in Roberts's story, the dominant boy is the more refined of the two.

Another man from the Maritimes, James Macdonald Oxley, began a long literary career with a story in which the schoolroom becomes the sole stage, and because the conflicts are more moral than physical, boys are tested for truth, loyalty, and spiritual leadership. In *Bert Lloyd's Boyhood* (1889) the hero, at first "a perfect pickle," develops into a boy reformer, "Dux" (top pupil) of his Nova Scotia school, wins a scholarship, works as a social activist, becomes a muscular Christian ready to discomfit the brutal Brannigan, and finally hears the call to join the ministry. This is the first of 29 novels by Oxley; some are historical fiction, but most present a boy's life as consisting in facing a series of recurring moral crises.

Marjorie Pickthall, a Toronto poet and short story writer, served younger boys similar bracing moral stories. Violent incidents are glossed over by a pious moral ending in her *Dick's Desertion* (1905). More inventively, in *The Straight Road* (1906) Pickthall shows the way working on a railroad can rouse a lazy discontented boy to energetic action. In another unconventional story, *Two Little Savages* (1903) by Ernest Thompson Seton, boy heroes become voluntary Crusoes. Yan, undervalued by his family, finds solace in the company of his friends Sam and Guy and in their forays into the glens and bushland near their Ontario homes. They "go Indian," master survival skills, and grow in awareness of the rich fauna and flora just outside the fenced-in farm. For them nature is friend not foe. Besides a wealth of illustrations and marginal decorations, this fat book includes an index that lists such items as "Dyeing—with butternuts / goldenrod / pokeweed / oak chips / dogwood" and "Fire—how to light without matches / right woods to use / signal," which makes this a realistic handbook for would-be savages.[8]

An unassuming but lively and readable story by Frances Wood, *The Old Red School House* (1913) adds evidence that the schoolroom can be the site of lively conflict. This story of early days in Canada East (Quebec) features a "Wild Boy" who terrorizes classes and burns down the schoolhouse.

Heroic Specimens

Most readers in the early 1900s continued to demand tougher stuff than backyard teepees and schoolroom discipline. A Canadian who published in New York (a common practice for many writers of boys' books) came up with titles that epitomize the kind of heroes readers wanted to hear about: *Trapper "Jim"* (1903) and *Sportsman "Joe"* (1904), both by Edwyn Sandys. Yankee villains, Moke the Indian, and a Portuguese make life in Assiniboia difficult in E. H. Burrace's *Never Beaten!* (1908). For English and Canadian readers of *Boy's Own Annual* and *Chums,* physical prowess and scorn of sentiment remained the required heroic qualities. In the prewar days demand stayed high for tales with titles such as *Boy Ranchers* (1910) by Bindloss, *Boy Trappers in the Rockies* (1913) by W. B. Anderson, *A Boy of the Dominion* (1913) by Captain Brereton, and *Rattlesnake Ranch* (1912) by Robert Leighton.

The best of these prewar stories of westward-questing young heroes is Christopher Beck's *Stronghand Saxon* (1910). Saxon helps an English lad who is being defrauded of his Canadian inheritance at Sunk River. Together they rout the bad guys, Lomax, Stark, and Jaxbe. This novel is also important because it introduces readers to yet another mythic Canadian figure, the Canadian Mountie. At the crucial moment, "the scarlet uniforms of the Mounted flared against the green. . . . Dead men littered the floor."[9] With the help of the Mounties boy and his stronghanded friend unravel the dastardly plot and move on to proprietorship of the ranch and the gold mine hidden beneath its sunken river.

Paleface and Indian become blood brothers on the Peace River in David Douglas's *On the Great Fur Trail* (1919). But the apparently endless list of stories of theatrical conflict comes to a sad finale with a series of stories about the real war of 1914–18. Clair Hayes's *The Boy Allies; or, With Haig in Flanders* (1918) transposes the adventure story formula to a grimmer initiation tale.

Many wartime boys' stories were played out in air battles, reflecting the new venue of battle. The pivotal book in the wartime genre is *The Flying Squad* (1927), coauthored by Rothesay Stuart-Wortley, and William Bishop, V. C. (Victoria Cross), Canada's most well known First World War flying ace who was also something of a prankster, something of a Coyote-figure. This novel tells of two boys who end their term at Upper Canada College in Toronto and undertake dangerous missions against Black Jude, Long Jim, and Rosenbaum—adventures climaxing in an aerial battle over Lake Ontario and the defeat of an American multimillionaire. The essential shift that occurs after the First World War is not a shift in the space through which the questers move but in the nature of the young hero.

After four years of war, and the very high loss of life, however, boys who read postwar books, like the men who survived the war to write them, could never quite regain the panache of the hero myth.

Boys between the Wars

In many postwar stories, the lad becomes a spectator of adult prowess; in most cases the adult is a Mountie. *Renfrew of the Mounties* (1922) by Laurie Erskine exemplifies the formula: young boys, enjoying their own lesser exploits, are drawn in by the mysterious man, their new neighbor, who tells his tales of the wild northwest and his adventures as a redcoat. The boy's petty mischief forms a frame for the man's tales of desperate courage and discipline.

Between the wars boys also had a wide range of mystery adventure series to draw from. Frank Packard's "Jimmie Dale" books, featuring a debonair millionaire for whom detecting crime is a hobby, ran from 1917 through 1935. The "Hardy Boys" books, which began to appear in 1926, many of them written by the Canadian Leslie McFarlane under the pen name Franklin W. Dixon, depict two indistinguishable boys who do the detecting.[10] *Wings of the North* (1932) by Harris Patten takes its pair of young heroes, Bert and Dick, into heroic conflict with evildoers in the air.

During the 1920s less theatrical adventures become the rule. For instance, G. H. Graham's *Larry* (1923) is a funny tale about Lakefield School near Peterborough; and there were camp stories such as E. H. Bennett's *Camp Ken-Jockety* (1923). The down-to-earth title *The Shack in the Coulee* (1932) introduces two localisms that foreshadow the regional realism in George Surrey's novel. Although like old *Boys' Own* stories this book is set on a western ranch, it features real-sounding back-chat between Canadian Don and English Harry, the "pupil rancher."

Some of the old stereotypes reappear in publications during the years between the wars. Dark and sinister strangers menace the boys with black magic in G. H. Grahame's *The Voodoo Stone* (1935), a rollicking tale of adventures away from school. The appeal of the Mounties continues in Jack O'Brian's *Corporal Corey of the Royal Canadian Mounted* (1936).

Initiation Stories

Boys in some stories of the 1940s—Jory in Clare Bice's depiction of Maritime life, *Jory's Cove* (1941), or Danny Whiteduck and Little Beaver, the Indian lads of Temagami in *The Red Canoe* (1940) by Harriet Evatt—are polite and friendly and solve problems in a mannerly rather than a muscular way. But soon after the Second World War ended, the glorification of the old virile pursuits of hunting and lonely wilderness travel resumed. Roderick Haig-Brown and Farley Mowat emerged, reviving the power of the Ballantyne and Butler line.

An initiation story that won an important Canadian award as best book of 1947 was Roderick Haig-Brown's *Starbuck Valley Winter*. Here as in a companion piece, *Saltwater Summer* (1948), Haig-Brown reinstates many of the conventions of the tale of heroic maturing. In the classic mold, Don is an orphan, and his kindly Uncle Joe puts him through ritual tests—building a water wheel, shooting a buck—before setting him free to follow the Shifting River up to a winter of endurance. Like the narrator of *Red Cloud*, Don has a comic comrade in Tubby Miller, and a dark mysterious woodsman named Lee Jetson enacts a tutelary role somewhat like that of Red Cloud. Don faces and conquers the wilderness. He becomes a trapper, a hunter, a builder of winter shelter and is rewarded, like the hero of Red Cloud, with the gift of gold. But unlike *Red Cloud, Starbuck Valley Winter* includes a girl among the major characters. At the central point of the novel, when Don comes back to the farm at Christmas time, Don's cousin Ellen tackles him on the huntsman's code.

"Do you really like trapping?" Ellen asked again.
"Sure," Don said. "I like it fine."
"But not the killing part," Ellen said. "Nobody could like that."
"You don't have to think about it," Don said. "Anyway, if I wasn't trapping somebody else would be."
Ellen sighed. . . ."But it does seem as if we just live by killing all the time—cougar and deer and bear and all the little animals in the woods. Salmon in the salt water, trout up the rivers. And even on the farm there's butchering beef and killing chicken and pigs when we have them." . . .The next day Don went up the river. He took the rifle. . . and two number four beaver traps.[11]

Like Red Cloud, Don has a clear code of behavior. He rarely says "I," always "A man has got to . . . ," "A man can hunt . . . ," or "'Tain't right for a man to . . . ." For boys in the wake of war, there was reassurance as well as elegy in the voicing of an old code.

One of the novels that most clearly adheres to the archetypes of initiation stories is Farley Mowat's *Lost in the Barrens* (1956). Important for its ecological message, this novel is also important for its use of the old theme of mutual dependence between white man and Indian. Jamie MacNair, the nephew of a trapper at the Pas, and Awasin Meewasin, a Cree, strike first into the land of the Chipewyans, and then, separated by mischance from the caribou-hunting band, they spend a whole winter in a Crusoe-like existence. In a hidden valley in the Barren Grounds, they build, cook, tame two huskies, and prepare for escape. In the end that escape depends on the aid of yet another band, Eskimos and their harbinger, a boy named Peetyuk. The relationship between the boys is the finest element in this convincing, exciting story. There are no girl characters, and there is no questioning of the native wisdom in the ways of the north: "If you fight against the spirits of the north you will always lose," says Awasin.[12]

A more complex use of the underlying motifs in Ballantyne and Butler comes in novels by David Walker, particularly *Dragon Hill* (1962) and *Pirate Rock* (1969). Walker, like Ballantyne, is a Scot. As in *The Young Fur Traders,* two young people, one born in Canada, the other in Scotland, set out together in *Dragon Hill.* This time, however, one of the questers is a girl. Physically, the quest covers less ground. William and Mary snake through woods, climb hills, cross water, but only in the distance between their summer home on Seal Point and old Captain McDurgan's barricaded stronghold nearby on the mainland. The children draw the "old Dragon" (as they call McDurgan) out of his misogyny, and a hurricane draws him up to Seal Point. Then a parallel more complex than anything in Ballantyne emerges: the Old Dragon connects with William's writer father, who in riding out his own storm of obsessive creativity has excluded the "real" world as stoutly as Captain McDurgan ever has. For William, and the boys who enjoy this story, there are three adult male role models: the abstracted father, the hostile Old Dragon, and Pugsy the hired man, who retains many of the old crafts and virtues of a simple woodsman. At the end of the quest, the expected treasure has been shattered by the hurricane, but the children, like Old Dragon, keep something from "the flotsam, the jetsam, the wreckage, the trash of the storm."[13]

This fine and subtle book was followed by *Pirate Rock* (1969), Walker's equally complex tale for slightly older fans of adventure stories. Two boys and a girl in *Pirate Rock* undergo the old initiation ordeals on land and sea. They face grim members of an international spy ring who are more murderous than the outlaws of the old western tales. They plunge to the depths of foggy waters and creep down dark tunnels, but they are also involved in convincing, complex family relations and develop confusing feelings for each other. Their language is fresh and funny. As in his books for adults, David Walker's stories, like John Buchan's, have an ability to raise the reader's blood pressure and speed the heartbeat.

A quieter initiation comes to the young hero in *A Boy of Taché* by Ann Blades. In trying to help his ailing grandfather, Charlie, a Carrier Indian boy, travels alone down the river to get medical aid and gains the respect of his tribesmen. The story is complemented by Blades's paintings, which suggest the spare beauty of northern British Columbia.

Enter the Antihero

In the 1970s and 1980s, many adult books debunked male prowess. The Angry Young Men of England and the Beat generation of the United States mocked the concepts of heroism traditionally held by adults; a spin-off of this view affected young readers also. Permissive schooling and homes opened the shelves of adult books to young readers, and there young readers found new images of male adolescence in *The Catcher in the Rye, A Separate Peace, What Makes Sammy Run?,* and *The Apprenticeship of Duddy Kravitz.* Boys stopped reading the designated boys' books. Then, from young authors who had themselves grown up in the era of black humor, new books began to emerge that were designed to give boys something of their own to read again, stories articulating a new myth, a new male archetype.

Least known of the new writers is Peter Davies. *Fly Away, Paul* (1974) derives from his heart-wrenching experience in a halfway house for boys. He details the residents' rivalries, fantasies, sexual and drug abuse. Reading this book, parents and teachers and librarians face the problem of unrestrained reportage of language and behavior. Although books like this one contain nothing more explicit than what appears in most adult fiction these days, and not much that differs from the language and behavior observable in most schools, some difficulties have arisen over the question of setting standards in the writing and publishing of books specifically designed for immature readers. A less insistently shocking tone softens Claire Mackay's *Exit Barney McGee* (1979). But this is an equally troubling story of family disruption and poverty in a run-down Toronto boarding house.

Such problems do not shadow the reader's joy in Gordon Korman's work. Having begun writing at a phenomenally young age, Korman has been publishing irreverent, inventive, irresistible school stories annually since 1978. Undimmed by the farce, the old archetypal phases of questing stories shine clearly—but usually with a trickster turn. Comrades Rudy and Mike pit themselves against dark forces in *I Want to Go Home* (1981)—but the dark forces are the enjoyment-bound directors of a summer camp. The escape route from camp involves the young heroes in slapstick situations, from which they emerge by absurd devices. In the Macdonald Hall school stories about Boots and Bruno, Korman again creates havoc by involving young protagonists in endeavors and projects that are perfectly proper for the young heroes of traditional stories, but that turn into disastrous improprieties. The boys have the flatness of comic book characters, but that trait has been a staple of the heroes of boys' books since the good old "boy trapper" days. Korman's *Who Is Bugs Potter?* (1980) is an easy-to-read travesty of the success story. A rock 'n' roll drummer, Bugs sides with the hoodlums who should be his antagonists and debunks the glamor of show business, which he should worship. In all Korman plots there is an underlying movement towards justice, but the comic misadventures en route reduce the questing drive to a humorous meandering.

Brian Doyle also published his first work in 1978. Thirty years older than Korman, Doyle is both slower in narrative movement and deeper in theme. *Up to Low* (1982), his third novel, is a poignant antiheroic initiation story. A motherless boy travels with his father and a rowdy drinking companion up to the father's old home in the Gatineau valley. Like all the certainties of life, the car and the companion gradually decompose before the boy's eyes. In a slowly maturing restorative relationship with a girl, Tommy makes a second voyage by boat up the river to perform a strange deed of charity for her and her disease-ridden father. Comic and tragic, the plot traces Tommy's twists and evasions as he moves toward responsible action. Doyle presents a flawed, beautiful world and a narrator-hero who is poetic, brash, and honest.

Angel Street, published later than *Up to Low,* presents a younger phase in Tommy's life—a time of school battles in the no-man's-land of Lowertown, Ottawa, battles between French Catholics, Jews, Irish, and Protestants; a time, also, when Tommy is living in an imagined world created by radio dramas and comic books, playing the boy detective in a world undreamed of by the Hardy Boys. In this new wilderness Brian Doyle's hero moves as a complex being, cocky, lonely, motherless yet acting as mother to his retarded sister. Like the hero in Kipling's *Kim,* he is a friend of all the world but in this world there is no "Great Game" of patriotic espionage, only squalid petty corruption and brutality.[14]

A different kind of game, the tussle between union organizers, bosses, and politicians, forms the background for Silver Donald Cameron's initiation story *The Baitchoppers* (1982). The two boys involved in the fight for a fisherman's union are idealized, but Cameron paints the east coast community in colors darker than those that appeared in other Atlantic coast writers such as Roberts and Walker.

The antihero tradition continues with Kevin Major, a Newfoundland writer whose first work appeared in the same year as Korman's and Doyle's. Major's *Hold Fast* (1978) and *Far from Shore* (1980) take the boys' book into new tensions and problems.

Kevin Major has a sharp ear for dialogue and a keen awareness of boys' interests and attitudes. In *Hold Fast* (1978) he presents a desolate young character whose childhood energy is held captive by misfortune. Michael, a Newfoundland outport boy whose parents are tragically killed, is sent to an uncle and aunt in the city, where he must share his life with a namby-pamby cousin. Without a comrade, he drags himself to an impersonal school, defends himself against bullies and the blandishments of a girl named Brenda. Although Michael appears as a victim in the first half of the novel, in the second half he emerges as a trickster in a picaresque travelogue. He lights out for his outport home, and en route he steals a car, poaches rabbits, lies, begs, and disguises himself. He also befriends the needy and assists a helpless old lady (whose car he later steals). Eventually he liberates his cousin from domination. This demonic dream of freedom and power offers vicarious release to all young readers, and particularly to those boys who have been dubbed "reluctant readers."

Chris in *Far from Shore* is a character with a wry twist—he is de-idealized and set against the models presented in earlier children's literature. He slides into wildness, defies his parents and his school, and slips away from his church, under pressure of forces not only beyond his control but also beyond the possibility of adult management. Chris's father drinks heavily and eventually leaves for the west in response to losing his job and his authority. His mother slips toward infidelity under the indignity of loneliness. His successful sister sets too good an example and alienates Chris by concentrating on her own problems.

Chris longs for order, and he is capable of sacrifice and devotion. Although the plot twist has assigned the traditional westward journey to the father rather than the son, Chris performs many of the other deeds of the questing hero. After a week that "has got to be one of the worse ones [he] ever punished through," he enters a green world at a church camp.[15] There, like the traditional quester, he dives for a "treasure," saving a drowning child who has begun to restore his capacity for loving. He fights a bully whose name, Earle, suggests ancient power. But Chris is defeated by newer dragons: beer, drugs, and a poor self-image. The ending seems overly hopeful: Chris's father returns from being "away," restoring the possibility of order and companionship; the intimidating sister leaves home; and a new girlfriend comes to meet the restored family. In the end, Chris and his dad go hunting together. Perhaps this episode is just a realistic report on the persistence of hunting as a male sport in a province that still has some frontier qualities, but more likely it is the resurfacing, through the bitter tide of ironies, of the old union of man and boy, prince and dying king, in a male mystique of wilderness life.

The female view voiced by Ellen in Haig-Brown's *Starbuck Valley Winter* is reiterated in Monica Hughes's *Hunter in the Dark* (1982). Her protagonist Mike lights out to the Freeman River, pursued by a new dragon, the life-menacing disease of leukemia. "Bear country, not people country,"[16] near Fort Assiniboine, is the setting for a struggle against the fear of death. Mike goes on a different kind of hunt, with emergency kit, paper packs of sugar, canned stew, granola bars, and an authorization metal tag to put on the antlers of the whitetail buck he is stalking. But this hunt ends when Mike remembers the tag that was clamped to his wrist at hospital Admitting, and he meets the darkness he has been trying to push away. This story features a new kind of hunter and is directed at a new kind of reader. It poses a question darker and more troubling than the question of the uncensored use of language. Should a boy reader be asked to live vicariously in this kind of dark hunt, this existential probing into death?

Marilyn Halvorson in *Cowboys Don't Cry* (1984) uses a southern Alberta setting for another controversial novel about the way a boy faces his feelings about his mother who has in effect been killed by his father's alcoholism. Shane Morgan's rodeo world is a harsh field of combat, like the Angel Square where Brian Doyle's Tommy dodges through his more urban battles. But Shane fights without any of Tommy's redeeming allies: imaginative fantasy, humor, and a father's shielding warmth and affection. The strain of Shane's feelings toward his parents recalls the Toronto boarding house tensions of Claire MacKay's *Exit Barney McGee*. The drift of all Halvorson's work is summarized in the title of a wilderness survival story she published in 1987: *Nobody Said It Would be Easy*.

One of the central characters in Halvorson's books is a Métis boy, Lance Ducharme. He faces contemporary problems: drug addiction, desertion by his mother, involvement in a custody case. Stories like Lance's give a last twist to the antihero stories: here the white man's "civilization" erodes native values, and the Métis boy turns trickster as a consequence. The plight of Canadian Indians and Métis had been reflected in other books such as John Craig's *No Word for Goodbye* (1969) and *Zach* (1972). The first of the two novels ends with a sad acknowledgment that Ken Warren's desire to help his Ojibway friends is doomed by the power of land developers. These new, privileged, faceless antagonists prove harder to wrestle than the old enemies—nature, ferocious animals, and hard-hearted outlaws. *Zach* presents an Indian boy, the last of his tribe, who loops through an American World of petty crime, drunkenness, and drugs, before heading back to his own country.

In the farthest north, however, young travelers are presented as still moving along the clear paths of heroism, as is apparent in the tragic novels of James Houston. Novels such as *Frozen Fire* and *River Runners* (1980) expand the traditional quest pattern, deepen the sense of white-native camaraderie, and set the tale against a finely realized Arctic world. Matthew Morgan in *Frozen Fire* is less like Halvorson's Shane Morgan and more like Don Morgan in Haig-Brown's *Starbuck Valley Winter.* These names, with the recurring echo of *morgen,* that is, *morning,* reinforce the emphasis on characters who are in an apprenticeship stage. Houston's Matthew, like Haig-Brown's Don, is the son of a wilderness prospector, but Mathew's story centers on survival in a remote Arctic world. Hunting to survive, accepting mutual dependence on his boy comrade the Inuit lad Kayak, Matthew endures problems essentially simpler than those posed by Monica Hughes and Marilyn Halvorson. Like Red Cloud, the native people in Houston's stories teach attitudes toward hunger and cold, toward animals, and toward human rivalries and enterprises that furnish strong guidance and lead to a final acceptance of goals other than the gold dreamt of by the white prospectors.

With computer games and videos offering new competition as nurturers of imagination, boys' books are no longer produced in great numbers in Canada. The recent stream, though narrow, is deep; and boys can keep a still deeper, older tide of value running by reading, in complement to the new antiheroic stories, some of the old epic adventure stories of Ballantyne and Butler, Haig-Brown and Houston.

10

Historical Fiction

In 1874 Agnes Machar published *For King and Country.* The country was Canada; the king was the king of England. Fired by dual loyalty, the young hero in Machar's book flashed his sword in gallant assault against the enemy—in this case the American armies that invaded Canada in the War of 1812. Over a hundred years later Janet Lunn published *The Root Cellar* (1983), a modern book of historical fiction in which an alienated young girl slips into a different kind of past: the 1860s, when the Civil War in the United States drew sympathetic Canadians into inglorious suffering. Between these two books stretches a complicated train of historical fiction for young Canadian readers.

Ideas about the function of historical fiction have changed in recent years; so, too, has the concept of a "real past" that is accessible through research and imagination. In other countries as well as in Canada, some historical fiction has witnessed something of a shift from hero to heroine, from glorification to denigration of conflict, and from untroubled patriotism to a sense of responsibility for people of other nationalities.

In spite of all such changes, historical fiction continues to hold interest and value for young readers on the threshold of adulthood. In *The Hurried Child,* American psychologist David Elkind writes of the special needs in late adolescence to find relief from the pressure to develop accomplishments for future use.[1] The need to relish present time as it passes can be met in part by books that re-create times past. Historical fiction gives full rein to reverie, to speculation about personal roots, to confrontation of social injustice at a safe unimperative distance, and to meditation on the mystery of time itself. All these mental experiences help the young adult develop a place to stand and an ability to resist the pressure to hurry into spiritually impoverished maturation.

Writers of historical fiction for young people fantasize about the past in order to develop a complex sense of national heritage. They also write with the aim of giving the present a fuller impact. As the English writer Leon Garfield wrote in the *Horn Book* in 1988, "Things familiar become invisible and it is only when we move them to another place and another time that they leap out at us."[2] Writers also create historical fictions for the sake of the future, choosing periods and heroes to aid cultural maturation in young people on the threshold of political and social responsibility.

"Literature . . . the living memory of a nation . . . preserves and kindles within itself a country's spent history," said the Russian novelist Aleksandr Solzhenitsyn when he accepted the Nobel Prize in 1972.[3] Canadian authors have felt strongly the urge to preserve their distinctive past. Frank Baird wrote in 1923 about the value of books "written at home, printed at home, and about people at home . . . for Canadians both East and West who love their country and are interested in its history and development."[4]

French Colonial Tradition

Unique qualities in Canada's internal politics and global situation have channelled Canadian history—and historical fiction—into some unusual patterns.

Most nineteenth-century stories of Canada's past focus on life in the French colonies. William Kirby was one of the first of the Victorian Anglophones who presented young readers with a picture of the French founders of the nation. *The Golden Dog* (1877) presents a political life, class structure, religion, and language all alien and exotic to most English-speaking Canadians. Kirby had done careful research, but although his choice of subject suggests sympathy and interest, his melodramatic plot emphasizes the tragic and horrible aspects of feudal, Catholic, French life. The murderous politics and debauched revelry of François Bigot, the historical intendant or administrator of the French colony, the choice of convent life by the beautiful Amélie, the defamation of her merchant brother by heartless Angélique who is in league with witchcraft—all imply that Kirby's values are at odds with the life he portrays so vividly. The Golden Dog, which is the sign of the merchant Bourgeois Philibert, symbolizes hope for a better future: "I'll bite him by whom I'm bit," says the inscription on the sign; the biting will mean the middle-class overthrow of corrupt aristocracy.[5] Kirby's novel, which created an image of the French regime as romantic, colorful, and corrupt, remained required reading for Anglophone high school students in Canada as late as the 1930s.

Another widely read story about the years before Wolfe conquered Quebec is Mary Catherwood's *A Romance of Dollard* (1888), which idealizes the patriotic self-sacrifice of Dollard in his lonely and doomed stand against the Iroquois at the Long Sault. But in 1887 the enormously popular boys' book writer G. A. Henty published *With Wolfe in Canada; or, The Winning of the Continent,* and Canadian novelists moved their focus from the preconquest years to the event that was glorified by British imperialists. Gilbert Parker in *The Seats of the Mighty* (1894) swung to the point of view of the English invaders, although he also, like Catherwood, glorified French courage in the face of unbeatable odds.

The Seats of the Mighty, a world best-seller in the 1890s, illustrates Anglophone chauvinism in plot, characterization, and theme. While imprisoned in the Quebec citadel, the seat of the mighty French in 1763, the Scottish soldier hero hears of the secret path by which Wolfe's forces could climb and conquer the city. In prison he also wins the heart of a French girl, the daughter of one of the governors of Quebec. The hero escapes from the citadel, makes his perilous way down the St. Lawrence to meet General

Wolfe, and guides him to the hidden path and to victory. For this storybook hero, the storybook heroine gives up her language, her loyalty, her religion, and her culture, and the couple lives happily every after in Quebec after the double conquest of the girl and the French nation.

In French-Canadian historical fiction the same elements of battle and romance recur with a dramatic difference. *Canadians of Old* by Philippe Aubert de Gaspé (1863) was translated by Charles G. D. Roberts and published in English in 1890. In its conclusion, the French heroine rejects her Scottish suitor, even though she loves him, because she cannot bear to abandon her race, her language, and her culture.[6]

The Seats of the Mighty became a great favorite with young people, even though it was originally intended for a general popular audience. Several other novels about Wolfe and the Seven Years War, such as Herbert Strang's *Rob the Ranger* (1907), were intended for boys and girls and were presented with lively colorful illustrations.

Another phase of French-English confrontation in the New World comes into focus in J. M. Oxley's *Fife and Drum at Louisbourg* (1899). Capitalizing on the popularity of Longfellow's *Evangeline,* Oxley concentrates not on the aristocratic aspects of French life, as dramatized by Kirby and Parker, but on the humbler realities of Acadian farm life which ended when the British expelled the Acadians from the Maritime colonies in 1755–58.

The American Border

Because Wilfrid Laurier held the prime ministership from 1896 to 1911, concentrating on the French-English conflict may have become politically unwise as the twentieth century opened. Furthermore the surge in British imperialist feelings in Canada around the turn of the century may have helped turn attention toward other past tensions, rising from British-Canadian opposition to the republican form of government of the United States. During the revolutionary war, British troops based in Canada had crossed the border to battle American forces; American Tories had crossed in the other direction to maintain allegiance to the British flag. By 1812, mutual distrust and grievances had led to the outbreak of border skirmishes that left a wake of hostile memories of raids and losses on both sides.

Robert Sellar, a Scots Canadian living in the small town of Huntingdon, in the Quebec border area south of the St. Lawrence River, published *Hemlock* in 1890 and *Morven* in 1911. The former deals with a British officer captured during the War of 1812 by Americans but freed by a friendly Indian band. The latter book traces the movement of Scots loyalists in the 1770s from Virginia up through the Adirondacks to a Canadian settlement.

Other writers picked up the same British-American tensions. H. A. Cody in *The King's Arrow* (1922), Jean McIlwraith in *Kinsmen at War* (1927), and E. A. Taylor in *Beatrice of Old York* (1929) wrote stories of divided loyalties during the War of 1812 among the United Empire Loyalists (UEL) who had moved up from the United States to the monarchist colonies north of Lake Ontario. The clustering of these titles in the 1920s leads one to speculate about the connection between this kind of fiction and the snobbish divisions that were being drawn during an urbanizing period between "old Canadians" and new ones.

Traditionally, however, in spite of the cachet of the "UEL," Scots had stood at the top of Canadian hierarchies in business and politics. Writers of Canadian historical fiction consistently chose Scots as protagonists. Perhaps the lingering literary influence of Sir Walter Scott also had some bearing on this emphasis in fiction. The titles tell the tale, from Oxley's *Fergus Mactavish* (1892), to McIlwraith's *The Curious Career of Roderick Campbell* (1901), to Frank Baird's *Rob Macnab* (1923), to mention only a few.[7]

Early Views of the Past

One essential feature of all these early historical romances is the travel motif. In all, a fictional character journeys through the "real" spaces of the past, that is, through a landscape really fixed in Canadian geography and re-created as it must have appeared

during a specific historic period. Reading these books, Canadian children travel in imagination not through a mythic land of magic mountains and fabulous rivers but through spaces that really are part of their own country, their native land.

In most of these historical fictions we can note another recurring attribute: in every case the quester is a young white male who plays a significant part in a momentous epoch of battle and public danger. Jean McIlwraith's novel *The Little Admiral* (1924) typifies the glorification of swashbuckling swordplay and espionage in a strong, high-minded lad—the sort of qualities that are epitomized in the Scottish Robert Louis Stevenson's *Kidnapped* (1886) and in Esther Forbes's story of American *Johnny Tremain* (1924). Even though E. A. Taylor's *Beatrice of Old York* is named for a girl, the principal action in this novel is undertaken by a Quaker boy who bravely decides to become a soldier. The old grandfather says, "Ladies shouldn't talk of war or politics," and although Beatrice objects, her involvement in both is slight.[8]

One charming little story by Helen Fuller, *The Gold-Laced Coat* (1934), places a small girl in action against the French-British-American military exploits around Fort Niagara and Buffalo and presents an Indian whose dialect runs to phrases like "Me never forget."

In *Susannah* (1936) Muriel Denison took the stories of Mounties and turned them upside down by making a little girl the pivotal figure in western history. Although *Susannah* was written originally for small children, its vigorous style and fine evocation of the northwest world of Mounties, trappers, Hudson's Bay Company factors, and Indians extended the reach of the book. Susannah's response to the western saga of the Riel and the North West Rebellion of 1885 is presented with imaginative sensitivity. Portraits of Almighty Voice, Spotted Calf, and Riel himself have surprising force. Denison foreshadows the use of native and Métis people in many later books such as Rudy Wiebe's *The Temptations of Big Bear* (1973), which characterizes Indians as representing a dark wisdom, an "otherness" contrary to the dominant white male world of order, power, and discipline. Susannah's friends in the Royal Mounted Police are also well differentiated. The plot denouement is slick, but the creation of a complex northern society justifies the book's popularity. Its effect was extended by three sequels (1938–40) and by an attractive movie version.

In the late 1930s Canadian writers began to change the tone and topics in historical fiction. Alan Dwight in *Drums in the Forest* (1936) and Charles Clay in *Young Voyageur* (1938) pay more attention to the interchanges between Indians and French settlers and re-create the earliest days of settlement in unheroic terms.

Emily Weaver's *The Only Girl: A Tale of 1837* (1938) turns to a major event in Canadian history involving none of the national conflicts. The Rebellion of 1837, launched by radicals infuriated by the abuse of power by the conservative elite (who were dubbed the "Family Compact"), was led in Quebec by Louis Joseph Papineau and in Ontario by William Lyon Mackenzie. Mackenzie is a pivotal character in Weaver's well-told tale, and Peggy, whose family's UEL conservatism holds them back from being inflamed by the radical atmosphere in Toronto, hides him at a crucial point.

A little girl plays a less dramatic but important role in *The Crimson Shawl* (1941), a story of the Acadian expulsion by Florence Choate and Elizabeth Curtis. *The Crimson Shawl*, which deals with the Evangeline legend familiar to American readers, was published by Lippincott of New York, while Weaver's *The Only Girl*, dealing as it does with a Canadian event of no special interest to Americans, came from Macmillan Press of Toronto. As Canadian publishers gathered strength after the war, they tended to publish novels reemphasizing differences between Canadians and Americans. John Hayes's *Treason at York*, about the War of 1812, was published in Toronto by Copp, Clark in 1949, followed by his *Rebels Ride at Night*, about the Rebellion of 1837, which was published by the same company in 1950. The American firm of Doubleday Doran, however, had published *His Majesty's Yankees* (1942), Thomas Raddall's fine adult novel about Nova Scotia privateers in action against American revolutionary forces, and when in 1950 Raddall revised the story for younger readers, it was published by the Philadelphia firm of Winston as *Son of the Hawk* (1950). This book was so well written it won the Boys' Club of America Junior Book Award.

Son of the Hawk, like the adult version of the same tale, reflects Raddall's sense of the significance of a single act by Nova Scotia Yankees who were the sons of settlers who had drifted north from New England. By firing at American privateers, they aligned themselves, the colony, and eventually the whole of Canada, on the British side, against the Americans. All historical fiction is teleological: it starts with a given historical act and then creates possible events leading up to that final "real" moment. Raddall had done a brilliant job of creating such a narrative sequence in the adult version of the novel. In *Son of the Hawk* he eliminates the most dramatic action—the shooting of the rebel Luke by his brother the Loyalist David. He also reduces hints of adolescent sexuality, brutal episodes such as Colonel Gorham's scalping of Indians, and also the complex legal arguments about the rights of loyalists in the courtroom scene. What is left seems choppy, yet the reader still has a sense that beneath the overenergetic surface story there are some deep messages about moderation, survival, and peace.

Raddall's message is conservative, of course, as are the implications of many other novels of the 1950s. Hayes's *Rebels Ride at Night,* like Lyn Cook's *Rebel on the Trail* (1953), to quote Sheila Egoff, treats the Rebellion of 1837 as "a pointless scheme of a foolish few" (Egoff, 84). Such novels inculcate in children an orthodox view of past events as exciting and directional, involving dramatic shifts in government, war, politics, and class conflict. They assume logical motivation, consequential acts, and the importance of the individual life as it interacts with the general life of the times. Such a view led to the flourishing of another genre, biography; the nonfictional rendering of the lives of real leaders appeared in series such as Canadian Portraits, published by Clark, Irwin in the 1960s.

Indian Memories

As anthropology was drawing attention to groups other than the Scots-Irish-English, major change in the views of the past was generated. White writers turned their attention to history as the

Indian peoples remembered it. Edith Sharp in *Nkwala* (1958) and Haig-Brown in *The Whale People* (1962) led the way in trying to catch the Indian perspective on time as well as to re-create past events in the life of the west coast tribes. Both authors convey a sense of time and causality that is very different from that of Europeans or European historians. *Nkwala* follows a Salish boy as he negotiates for his Spokan tribe with Okanogans in a time of hunger. The author's research at the Smithsonian Institute is applied to a fictional re-creation of the mind-set of a youth on the threshold of manhood, in the days before contact with white culture. Haig-Brown also turns to precontact times with his protagonist, a young man of the West Coast Nootkas, who moves toward chieftainship in *The Whale People*. The title suggests a shift of emphasis from the individual to the group, but in fact, the emphasis is still on the individual prowess of the youth Atlin.

Raven's Cry (1973) by Christie Harris continues the stream of Indian history, significantly reducing the emphasis on the force of a single hero. This record of the struggles and rituals of the Haida people in their period of decline is magnificently illustrated by Bill Reid, a Haida whose graphic work furthers the sense of a different perspective on time and individual responsibility.

Fiction concerned with the relations between native peoples and whites, such as W. Towrie Cutt's *Carry My Bones Northwest* (1973), a novel about the 1794 massacre at a Hudson's Bay Company post, also presents a deepening awareness of the subtleties in the clash of cultures. Tony German's *A Breed Apart* (1985) fosters understanding of the psychological tensions in a boy whose parents are a Scot and a Cree, and German's treatment of half-breeds is more perceptive than earlier stereotypical presentations.

Social Mythology

Partly under the influence of Marxist theory, formal historians and writers of fiction over the past quarter century have swung their emphasis from international wars and treaties to class struggle and to documenting the lives of alienated and exploited groups. This second major shift began with James Reaney's *The Boy with an R in His Hand (1965),* a modern myth in which Reaney filters to a young audience some of the views of revisionist historians.

The Boy with an R in His Hand (1965) presents an account of the Rebellion of 1837 that runs counter to convention. In this case, the story of William Lyon Mackenzie, the firebrand who challenged the Family Compact, presents an archetype of insurgent change. Reaney's "boy," Alec, works as an apprentice in Mackenzie's printshop, helping produce radical anti-authoritarian pamphlets. He holds in his hand not a sword but a letter from a handset press, which is the real weapon of class strife in the 1830s. Although the central character is the boy Alec, there is also a girl with an *R* on her hand. Servant-girl Rebecca is branded as a robber, in an era when a workingman could be hanged for stealing a cow, whereas a gentleman could kill a man in a duel and walk free.

Mackenzie says of a stick of type, "There's freedom and liberty, lad. There's the mind of man. All his thoughts that thousands of people will read and find helpful—all these in thousands of wee bits of lead stuck together."[9] But the forces of conservatism break up Mackenzie's print shop, singing, "Since he prints tripe, / We'll smash his type, / All for King and Country" (*BRH,* 77). The story ends gloriously, however, with the discomfiture of the Tories. Reaney does not follow the story through to the defeat of Mackenzie and his followers; instead, he gives young Alec the ending traditional in older Canadian adventure stories—a return to Scotland, where the lad comes into his inheritance. Perhaps this evasive ending reflects the fact that Reaney was working for an audience younger than that for most historical fiction.

A more familiar myth underlies Mary Alice and John Downie's very popular *Honor Bound* (1970). In this story of a Philadelphia loyalist family that comes to a bush farm in Ontario, hot-headed Miles plays the traditional part of the questing hero. He undertakes a long journey, failing at first, but surviving to learn a new moral code and to win through to a new "kingdom," in the mythic rather than the political sense. The American border is seen as a marker of significant space. Crossing the border represents a radical change in loyalty. In literary terms, for the Downies as for many other Canadian writers, crossing the border also means crossing from a vaguely imagined country peopled with stereotypical characters into a well-realized setting in which characters are conceived with more psychological depth and complexity. American revolutionists are depicted as victimizers, tyrants, and opportunists, moving through a land racked by fire and pillage; the Canadian life is presented in more recognizable topographical detail and with characters who exemplify complex traits of endurance, humor, ingenuity, and cooperation. These Canadian qualities are not macho male ones, even though these books place young boys at the center of the historic unfolding of events.

The Canadian approach to social problems and responsibilities is suggested in Bill Freeman's *Shantymen of Cache Lake* (1975). This story of union organization in the 1870s conveys the deep undercurrent of socialistic tendencies in Canada, reflected today in medicare, a free public education system, unemployment insurance and baby bonus, old age security and other programs, and based on the recognition of the need for safety nets in a land where climate and economic interdependence make self-sufficiency very hard to attain. The shantymen of Freeman's title work in Ottawa Valley lumber camps. Two youngsters, a boy and his sister, help the lumbermen organize a union in spite of the company bosses, and they also help with a group effort to bring logs down the river towards Ottawa, the capital city of the new Dominion of Canada. Tony German's "Tom Penny" stories, such as *River Race* (1979), are also well-researched stories of working-class life. Notably, the use of Scots as heroes in these works has diminished.

A very different study of the disadvantaged carries its protagonist up the rivers of the United States, across Lake Erie, to freedom. Barbara Smucker, a Mennonite, had been involved with the activist movement led by Martin Luther King during her American childhood and youth. When she moved to Canada, she became interested in the story of the "Underground Railroad," which convoyed runaway slaves to Canada in the years before the American Civil War.

Underground to Canada (1977) begins in Virginia, moves to darker Mississippi when the slave child Julilly is sold to a harsher owner, and follows the route of her terrifying flight up the Mississippi, through Tennessee and Ohio, and across Lake Erie to a harbor near Dresden, Ontario. Although Canada is mentioned in every chapter in the book, the novel gives no real sense of the country Julilly is traveling toward. Nevertheless, all children can gain from the novel some sense of the human dimension of a social evil. And most can identify with Julilly's plight as, stowed in a cave, disguised in a boy's ragged clothes, cabined, carried in a sack, and finally hidden in a lifeboat, she is borne northward. The very helplessness of her "underground" spirit is moving and serves as a powerful symbol of the theme of enslavement.

A social problem more specific to Canada but still involving the problems of children victimized by social inequity is *The Tin-Lined Trunk* (1980). Mary Hamilton tells the story of the Barnardo children, slum dwellers sent to Canada in the 1880s who all too often find ill-treatment and exploitation in their new country. The plight of city children in another era before social agencies were available to protect the poor and the orphaned is also explored in Geoffrey Bilson's *Death over Montreal* (1982), which covers the cholera epidemics of the 1830s, and in Marianne Brandis's *The Quarter-Pie Window* (1985), in which a 10-year-old boy and his 14-year-old sister face the drudgery of work as livery boy and chamber maid in an 1830s hotel in York. Another novel published in 1985, *Redcoat* by Gregory Sass, reexamines the War of 1812 in terms of the social problems and poverty that plagued that period. Although less melodramatic than *Underground to Canada,* these novels honestly probe the lesser slavery of an exploitative economic system.

Feminist Perspectives

Besides becoming open to pluralist concepts of time especially as manifested in Indian versions of the past, and besides shifting from war and treaty stories to dramatizations of class struggles, Canadian historical fiction has changed course recently in yet another way. This third major change involves a different kind of politics—what feminists have called "sexual politics." Girls emerge as the heroes of recent novels, not as romantic objects but as people who are torn by difficult decisions and play significant and central roles.

Suzanne Martel's sprightly romance *A King's Daughter* (1982; translated from the original French version published in 1974) is an excellent example. Martel returned to the old colorful stories of preconquest New France, and Jeanne Chatel, her heroine, brings intelligence and courage to the traumatic experience of being shipped to Quebec as the wife for an unknown settler. Jeanne reflects a total break from the assumptions about women's roles that led William Kirby to create his Amélie in *The Golden Dog* and Gilbert Parker his Alixe in *The Seats of the Mighty*.

Jeanne was among the "King's Daughters," young girls brought to the colony by the government of France to satisfy the male colonists' needs. Jeanne's relations with the taciturn man who accepts her as a bride develop with convincing sublety.

At home in France Jeanne has had romantic dreams about another young man, but when her girlhood hero reappears at the Rouville clearing she recognizes the thinness of her sentimental attachment. Jeanne recognizes her husband's apparently endless mourning for his first wife, yet she learns to love Simon Rouville's motherless children. In a powerful scene she tramps the woods to an Indian camp to beguile Indian captors into releasing her little foster daughter. While her husband is away at the frontier, she masters Indian lore and the traditional use of herbal medicines, and then to protect her husband's land claims she cuts off her beautiful hair, disguises herself as a boy, and beards Montreal officialdom. When Simon returns he accepts the brave *"fille du roi"* as a beloved wife.

Martel, however, does not move from this point to a traditional romantic ending. The potential love scene is aborted when Jeanne hears the note of command in her husband's voice, indicating "that the master had returned"[10] and she rejects the "trap of blissful dependence" (*KD*, 175). The story moves on to three more scenes in which Jeanne plays the dominant part. First she fights off Iroquois raiders with firebrand, mustard powder, and a frying-pan. Next she moves through the forests to heal Simon's deadly wounds by exercising all her medical skill. Third, when Iroquois attack again, she ingeniously deceives them and survives, with the children, by hiding in a secret root cellar. At every stage of an exciting plot Martel remembers and reverses all the clichés of romantic historical fiction, while simultaneously creating an unforgettable picture of real frontier conditions as experienced by a strong-minded young woman with a piquant temperament.

In stories of native peoples there is a similar change. In place of the epics of male maturation in Haig-Brown's *The Whale People* and Sharp's *Nkwala,* Jan Hudson's *Sweetgrass* (1984) presents the moving story of a Blackfoot girl. Sweetgrass narrates in idiosyncratic fashion her heroic efforts to help her people cope with smallpox, starvation, drunkenness, and debilitating taboos and to find a life that is acceptable to her. Part of her story details the changes brought into the life of her tribe by the white traders, but part also traces her private rebellion against her position as a female in a deteriorating culture.

Finally, a story of border crossing, Janet Lunn's *The Root Cellar* (1983), recalls the old tensions between American and British values, dissolves them into a new interpretation of the border, and shifts our attention to the story of Rose Larkin, a girl at the psychological borderline of maturity. Rose has been racked by the modern problems of alienation, rootlessness, immigration, and orphanhood. She slips through the root cellar on the old Lake Ontario farm and finds herself magically transported to a past of equally real, more political problems—the 1860s, when young Americans were being called up to fight in the Civil War and Canadian boys were pulled by idealism to cross over and join the Union forces.

Rose disguises herself as a boy and travels across the border through wartime scenes of desolation to find a neighbor lad who has joined the Union army. Not an orthodox young hero, Rose is dogged, bad-tempered, but persistent and able to persuade or beguile others into helping her along the way.

In the modern setting Rose is obstreperous, disturbed, and disturbing. Underground, in the past, another side of her nature emerges: Rose develops independence and courage and also becomes a loyal, nurturing friend. She returns from the war to make peace in her modern Canadian world, and the story concludes with her acceptance of her new home and her family. Having rediscovered history, Rose can extend love to present-day people.

Janet Lunn uses historical fiction to emphasize the complexities of social action and the sadness and suffering of past times. She uses the traditional device of disguise to point to the marginalization of girls in the male worlds of politics and war. She uses the plot about crossing the Canadian-American border to imply the need of movement from one value system to another for an enlargement of spirit. And she uses the time-shift formula—transition from one period to another—to reveal a deep and relevant truth. An access to the past, to history, can help a character to coalesce in the present. Rose uses magic to reach the past; but any young person reading historical fiction can develop more oblique access to the same enriching sense of roots and a nurturing awareness of meaningful human life in the "underground" of history.

11

Young Adult Readers
From Place to Space

A study that concerns itself with Canadian children's literature must reflect a sense of place. On the map of the real world, Canadian terrain is a northern continental stretch of coastline, farmland, prairies, tundra, and mountains, netted by rivers, darkened by forests, blanked by barrens, and illuminated by the lights of cities, towns, villages, and farmsteads. Much of Canadian literature clarifies the life of that land. Yet it is hard to see the connection between this real world and the realms presented in Canadian books designed for young adult readers.

At 18 young men and women will be enfranchised, empowered to drive a car, to fly a plane, to leave home, to form permanent responsible relations with others, to enter a profession, and to obtain full-time productive and remunerative work. But at 16 or 17, rather than looking in books for road maps into the imminent adult sphere, readers prefer to swerve into other paths: to plunge into occult realms like Poe's "misty mid-regions of weir," or to leap into interstellar space via science fiction.

The preference for these genres signifies the attainment of a preadult stage in reading response. To return to the theory of aesthetic response, all texts are now "legible" to the person at the borderline of maturity. That is, full cognitive power allows the young person to decode the text to compensate for narrative gaps, to balance disrupted time sequences, to tolerate disturbances in point of view, to enjoy hermeneutic references to enigmas, to discriminate ironies and subtexts, and to cope with other structural and semantic oddities that would have bothered younger, less developed readers.[1] Yet although all books are now "legible," not all are "readable," again, in the sense of being pleasurable and interesting. Only from certain books do young adults carry away meanings and emotions valuable to them. They still bring limited experience to the reading, and they also bring needs that will gradually disappear with further maturity.

Young adults are at the height of sensory acuteness, energized by new hormonal and glandular suffusions; they bring to their reading intellectual and emotional energies already dimmed in older readers. Yet young adult readers' experience is still thin, and they carry from childhood a naïvete, a lingering insecurity about the limits of human capacity and the stability of the self.[2]

Both the positive strength of the young person's mind and the peculiar limitations imposed by being only on the threshold of adulthood have at different historical times led to odd reading addictions: to mystery and detective stories, fabulations of prehistory, stories of political corruption, wild west action stories, occult fantasies, and science fiction. All such fiction questions, deforms, and reconstitutes reality. All open doors of consciousness and invite readers into centrifugal reading, projecting the reader away from the known self. Of all these genres, occult fantasy and science fiction seem to hold most appeal to young adult readers in Canada.

Canadian works of speculative fiction throw light on the places to which all readers travel when in imagination they leave their homeland. *The Wind in the Willows* names two worlds that beckon when small beings sally forth from home: the Wide World and the Wild Wood. Young people reading Canadian science fiction can travel outward, taking the open road of knowledge about the real world's width and moving beyond places on all the maps ancient and modern, into galactic space. Reading Canadian fantasies of the occult, they can also pierce inward, opening the trail of self-awareness to the wild woods of the mind, the recesses of the heart, the hollows and heights of the spirit.

Occult Fantasy

Reading tales of the occult means dropping into the world of nightmare. Small children's games played at dusk with wavering cries of "bloody bones" and campfire whisperings about haunted houses are forerunners of the delightful frisson of terror brought to teenage addicts of the occult by horror movies and miasmic videos. Many of the old ghost stories passed along from child to child in playtime lore came from Europe along with other gentler traditional tales in early days. Recently, imaginative writers have superimposed on these tales elements from Canadian Indian lore, which give a primitive intensity to stories of demonic possession.

L. M. Montgomery made tales of weird and inexplicable events part of her repertoire and part of the reading experience of most Canadian girls. *Kilmeny of the Orchard* (1910), one of her earliest novels, in the uncanny story of a girl born mute because of her mother's proud and angry silence, then strangely given the power of speech in a moment of psychic crisis. Montgomery uses several regional tales of the uncanny in *The Story Girl* (1911). Many of her stories in this book and in its sequel *The Golden Road* (1914), tales of witches, ghostly bells, macabre weddings, terrifying prophecies, and mysterious dreams, were drawn from memories of stories told by a great-aunt.[3] *Rilla of Ingleside* (1921) ties events in the First World War to the strange prophetic dreams of one character. Montgomery based this motif on her belief in the deep significance of her dreams. She also promulgated the widely held Canadian conviction, preserved in many records of beliefs of the time, that an angel had appeared at Mons and turned the tide of battle at a crucial moment of the war.

Ghost stories are presented in Montgomery with irony—the Story Girl's promise to freeze the marrow and chill the blood of her listeners typifies the mock-heroic tone. But there is always also a touch of terror in the treatment of inexplicable psychic experiences by Montgomery who attributed her interest in the supernatural to her Celtic heritage.

Ruth Nichols, whose earlier fantasies for young children (*The Marrow of the World* and *A Walk out of the World*) continue to be reread and discussed by young adults, ventured into more serious speculation in two offbeat works in the 1970s: *Song of the Pearl* (1976), a fantasy of reincarnation, and *The Left-Handed Spirit* (1978), a novel that follows a young woman through a time quest into a confrontation with ancient supernatural forces and acceptance of her own strange power of healing.

Immersion in mysterious aspects of the past also preoccupies O. R. Melling in two novels, *Druid's Tune* (1983) and *The Singing Stone* (1986). Cuculann, the 17-year-old hero of ancient Ireland, looms as a figure strangely blending menace and attraction in *Druid's Tune*. Cuculan, the youthful defender of Ulster against a menacing warrior queen, charms the time-travelers yet dismays them with his blood-lust and mindless killings. In *The Singing Stone* a modern girl, shifted into a mythic world ruled by a goddess, searches for the treasure that opens the way to infinity.

Like Melling, Welwyn Katz presents a confrontation with evil forces rooted in a British setting in *Witchery Hill* (1984) and *Sun, God, Moon Witch* (1986), and like Melling she invokes the shadows of Celtic Britain in *Third Magic* (1988). In the latter story young people are transported to Arthurian times through a psychic affinity with beings of another world. In all these novels, Canadian protagonists find and confront occult forces of evil in old-world settings.

More effective and more chilling is Welwyn Katz's *False Face* (1987), in which evil is brought home to London, Ontario, and home to the family life of a Canadian girl. In this novel Katz uses a traditional Iroquois mask to release evil power and deepen the chasm between a girl and her mother. This book is one of a group of contemporary stories in which ghostly Indian legends have risen to haunt the imagination of author and reader. *False Face* is linked with two books by Joan Clark, *Wild Man of the Woods* (1985), in which a threatened boy learns to release defensive power through donning an Indian mask, and *The Moons of Madeleine* (1987), in which a girl slips into a silvered world under the spell of an old Indian moon mask and begins a frightening search for First Woman, the female spirit of night. *The Moons of Madeleine* also effectively ties female adolescent tension to the mysteries of the moon. Madeleine finds in the mysterious world conjured by the moon mask a second self, deeply antagonistic.

The fusion of stylish occultism with traditional Indian lore by Katz and Clark is a noteworthy innovation. The focus on Indian masks may stem from the visual impact of a powerful National Film Board movie on this subject, made in 1958, which draws on the current psychological emphasis on masks and personae. Possibly the original suggestion that an Indian underlay could add local depth and suggestiveness to occult fiction came from Leonard Cohen's adult novel *Beautiful Losers* (1966). Cohen used the Indian Catherine Tekakwitha, saint and mystic, as the pivotal figure in his novel, which in its time held a powerful interest for young writers.[4]

The time-shift form is used in Katz's *False Face* as in other novels of this type not for the simple mind-stretching effect of enabling a confrontation with people of a different era and not to unfold a happy ending in a morning scene in the present. The occult cross-temporal experience conveys an insidious sense of the dominance of evil forces in the present as well as in the past. The tie-in to Indian lore may account for some of the darkness of tone in Canadian occult fantasy.

A book deeper and more sophisticated than these "mask of evil" stories is Donn Kushner's *Uncle Jacob's Ghost Story* (1985). Totally different in its gritty urban setting from Montgomery's pastoral stories, it nevertheless blends the same combination of genuine folkloric materials, ironic byplay, and ultimate acceptance of the oddities of psychic experience. One of the pleasures this book offers a reader is intertextuality. The frame, two old people telling stories to a boy, recalls many earlier stories that use traditional materials—Maria Campbell's *Little Badger and the Fire Spirit,* for example—and, indeed, the values presented here are close to those of that gentle, humorous fable about an antihero. The rich, quick, inventive narrative has a movement comparable to *Jacob Two-Two* (and maybe Kushner's Sergeant O'Toole is related to Richler's Fearless O'Toole?) The guitar-playing ghosts in Kushner's story are joined by a mannequin from Macy's window, perhaps an allusion to the marionettes in Myra Paperny's *The Wooden People;* the histrionic family encounters also recall the drama of Paperny's book. In its own right *Uncle Jacob's Ghost Story* plays poignantly with the idea of the persistence of past life in the present. Whimsy and sadness work together to evoke a pensive enriching response. Kushner authenticates the ghost story as part of the obligatory preservation of memories of the past, and he also humanizes his ghosts by placing them in the settings of show business and the steamy hype in downtown New York. This sophisticated, surrealistic novel, like Kushner's fantastic *A Book Dragon* and his folkloric *Violin Maker's Gift,* comes from an author who quietly offers great value to young readers.

Science Fiction

One might expect the imagined world of science fiction to be without national coloration. The future as conceived by experts in computers, robotry, lasers, nuclear power, and intergalactic travel should be a life without Balkan boundaries. Yet the science fiction of British and American writers such as Ursula Le Guin, Madeline L'Engle, and Robert Heinlein reveals the pressures of national biases even in imaginative voyages to postnational universes. Science fiction reveals both the national attitudes toward priorities in science and also the national trends and fashions in narrative and character creation.

Canada has maintained very supportive policies toward innovative research, through national research councils in science and medicine, social sciences and humanities. Partly as a consequence, Canadians have broken barriers in theory and experiment, and the country honors technological and intellectual

pioneers such as Alexander Graham Bell, Frederick Banting, and Wilder Penfield. Strong work in science fiction for the young might be expected from such a society. Because so many of the technological breakthroughs have been achieved by men, it might also be assumed that men would write the science fiction novels and that boys would appear as the heroes of the imaginary spaceships and laboratories.

In fact, however, very little science fiction has come from Canadian pens—or word processors, and the two most interesting achievers in the field are Monica Hughes and Suzanne Martel. Hughes, like so many Canadian writers, is not a Canadian by birth or education; Martel, a Quebecoise, writes in French, and her prose reaches English readers in translations in a form that is weakened in both tone and cadence. The popularity of these two writers with both English and French Canadians is perhaps an appropriate indicator of the movement of fiction beyond particular places and languages. Yet Hughes and Martel have produced works that capture many of the particular pressures and problems of modern Canada, and they have extrapolated from the present state of our technology and culture a future world that they finely communicate in fictional forms.

Earlier Canadian authors had written some science fiction but not for children. Yet science fiction is a genre in which the border between childhood and maturity is obscure. Perhaps James De Mille's *A Strange Manuscript Found in a Copper Cylinder* (1888) could be resurrected as an early example of Canadian science fiction that is accessible to young readers. *A Strange Manuscript* recounts a voyage through the terrifying ice barrier of Antarctica into a tropical world where an alien group have founded a dystopia based on strange distortions of Judeo-Christian values. De Mille's story is science fiction rather than pure fantasy. Although, as in fantasy another world is accessed, in the world created by de Mille it is science rather than magic that impels growth, shrinkage, flight, and paralysis. *A Strange Manuscript* asks us to accept the power of science—rationally devised and directed by man—to activate change; then we are set to puzzle out whether science can halt or redirect the changes it has instigated.

Other more recent science fiction novels written for adults but likely to be accessible to young adults include David Walker's *The Lord's Pink Ocean,* which might catch the eye of a young reader who has earlier enjoyed Walker's boys' adventure stories such as *Pirate Rock* and *Dragon Hill.* Gordon Dickson, generally acclaimed as a major science fiction writer, now lives in the United States, but his works, such as *Dorsai* (1959), show traces of his Canadian upbringing.[5]

Of the more chilling variety of science fiction, Phyllis Gottlieb has concocted several stories that focus on child life in the supposed future, including *O Master Caliban* (1976). Although her short stories fantasizing about young planetoids, alien telepaths, and mutants were clearly intended for an older audience, young adults join that audience in admiring her sensitive confrontation of the evolving problems of biological engineering.[6]

Among works of science fiction specifically intended for younger readers, Christie Harris's *Sky Man on the Totem Pole?* (1975) rather ineffectually blends science fiction with native legends, which have been Harris's stronger suit. Three groups of space epics by Douglas Hill, a Canadian who lives and writes in England, include the Warlord Series (1979–82), the Huntsman Series (1982–84), and the Colsec Series (1984–85). In all these stories, young humans carry their troubles into space, encounter there the chilling scientific arrogance of aliens, and fight against and conquer evil in outer space. Although Hill's adventures are exciting, they convey little sense of the battles that are waged within the human consciousness.

The work of Suzanne Martel offers a richer moral ambivalence. Her dwellers in future worlds are locked in more complex and evenly matched battles. In *The City under Ground* (1964) Martel shows the confusions as well as the achievements of a group of boys who emerge from an underground world where they have lived since surviving a nuclear holocaust. The boys challenge and are challenged by the concepts and life-style of the strangely adapted survivors above ground. The two worlds, scientific and primitive, interact and, indeed, complement each other. The notion of complementarity becomes even more complex in Martel's more recent *Robot Alert* (first published as *Nos Amis robots* in 1982, and in English translation in 1985). Adam in Vancouver and Eve in Montreal represent western, male, Anglophone rationality, and eastern, female, Francophone intuition, respectively; together they form a human pair of communicators who respond to the admirable robotry of science.

Monica Hughes and Suzanne Martel have both won awards presented by the Canadian Authors' Association for a body of work that appeals to young readers. Martel has also won a major prize as a writer of historical fiction, whereas Hughes has won Canada Council awards twice for best book of the year in English—one of the awards being for the boys' initiation story *Hunter in the Dark* (1982), the other for *Guardian of Isis* (1981), part of a science fiction trilogy. Of Hughes's 10 works of "speculative fiction"—her term for science fiction—*The Keeper of the Isis Light* (1980) is probably most representative of the genre and is revelatory of recurring themes in the whole sequence of Canadian books for young people.

The keeper of the light in a distant planet in some space world future is Olwen. Through biological engineering Olwen has been adapted for survival in the ultraviolet nonozone of the planet Isis. Consequently, though she has (like so many young Canadian heroines) a marvellous head of red hair, her other features are startlingly unexpected: she has wide nostrils, a heavy brow, a lizardlike nictitating membrane over her eyes, claws, thick ankle bones, and green, scaly skin. Olwen's 15 years of isolation on Isis are broken when an interstellar shipload of people arrive, and among the new settlers is Mark London, a boy just a little older than her. Although she "functions perfectly," Olwen is rejected; Mark London, like Prince Ronald in Robert Munsch's picture book *The Paper Bag Princess,* is horrified at her appearance. She in turn rejects the newcomers and sets out for the higher ground of freedom.

Besides its feminist import, this book has a peculiarly Canadian relevance. It is an allegory of the encounter between beings adapted to the New World and a race of newcomers ill fitted to survive there. This dream of the future recalls the facts of the past—the clash between European settlers and the native peoples—a clash, like that on Isis, still unresolved. Olwen's antagonist is neither the newly spun evil of science nor the ancient evil dragon of sin and corruption. (Indeed, the dragon of old has been reduced to a strange-looking beast that has become her pet.) Her enemy is insensitivity, the inability to recognize pluralism or alternative ways of moving through life.

Another recurring motif, underplayed here as in traditional books for girls, is the motif of motherhood. In a cosmic storm, Olwen pulls an infant out of a crevasse, and this act leads to her being pulled up into the community of the space ship. Her mothering instinct makes possible her reintegration with the human community.

Keeper of the Isis Light extrapolates from our modern development in biological engineering a story of what the world may be like in the future. It makes the fantastic seem real by introducing inversions of familiar detail. Such a book may help a young person prepare for the future by foreshadowing probable technological advances. It may also, of course, prepare a more important readiness for the future by suggesting to the young reader that scientific advances hinge on ethical decisions, and that human stories, the boy-and-girl stuff, the defeat-the-dragon stuff, will probably not change in spite of technological revolutions. *Keeper of the Isis Light* implies that the young person will still need certain nonscientific gifts in the future—imagination, idealism, sympathy—gifts that can be developed through reading. Choice based on rich experience both direct and vicarious will continue to be the hinge of human life.

The Study of Children's Literature

The popularity of science fiction is an epic sign of a transitional movement beyond nationalism not just to a global but to a galactic village. Many seers besides Marshall McLuhan have prophesied a movement beyond the "Gutenberg galaxy"—the world of the book and book literacy—to a universe of electronic interactive composition, editing, dissemination, and reception of communication. Electronic, instantaneous, and international, such communication would make obsolete nonsense of the books we have saved from the past. No longer would we conceive of a national culture slowly incubated by individual creators. In the world predicted by much science fiction, fiction, and, indeed, literature in general would be inconceivable.

Children's literature has had a short history. Maybe that history will end soon, or maybe it will subside into a residue of half-remembered nursery rhymes, crooned to a human baby before it first toddles toward an interactive video game.

But when we fantasize such an end to literacy, memory—not prophecy—takes over. The memory of childhood reading, of participating in a process of complexity and intensity beyond any subsequent experience of film, television, radio, or video, rises to protest against and to resist the erosion of the book world.

One encouraging and significant phenomenon that buttresses this protest is the recognition that the study of children's literature is a field of great intellectual and social significance. Students who somehow missed reading children's classics enroll in great numbers today in courses on children's literature. They find in *Charlotte's Web* or *Winnie-the-Pooh* or *Anne of Green Gables* myths crying for analyses, cadences calling up undeveloped abilities and sympathies and perceptions. Many of the students of children's literature move on to teach and study and spread knowledge of these newfound mysterious resources.

Grown-ups find in the children's literature of their country a root cellar where national memories are stored. General readers, starved for the old literary gifts of laughter, vision, vicarious adventurous action, romance, and sympathy, find these gifts in children's books, either familiar or newly encountered. For children's literature takes readers back to their childhood memories and recalls their country's past as well.

Canadians in particular, at a moment when the concept of nationalism is in a volcanic state, turn to the novels and poems written for and about Canadian children, from colonial days to this free trade time, as invaluable texts. Canadian children's literature invites readers to slip on the olden-days coat, go down into the root cellar, turn on the Isis lights, put on a paper bag—and eat a little alligator pie.

The ability to reexperience the art of children's books offers the hope of a paradisal power, "childhood regained." This is not a vain hope: despite technology, there still exists a city under ground— a mysterious, magic, fantastic, amusing world of books to which any child and every adult can find access.

Notes and References

Chapter One

1. Pierre Trudeau, speech to Parliament. House of Commons Debates, Vol. III, 1971 (Ottawa: Queen's Printer, 1971), 8545-6.

2. Dennis Lee, "Ookpik," in *Nicholas Knock and Other People* (Toronto: Macmillan, 1974), 63.

3. Sheila Egoff, *The Republic of Childhood: A Critical Guide to Canadian Children's Literature,* (1967; rev. ed., Toronto: University of Toronto Press, 1975), hereafter cited in the text.

4. Founded in 1975, this journal appeared as *Canadian Children's Literature* until 1983, when the title was changed, to emphasize its bilingual quality, to *Canadian Children's Literature / La littérature canadienne pour la jeunesse*; hereafter the journal will be cited as *CCL*.

5. Sigmund Freud, "Creative Writers and Day-Dreaming," *The Complete Psychological Works of Sigmund Freud,* standard ed. (London: Hogarth, 1978), III, 215.

6. Norman Holland, *Dynamics of Reading* (New York: Oxford University Press, 1968), chapter 5.

7. Gerald Prince, *Narratology: The Form and Functioning of Narrative* (Berlin: Mouton, 1982), 103.

8. Jean Piaget, *The Psychology of Intelligence,* trans. M. Percy and D. E. Berlyne (London: Routledge & Kegan Paul, 1950).

9. Erik Erikson, *Childhood and Society* (New York: Norton, 1963); see also *The Complexities of Childhood,* ed. Mary Taylor, Clare McIntyre and Murray Wood (Toronto: Ministry of Education, 1987).

10. Jack Zipes, *Breaking the Magic Spell: Radical Theories of Folk and Fairy Tales* (New York: Routledge and Chapman Hall, 1982), 22.

11. Susan Sugarman, *Piaget's Construction of the Child's Reality* (Cambridge, England: Cambridge University Press, 1987), 244.

12. Jill May, *Children and Their Literature: A Readings Book* (West Lafayette, Ind.: ChLA Publications, 1983), 7.

Chapter 2

1. Laurie Ricou, *Everyday Magic: Child Languages in Canadian Literature* (Vancouver: University of British Columbia Press, 1987), ix; hereafter cited in the text.

2. See Wilder Penfield and L. Roberts, *Speech and Brain Mechanism* (Princeton, N.J.: Princeton University Press, 1959).

3. Dorothy Butler, *Babies Need Books* (London: Bodley Head, 1980; reprint London: Penguin, 1988), xii–xiii.

4. See M. Bernstein, ed., *Sensitive Periods in Development: An Interdisciplinary Perspective* (Hillsdale, N.J.: Erlbaum, 1986).

5. Amelia Howard-Gibbon, *An Illustrated Alphabet, 1859* (Toronto: Oxford University Press, 1966), unpaginated.

6. *ABC of Good Conduct* (London, Ont.: London Life Company, 1933), unpaginated.

7. Dorothy Allison, *A Fairy's Garland of B. C. Flowers* (Vernon, B. C.: *The Vernon News*, 1947), unpaginated.

8. R. M. Walts, *ABC's of Forest Fire Prevention* (Ottawa: Department of Resources and Development, 1950).

9. Iona and Peter Opie, compilers, *The Oxford Dictionary of Nursery Rhyme* (Oxford: Oxford University Press, 1963), hereafter cited as Opies).

10. *Young Canada's Nursery Rhymes* (London: Warne [1881]), 66.

11. "Mary Susan Goose," *Mother Goose's Bicycle Tours* (London: Briggs, 1900), 14.

12. David Boyle, *Uncle Jim's Canadian Nursery Rhymes,* illus. C. W. Jefferys (Toronto: Musson, 1908), 63, 47; hereafter cited in the text.

13. Dennis Lee, *Jelly Belly,* illus. Juan Wijngaard (Toronto: Macmillan, 1983), 22; hereafter cited in the text as *JB.*

14. Helen Shackleton, *Saucy and All* (Toronto: Macmillan, 1929), unpaginated.

15. A. M. Klein, "Orders," in *The Wind Has Wings: Poems from Canada,* Mary Alice Downie and Barbara Robertson, ed., illus. Elizabeth Cleaver (Toronto: Oxford University Press, 1968), 5.

16. For a different selection of Canadian poets, see, for instance, T. R. Lower and Fred Cogswell, *The Enchanted Land: Canadian Poetry and Young Readers,* illus. Peggy Steel (Toronto: Gage, 1967).

17. Dennis Lee, "Friends," in *Alligator Pie,* illus. Frank Newfeld (Toronto: Macmillan, 1974), 58; hereafter cited in text as *AP.*

18. Michele Landsberg, *Michele Landsberg's Guide to Children's Books* (London: Penguin, 1985), 68.

19. Dennis Lee, "Roots and Play: Writing as a 35-year-old Children," *CCL* 4 (1976): 34.

20. Quoted in Wayne Grady, "A Man's Garden of Verse," *Saturday Night* (November 1983): 73.

21. Perry Nodelman, "The Silver Honkabeest: Children and the Memory of Childhood," *CCL* 12 (1978): 32; see also Nodelman's "Who's Speaking? The Voices of Dennis Lee's Poems for Children," *CCL* 25 (1982): 4–17.

22. Gilles Vigneault, "Petite berceuse du début de la colonie," in *Comptine pour endormir l'enfant qui ne veut rien savoir,* illus. Claude Fleury (Montreal: Nouvelles éditions de l'arc, 1983).

Chapter Three

1. Bruno Bettelheim, *The Uses of Enchantment* (New York: Knopf, 1976); Jack Zipes, *Fairy Tales and the Art of Subversion: The Classical Genre for Children and the Process of Civilization* (New York: Routledge, 1981); see also Roger Sale, *Fairy Tales and After* (Cambridge, Mass.: Harvard University Press, 1978).

2. Constance Hieatt, "Analyzing Enchantment: Fantasy after Bettelheim," *CCL* 15/16 (1980): 6–14.

3. *A Mohawk Song and Dance . . . a Tune to an Indian Drum . . . Printed for Little Master Caldwell* (Quebec: Wm. Brown, 1780). This broadside is held at the British Museum, London.

4. Anne Cameron, "Notes," *CCL* 56 (1989): 120–21.

5. Gordon Johnston, "Obiquadj: Instruction and Delight for Children in White Versions of Indian Stories," *CCL* 31/32 (1983): 91.

6. Perry Nodelman, "'Little Red Riding Hood' as a Canadian Fairy Tale," *CCL* 20 (1980), 17–27.

7. Agnes Grant, "A Canadian Fairy Tale: What is it?", *CCL* 22 (1981), 77–35.

8. James M. Barrie, *Peter Pan; or The Boy Who Would Not Grow Up* in *The Plays of J. M. Barrie* (London: Hodder and Stoughton, 1928), 72.

9. Muriel Whitaker, *Pernilla in the Perilous Forest,* illus. Jetska Ironside (Ottawa: Oberon, 1979), unpaginated.

10. See Lorrie Andersen, Irene Aubrey, and Louise McDiarmid, *Storytellers' Rendezvous: Canadian Stories to Tell Children,* illus. BoKim Louie (Toronto: Canadian Library Association, 1979); Irene Aubry, Louise McDiarmid, and Lorrie Andersen, *Storytellers' Encore* (Toronto: Canadian Library Association, 1984); Bob Barton, *Tell Me Another: Storytelling and Reading Aloud at Home, at School and in the Community* (Pembroke, s.n., 1986).

11. Ellen Bryan Obed, *Borrowed Black,* illus. Jan Mogensen (St. Johns, Newfoundland: Breakwater), unpaginated. Reissue of a 1979 publication, illus. Hope Yandell.

Chapter Four

1. See Lloyd Ollile and Joanne Nurss, "Beginning Reading in North America," in *Beginning Reading Instruction in Different Countries,* ed. Lloyd Ollila (Newark, N.J.: International Reading Association, 1978).
2. See Ken Goodman, *What's Whole in Whole Language?* (Toronto: Scholastic-TAB, 1986).
3. Good regional collections of early primers are held at the University of Prince Edward Island, Mount Allison University, McGill University, University of Western Ontario, University of Alberta, and University of British Columbia. One of the earliest Canadian imprints in English, held at Boys and Girls House of the Metropolitan Toronto Public Library, is Daniel Claus's *A Primer for the Use of the Mohawk Children* (Montreal: Fleury Mesplets, 1781).
4. William Corry, *Spelling Book* (St. John, New Brunswick: Chubb, 1841), 2.
5. *The Small Preceptor; or, a New Set of Lessons for Children* (Montreal: Starke, 1835), 7.
6. *A First Book of Lessons for the Use of the Schools* (Toronto: Rob't McPhail, 1859), 2.
7. *First Book of Reading Lessons* (Toronto: Canada Publishing, 1867), 11.
8. Grace Duffie Boylan, *Our Little Canadian Kiddies* (New York: Hurst, 1901), unpaginated.
9. Emma Lorne Duff, *A Cargo of Stories for Children* illus. Ike Morgan (Toronto: McClelland & Stewart, 1929), 256.
10. Books mentioned in this section were examined at the National Library of Canada in Ottawa or in Boys and Girls House in Toronto. Both have excellent catalogues arranged in chronological order.
11. Margaret Evans Price, *The Angora Twinnies* (Rochester, N.Y.: Stecher, 1919), unpaginated.
12. Margaret Atwood, *Up in the Tree* (Toronto: McClelland & Stewart, 1978), unpaginated; hereafter cited in the text.
13. Marie-Louise Gay, *Moonbeam on a Cat's Ear* (Toronto: Stoddart, 1986), unpaginated.
14. bp Nichol, *To the End of the Block,* illus. Shirley Day (Windsor: Black Moss, 1984), unpaginated.

15. Kathy Stinson, *Red Is Best,* illus. Robin Baird Lewis (Toronto: Annick, 1982, unpaginated; hereafter cited in the text.

16. Heather McKend, *Moving Gives Me A Stomach Ache,* illus. Heather Collins (Erin, Ont.: Press Porcepic, 1989), unpaginated.

17. Margaret Laurence, "Upon a Midnight Clear," in *Heart of a Stranger* (Toronto: McClelland & Stewart, 1976), 199.

18. Fred Inglis, *The Promise of Happiness* (Cambridge, England: Cambridge University Press, 1981), 4; hereafter cited in the text.

19. Margaret Laurence, *Six Darn Cows,* illus. Ann Blades (Toronto: Lorimer, 1979), unpaginated.

20. Chinua Achebe, quoted by Jonathan Cott, in *Pipers at the Gates of Dawn: The Wisdom of Children's Literature* (New York: McGraw-Hill, 1981), 174.

21. Bruce Kidd, *Hockey Showdown* (Toronto: Lorimer, 1979), unpaginated.

22. Robert Munsch, *David's Father,* illus. Michael Martchenko (Toronto: Annick, 1980), unpaginated.

Chapter Five

1. Mordecai Richler "The Great Comic Book Heroes," in Margaret Meek, Aidan Warlow, Griselda Barton, eds., *The Cool Web* (New York, Atheneum, 1978), 300.

2. Jean Piaget, *The Language and Thought of the Child,* trans. Malcolm Piercy and D. E. Berlyne (London: Routledge, 1932).

3. Maria Nikolajeva, *The Magic Code* (Stockholm: Almqvist and Wiksell, 1988).

4. Catherine Anthony Clark, *The Golden Pine Cone* (Toronto: Macmillan, 1950), 134.

5. Ruth Nichols, *A Walk out of the World* (New York: Harcourt Brace, 1969), 64, 66; cited hereafter in text as *WOOW.*

6. Marisa Bortolussi, "Fantasy, Realism, and the Dynamics of Reception: The Case of the Child Reader," *CCL* 41 (1986): 32–43.

7. Ruth Nichols, "Fantasy and Escapism," *CCL* 4 (1976): 20–27; see also Jon Stott, "An Interview with Ruth Nichols," *CCL* 2 (1978): 5–19.

8. Hilary Thompson, "Doorways to Fantasy," *CCL* 21 (1981): 8–16.

9. Gaston Bachelard, *The Poetics of Reverie,* trans. Maria Jolas (New York: Orion, 1969), 217.

10. Wolfgang Iser, *The Act of Reading:* (Baltimore: Johns Hopkins University Press, 1978), 37.

11. See the two double issues on Canadian children's drama and theater: *CCL* 8/9 (1977) and *CCL* 57/58 (1990).

Chapter Six

1. Lawrence Kohlberg, "Moral Stages and Moralization: the Cognitive-Developmental Approach," in *Moral Development and Behavior: Theory, Research and Social Issues,* ed. Thomas Lickona (New York: Holt, Rinehart and Winston, 1976), 34–35.

2. Richard Hersh, Diana Paolitto, and Joseph Reimer, *Promoting Moral Growth* (New York: Longman, 1979), 58–61. See also Bob Dixon, *Catching Them Young: Sex, Race, and Class in Children's Fiction* (London: Pluto, 1977).

3. Louise Rosenblatt, *The Reader, the Text, the Poem: The Transactional Theory of the Literary Work.* (Carbondale: Southern Illinois University Press, 1978), 25–27.

4. Margaret Cutt, *Ministering Angels: A Study of Nineteenth-Century Evangelical Writing for Children* (Wormley, Herts.: Five Owls, 1979).

5. Adrienne Kertzer, "Painful Stories: Narrative Strategies of Immigration," *CCL* 35/36 (1984): 14–26.

6. See Northrop Frye, *The Educated Imagination* (Toronto: CBC Publications, 1963), 45, 53.

Chapter Seven

1. Juliet Dusinberre, *Alice to the Lighthouse* (London: Macmillan, 1987), chapter 1.

2. Sigmund Freud, *Totem and Taboo,* trans. James Strachey, *The Complete Psychological Works of Sigmund Freud* standard ed. (London: Hogarth, 1978), XIII, 127.

3. Robert Burns, "To a Mouse" in *The Poems of Robert Burns,* ed. DeLancy Ferguson, illus. Joan Hassall (New York: Heritage, 1965), 35.

4. Robertson Davies, [Samuel Marchbanks"], "Diary of a Poet," *Peterborough Examiner,* 29 January 1949, 4.

5. John Rowe Townsend, *Written for Children,* 2nd rev. ed. (New York: Lippincott, 1983), 123.

6. Charles G. D. Roberts, *The Kindred of the Wild: A Book of Animal Life* (Boston: Page, 1902), 29.

7. Charles G. D. Roberts, *Eyes of the Wilderness* (New York: Macmillan, 1933), 253.

8. Joe Gold, "The Precious Speck of Life," *Canadian Literature* 16 (1965): 22–23.

9. Clarence Hawkes, *Shaggycoat, the Biography of a Beaver,* illus. Charles Copeland (Toronto: Musson, 1906), 25.

10. Glenys Stow, "A Conversation with Roderick Haig-Brown," *CCL* 2 (1975): 20; see also Alec Lucas, "Haig-Brown's Animal Biographies," *CCL* 11 (1978): 21–38.

11. Alec Lucas, "Nature Writers and the Animal Story," in *Literary History of Canada,* ed. C. F. Klinck (Toronto: University of Toronto Press, 1965), 388.

12. Morley Callaghan, *Luke Baldwin's Vow* (Philadelphia: Winston, 1948), 187.

13. Farley Mowat, *The Dog Who Wouldn't Be* (Boston: Little, Brown, 1957), 195.

Chapter Eight

1. Herbert Ginsberg and Sylvia Opper, *Piaget's Theory of Intellectual Development* (Englewood Cliffs, N.J.: Prentice-Hall, 1969). Adolescent cognitive development involves mastery of Piaget's INRC group: identity, negation, reciprocity, and correlativity.

2. In Freudian theory adolescent identity crisis is viewed as affecting the search for consistent self-definition. Erik Erikson and other students of adolescent psychology emphasize the integrative process but postulate that gender-based differences, including the sense of "inner space" in females, affect identity development. Feminist critics postulate that male-dominated social institutions negatively affect young women's sense of identity.

3. Juanita Williams, *Psychology of Women,* 3rd ed. (New York: Norton, 1987), 195–97; see also Max Sugar, *Female Adolescent Development* (New York: Brunner/Mazel, 1979).

4. Rachel Du Plessis, *Writing Beyond the Ending* (Bloomington: University of Indiana Press, 1985).

5. A copy of *Pen Tamar; or, The History of an Old Maid* (London: Longman, Rees, Orme, Brown, Green, 1830) is held in the Lawrence Lande Room, McGill University. Other early girls' books mentioned in this chapter were consulted in the National Library of Canada; some are held in the children's section, and others are in the main library.

6. Douglas Lochhead, Introduction to Julia Beckwith Hart, *St. Ursula's Convent,* The Maritime Literature Reprint Series (Sackville, N.B., 1978), 8.

7. L. G., *Jessie Grey: or The Discipline of Life, A Canadian Tale* (Toronto: Campbell, 1870), vii, 110.

8. Henrietta Skelton, *Grace Morton* (Toronto: Irving, 1873), 18.

9. Mary Cadogan and Patricia Craig, *You're a Brick, Angela!* (London: Gollancz, 1976).

10. A selection of this poetry appears in *Poets of the Confederation,* ed. Malcolm Ross (Toronto: McClelland & Stewart, 1960). These poems appeared in Canadian school readers from the 1880s on.

11. E. E. Cowper, *Girls on the Gold Trail* (London: Nelson, n.d.), 327.

12. Annis Pratt, *Archetypal Patterns in Women's Fiction* (Bloomington: University of Indiana Press, 1981). Pratt notes that images of enclosure, dwarfing, and flight, rather than images of expansion and assurance, characterize the archetypal reveries of young girls.

13. Alice Munro, "Afterword" in L. M. Montgomery, *Emily of New Moon* (Toronto: McClelland & Stewart, 1988), 359. The novel was first published in 1923.

14. Margaret Atwood, *Surfacing* (Toronto: Anansi, 1972); *Survival* (Toronto: Anansi, 1972).

15. Robert Kroetsch, "Disunity as Unity" in *The Lovely Treachery of Words* (Toronto: Oxford University Press, 1989), 28.

Chapter Nine

1. Joseph Campbell, *Hero with a Thousand Faces* (New York: World, 1956). See also C. J. Jung and C. Kerenyi, *Essays on a Science of Mythology: The Myths of the Divine Child and the Divine Maiden* (New York: Harper, 1949).

2. Pierre Radin, *The Trickster* (New York: Greenwood, 1956); Douglas Hill, *Coyote the Trickster: Legends of the North American Indians* (London: Chatto and Windhus, 1975).

3. R. M. Ballantyne, *Sunbeams and Snowflakes; or, The Young Fur Traders* (London: Ward, Locke, 1856), 393.

4. Jon Stott, "The Circle and the Square," *CCL* 31/32 (1983): 2–4.

5. Eleanor Stedder, *Lost in the Wilds: A Canadian Story* (London: Nelson, 1893), 67.

6. J. M. Oxley, *The Wreckers of Sable Island* (London: Nelson, 1907), 41.

7. James De Mille, *Lost in the Fog* (Boston: Lee & Shepard, 1873), 30.

8. Ernest Thompson Seton, *Two Little Savages: Being the Adventures of Two Boys Who Lived as Indians and What They Learned* (Montreal: Montreal News, 1903), 545.

9. Christopher Beck, *Stronghand Saxon* (Philadelphia: Lippincott, 1910), 254.

10. The 21 "Hardy Boys" books by Leslie McFarlane (Franklin W. Dixon) include *The Tower Treasure* (New York: Grossett and Dunlap, 1927). See David Palmer, "A Last Talk with Leslie McFarlane," *CCL* 11 (1978): 5–19.

11. Roderick Haig-Brown, Starbuck Valley Winter (New York: Morrow, 1943), 207.

12. Farley Mowat, *Lost in the Barrens* (Boston: Little, Brown, 1956), 219.

13. David Walker, *Dragon Hill* (London: Collins, 1962), 139.

14. Rudyard Kipling, *Kim* (London: Macmillan, 1901), 250.

15. Kevin Major, *Far from Shore* (Toronto: Clarke, Irwin, 1980), 88.

16. Monica Hughes, *Hunter in the Dark* (Toronto: Irwin, 1981), 2.

Chapter Ten

1. David Elkind, *The Hurried Child* (Don Mills, Ont.: Addison, Wesley, 1981), 85.

2. Leon Garfield, "Historical Fiction for Our Global Times," *Horn Book* November/December (1988): 741.

3. Aleksandr Solzhenitsyn, *Nobel Prize Lecture,* trans. Nicholas Bethell (London: Stenvalley, 1973), 31.

4. Frank Baird, Preface to *Rob MacNab* (Halifax: Royal Print and Litho, 1923), iii.

5. William Kirby, *The Golden Dog: A Legend of Quebec* (Boston: Page, 1896), authorized ed., 132.

6. See Elizabeth Waterston, "The Politics of Conquest in Canadian Historical Fiction," *Mosaic* 3 (1969): 116–24.

7. See *The Scottish Tradition in Canada,* ed. Stanford Reid (Toronto: McClelland & Stewart, 1976).

8. E. A. Taylor, *Beatrice of Old York* (Toronto: Musson, 1929), 79.

9. James Reaney, *The Boy with an R in his Hand,* illus. Leo Rampen (Erin, Ont.: Porcupine's Quill, 1984), 48; hereafter cited in text as *BRH.*

10. Suzanne Martel, *The King's Daughter* (Vancouver: Douglas & McIntyre, 1982), 173; hereafter cited in text as *KD.*

Chapter Eleven

1. Gerald Prince, *Narratology;* see also Barbel Inhelder and Jean Piaget, *The Growth of Logical Thinking* (New York: Basic Books, 1962).

2. D. W. Winnicott, *Sense of Self: Playing and Reality* (Harmondsworth: Penguin, 1980).

3. *The Golden Road* is dedicated to "Aunt Mary Lawson"; for more details about the tradition of storytelling in the Macneill family, see *The Selected Journals of L. M. Montgomery,* 2 vols., ed. Mary Rubio and Elizabeth Waterston (Toronto: Oxford University Press, vol. 1, 1985; vol. 2, 1987).

4. Leonard Cohen, *Beautiful Losers* (New York: Viking, 1966).

5. Gordon Dickson's Dorsai stories began appearing in 1952; see Raymond H. Thompson, "Gordon R. Dickson: Science Fiction for Young Canadians," *CCL* 15/16 (1980): 38–46.

6. See David Ketterer, "Canadian Science Fiction: A Survey," *CCL* 10 (1977): 18–23.

Selected Bibliography

Primary Sources Works

*Alderson, Sue Ann. *Bonnie McSmithers, You're Driving Me Dithers*. Illustrated by Fiona Garrick. Edmonton Alberta: Tree Frog, 1974.

Allison, Rosemary. *Ms. Beaver Travels East*. Toronto: Women's Press, 1978.

Anastasiu, Stephane, *My House/Chez moi*. Toronto: Lorimer, 1984.

Andrews, Jan. *Very Last First Time*. Illustrated by Ian Wallace. Vancouver: Douglas & McIntyre, 1985.

*Anfousse, Ginette. *Hide and Seek*. Illustrated by author. Translated by Mayer Romaner. Toronto: NC, 1978.

———. *My Friend Pichou*. Illustrated by author. Translated by Mayer Romaner. Toronto: NC, 1978.

*Aska, Warabé. *Who Hides in the Park?/Les mystères du parc*. Montreal: Tundra, 1986.

———. *Who Goes to the Park?* Montreal: Tundra, 1984.

Assathiany, Sylvie and Louise Pelletier. *Grandma's Visit*. Illustrated by Philippe Béha. Toronto: Lorimer, 1985.

*Atwood, Margaret. *Up in the Tree*. Toronto: McClelland & Stewart, 1978.

———, and Joyce Barkhouse. *Anna's Pet*. Toronto: Lorimer, 1980.

Aubry, Claude. *The Christmas Wolf*. Illustrated by Edouard Perret. Translated by Alice Kane. Toronto: McClelland & Stewart, 1965.

———. *The Magic Fiddler and Other Legends of French Canada*. Translated by Alice Kane. Toronto: Peter Martin, 1968.

Baird, Frank. *Rob MacNab*. Halifax, Nova Scotia: Royal Print and Litho, 1923.

Baker, Olaf. *Heart o' the West*. London: Cassell, 1912.

*Ballantyne, R. M. *Sunbeams and Snowflakes; or, The Young Fur Traders*. Illustrated by author. London: Ward, Locke, 1856.

———. *Ungava; a Tale of Esquimeaux Land*. Illustrated by author. London: Ward, Locke, 1857.

*Discussed in some detail

*Barbeau, Marius. *The Golden Phoenix*. Retold by Michael Hornyansky. Toronto: Oxford University Press, 1958.

Bayley, Diana. *Henry; or, The Juvenile Traveller, a Faithful Delineation of a Voyage Across the Atlantic*. London: Simpkin, Marshall, 1836.

*Beck, Christopher. *Stronghand Saxon*. Philadelphia: Lippincott, 1910.

Béha, Philippe. *The Tree/L'Arbre*. Toronto: Lorimer, 1984.

————. *The Sea/La Mer*. Toronto: Lorimer, 1984.

Beissel, Henry. *Inook and the Sun*. Toronto: Playwrights Co-op, 1974.

Belaney, Archibald ("Grey Owl"). *The Adventures of Sajo and her Beaver People*. Toronto: Macmillan, 1935.

Bellegarde, the Adopted Indian Boy. London: Saunders and Otley, 1833.

Bennett, E. H. *Camp Ken-Jockety*. Toronto: Thomas Allen, 1923.

Bennett, Mary. *The Canadian Girl; or, The Pirate's Daughter: A Story of the Affections*. London: John Bennett, 1838.

*Berton, Pierre. *The Secret World of Og*. Toronto: McClelland & Stewart, 1971.

Bevans, Florence ("Jemima Revington"). *Percival, Plain Dog, Everyday*. Toronto, s.n., 1924.

Bice, Clare. *Jory's Cove. A Story of Nova Scotia*. New York: Macmillan, 1941.

Bindloss, Harold. *Boy Ranchers*. London: Blackie, 1910.

Bilson, Geoffrey. *Death Over Montreal*. Toronto: Kids Can, 1982.

Bishop, William, and Rothesay Stuart-Wortley. *The Flying Squad*. New York: Sundial, 1927.

*Blades, Ann. *Mary of Mile 18*. Montreal: Tundra, 1971.

*————. *A Boy of Taché*. Montreal: Tundra, 1984.

Bonnefons, Amable. *Le petit livre de vie, qui apprend à bien vivre et bien prier Dieu, à l'usage de diocèse de Quebec*. Montréal: Fleury Mesplet & Charles Berger, 1777.

Bonnell, M. *Mother Goose's Bicycle Tour*. Toronto: Briggs, 1900.

Bonner, Marjorie. *Rainbow at Night*. New York: Scribner, 1935.

Bourgeois, Paulette. *Franklin in the Dark*. Illustrated by Brenda Clark. Toronto: Kids Can, 1986.

Bowman, Anne. *The Bear Hunters of the Rocky Mountains*. London: Routledge, 1875.

Boylan, Grace Duffie. *Our Little Canadian Kiddies*. New York: Hurst, 1901.

Boyle, David. *Uncle Jim's Canadian Nursery Rhymes*. Illustrated by C. W. Jefferys. Toronto: Musson, 1908.

Brandis, Marianne. *Quarter-Pie Window*. Illustrated by G. B. à Brandis. Erin, Ontario: Porcupine's Quill, 1985.

Brereton, Captain. *A Boy of the Dominion*. London: Blackie, 1913.

Buchan, John (Lord Tweedsmuir) *Lake of Gold*. Illustrated by S. Levenson. Toronto: Musson, 1941; published in England as *The Long Traverse*, London: Hodder and Stoughton, 1941.

Buchan, Susan (Lady Tweedsmuir). *Mice on Horseback*. London: Oxford University Press, 1940.

Burkholder, Muriel. *Before the White Man Came*. Illustrated by C. M. Manly. Toronto: McClelland & Stewart, 1923.

*Burnford, Sheila. *The Incredible Journey*. Boston: Little, Brown, 1961.

Burns, Florence. *Jumbo, the Biggest Elephant in All the World*. Toronto: Scholastic-TAB, 1978.

Burrace, E. H. *Never Beaten!* London: Partridge, 1908.

*Butler, W. F. *Red Cloud*. London: Low and Marston, 1882.

*Callaghan, Morley. *Luke Baldwin's Vow*. Philadelphia: Winston, 1948.

Cameron, Anne. *How Raven Freed the Moon*. Illustrated by Tara Miller. Madeira Park, British Columbia: Harbour, 1985.

————. *How the Loon Lost Her Voice*. Illustrated by Tara Miller. Madeira Park, British Columbia: Harbour, 1985.

*Cameron, Silver Donald. *The Baitchoppers*. Toronto: Lorimer, 1982.

*Campbell, Maria. *Little Badger and the Fire Spirit*. Illustrated by David MacLagan. Toronto: McClelland & Stewart, 1977.

Campbell, Mary. *Sundays in Yoho: Twelve Stories for Children and Their Friends*. Montreal: Drysdale, 1884.

The Canadian Brothers: A Tale of the Western World. London: Darton, 1847.

Carlson, Natalie. *The Talking Cat and Other Stories from French Canada*. Illustrated by Roger Duvoisin. New York: Harper and Row, 1952.

*Carr, Emily. *Klee Wyck*. Toronto: Oxford University Press, 1941.

*Carrier, Roch. *The Hockey Sweater*. Illustrated by Sheldon Cohen. Translated by Sheila Fischman. Montreal: Tundra, 1984.

Catherwood, Mary. *The Romance of Dollard*. New York: Century, 1888.

Chetin, Helen. *The Lady of the Strawberries*. Illustrated by Anita Kunz. Toronto: Irwin, 1978.

Choate, Florence, and Elizabeth Curtis. *The Crimson Shawl*. New York: Lippincott, 1941.

*Clark, Catherine Anthony. *The Golden Pine Cone*. Illustrated by Clare Bice. Toronto: Macmillan, 1950.

*Clark, Joan. *The Moons of Madeleine*. New York: Viking, 1987.

————. *Wild Man of the Woods*. New York: Viking, 1985.

Clay, Charles. *Young Voyageur*. London: Oxford University Press, 1938.

*Cleaver, Elizabeth. *ABC*. Toronto: Oxford University Press, 1984.

Cleaver, Nancy. *How the Chipmunk Got Its Stripes*. Toronto: Scholastic-TAB, 1975.

Climo, Linda. *Chester's Barn*. Illustrated by author. Montreal: Tundra, 1982.

*Clutesi, George. *Son of Raven, Son of Deer: Fables of the She-Shaht People*. Sidney, British Columbia: Gray's, 1967.

Coatsworth, David and Emerson, eds. *The Adventures of Nanabush:*

Ojibway Indian Stories. Illustrated by Francis Kakige. Toronto: Doubleday, 1979.

Cody, H. A. *The King's Arrow.* Toronto: McClelland & Stewart, 1922.

Cole, Carol Cassidy (Carol Manchee). *Downy Wings and Sharp Ears: Adventures of a Little Canadian Boy among Little Wild Friends in Nature's Wonderland.* Toronto: Musson, 1923.

————. *Little Big-Ears and the Princess.* Toronto: Musson, 1926.

————. *Velvet Paws and Shiny Eyes: Adventures of a Little Canadian Boy in Nature's Wonderland.* Toronto: Musson, 1922.

Coleman, H. I. J. *A Rhyme for a Penny.* Toronto: Dent, 1929.

Frank Conibear. *Devil Dog.* Illustrated by John Scott. New York: Sloane, 1944.

———— and F. L. Blundell. *The Wise One.* Illustrated by Michael Bevans. London: Davies, 1949; Toronto: Scholastic-TAB, 1980.

———— and Kenneth Conibear. *Husky, the Story of Cap.* London, Davies, 1940.

Conibear, Kenneth. *North Land Footprints.* London: Dickson, 1936.

*Connor, Ralph (Charles Gordon). *Glengarry Schooldays.* Chicago: Revell, 1902.

Craig, John. *No Word for Good-bye.* Toronto: Clark, Irwin, 1969.

————. *Zach.* New York: Coward, McCann & Geoghegan, 1972.

*Cook, Lyn. *The Bells on Finland Street.* Illustrated by Stanley Wyatt. Toronto: Macmillan, 1950.

————. *The Little Magic Fiddler.* Illustrated by Stanley Wyatt. Toronto: Macmillan, 1951.

————. *Rebel on the Trail.* Illustrated by Ruth Collins. Toronto: Macmillan, 1953.

Coté, Marie-Josée. *My Street/Ma rue.* Toronto: Lorimer, 1984.

Cowper, E. G. *Girls on the Gold Trail.* London: Nelson, 1911.

————. *Witch of the Wilds.* London: Nelson, 1910.

Cox, Palmer. *The Brownies' Primer.* Chicago: Hill, 1901.

Crawford, Isabella Valancy. *Fairy Tales.* Edited by Penny Petrone. Ottawa: Borealis, 1977.

*Cutt, W. Cowrie. *Message from Ardmae.* Toronto: Collins, 1972.

————. *Seven for the Sea.* Toronto: Collins, 1973.

————. *Carry My Bones Northwest.* London: Collins, 1973.

Daunt, Achilles. *The Three Trappers.* London: Nelson, 1882.

Davies, Peter. *Fly Away, Paul.* New York: Crown, 1974.

de Gaspé, Philippe Aubert. *Canadians of Old.* Trans. C.G.D. Roberts. New York: Appleton, 1890.

*De la Roche, Mazo. *Jalna.* Boston: Little, Brown, 1927.

————. *Bill and Coo.* Toronto: Macmillan, 1958.

————. *Lark Ascending.* Boston: Little, Brown, 1932.

*De Mille, James. *The "B.O.W.C." Club: A Book for Boys.* Boston: Lee and Shepard, 1869.

*———. *The Boys of Grand Pré School.* Boston: Lee & Shepard, 1870.

———. *Fire in the Woods.* Boston: Lee & Shepard, 1872.

———. *Picked Up Adrift.* Boston: Lee & Shepard, 1872.

*———. *A Strange Manuscript Found in a Copper Cylinder.* New York: Harper, 1888.

Denison, Muriel. *Susannah.* New York: Dodd, Mead, 1936.

Dewdney, Selwyn. *The Hungry Time.* Illustrated by Olena Kassian. Toronto: Lorimer, 1980.

*Dickie, Donalda. *Sent to Coventry.* Toronto: Dent, 1929.

Dillon, Wallace. *Grit Aplenty.* New York: Revell, 1918.

Douglas, David. *On the Great Fur Trail.* London: Boy's Own Paper, 1919.

*Downie, Mary Alice. *How the Devil Got His Cat.* Illustrated by Jillian Gilliland. Kingston: Quarry, 1988.

———. *The King's Loon.* Illustrated by Ron Berg. Toronto: Kids Can, 1979.

———. *The Witch of the North: Folk Tales of French Canada.* Illustrated by Elizabeth Cleaver. Ottawa: Oberon, 1975.

Downie, Mary Alice and John. *Honor Bound.* Toronto: Oxford University Press, 1980.

*Downie, Mary Alice, and Barbara Robertson, eds. *The Wind Has Wings: Poems from Canada.* Illustrated by Elizabeth Cleaver. Toronto: Oxford University Press, 1968; 1978.

*Doyle, Brian. *Angel Square.* Vancouver: Douglas & McIntyre, 1984.

*———. *Up to Low.* Vancouver: Douglas & McIntyre, 1982.

Dragland, Stan. *Simon Jesse's Journey.* Vancouver: Douglas & McIntyre, 1983.

Drawson, Blair. *I Like Hats!* Illustrated by author. Toronto: Gage, 1977.

Duff, Emma Lorne. *A Cargo of Stories for Children.* Toronto: McClelland & Stewart, 1929.

*Duncan, Frances. *Kap-Sung Ferris.* Toronto: Macmillan, 1977.

———. *The Tooth-Paste Genie.* Toronto: Scholastic-TAB, 1981.

*Duncan, Norman. *The Adventures of Billy Topsail.* New York: Revell, 1906.

*———. *The Suitable Child.* Illustrated by Elizabeth Green. New York: Revell, 1909.

Dunham, Mabel. *Kristli's Trees.* Illustrated by Selwyn Dewdney. Toronto: McClelland & Stewart, 1948.

Dwight, Alan. *Drums in the Forest.* New York: Macmillan, 1936.

E., J. *The Old Home and the New.* Toronto: Campbell, 1870.

Embree, Beatrice. *The Girls of Miss Cleveland's.* Toronto: Musson, 1920.

Engel, Marian. *My Name is Not Odessa Yarker.* Illustrated by Laszlo Gal. Toronto: Kids Can, 1977.

Erskine, Laurie. *Renfrew of the Royal Mounted.* New York: Grosset & Dunlap, 1922.

Evans, Hubert. *Derry, Airedale of the Frontier.* New York: Dodd Mead, 1928.

Evatt, Harriet. *The Red Canoe.* New York: Bobbs, Merrill, 1940.

Finnigan, Joan. *Look! The Land Is Growing Giants: A Very Canadian Legend.* Montreal: Tundra, 1983.

Fortier, Caroline. *Unknown Fairies of Canada.* Toronto: Macmillan, 1926.

*Fowke, Edith. *Sally Go Round the Sun.* Toronto: Oxford University Press, 1969.

Foster, Janet. *The Wilds of Whip-poor-will Farm: True Animal Stories.* Illustrated by Olena Kassian. Toronto: Greey de Pencier, 1982.

Fox, Mary Lou. *Why the Beaver Has a Broad Tail.* Illustrated by Martin Panamik. Cobalt: Highway Bookshop, 1974.

Franko, Ivan. *Fox Mykyta.* Illustrated by William Kurelek. Montreal: Tundra, 1978.

Fraser, Joshua. *Three Months among the Moose.* Montreal: Lovell, 1881.

*Fraser, W. A. *Mooswa & Others of the Boundaries.* New York: Scribner, 1900.

Frazer, Frances. *The Bear Who Stole the Chinook and Other Stories.* Illustrated by Lewis Parker. Toronto: Macmillan, 1959.

Fréchette, Annie Howells. *On Grandfather's Farm.* Philadelphia: American Baptist Society, 1897.

*Freeman, Bill. *Shantymen of Cache Lake.* Toronto: Lorimer, 1975.

Frith, Henry. *The Opal Mountain.* London: Griffith, Farrar, 1889.

"G., L." *Jessie Grey.* Toronto: Campbell, 1870.

*Gay, Marie-Louise. *Moonbeam on a Cat's Ear.* Toronto: Stoddart, 1986.

———. *The Garden/Le potager.* Toronto: Lorimer, 1984.

German, Tony. *River Race.* Toronto: Lorimer, 1979.

———. *A Breed Apart.* Toronto: McClelland & Stewart, 1985.

Gilman, Phoebe. *The Balloon Tree.* Illustrated by author. Toronto: North Winds, 1984.

Godfrey, Martyn. *Here She Is, Miss Teeny Wonderful.* Toronto: Scholastic-TAB, 1984.

Gotlieb, Phyllis. *O Master Caliban.* New York: Harper & Row, 1976.

Grahame, G. H. *Larry, or The Avenging Terrors.* Toronto: Musson, 1923.

———. *The Voodoo Stone.* Toronto: Ryerson, 1935.

Grannan, Mary. *Just Mary.* Toronto: Gage, 1941.

———. *Maggie Muggins.* Toronto: Allen, 1944.

Grant, J. M. ("Grant Balfour"). *The Fairy School of Castle Frank.* Toronto: Poole, 1889.

———. *On Golden Wings through Wonderland.* Toronto: Poole, 1899.

Grisdale, Alex. *Wild Drums: Tales and Legends of the Plains Indians.* Ed. Nan Shipley. Winnipeg: Peguis, 1974.

Guelton, Elizabeth. *The Story of Peter, a Canadian Cat.* Toronto: Briggs, 1904.

*Haig-Brown, Roderick. *Ki-Yu: A Story of Panthers*. Boston: Houghton Mifflin, 1934.

———. *Return to the River: A Story of the Chinook Run*. New York: Morrow, 1941.

*———. *Starbuck Valley Winter*. New York: Morrow, 1943.

———. *The Whale People*. Illustrated by Mary Weiler. London: Collins, 1962.

Hall, Pamela. *On the Edge of the Eastern Ocean*. Illustrated by author. Toronto: GLC, 1982.

*Halvorson, Marilyn. *Cowboys Don't Cry*. Toronto: Irwin, 1984.

———. *Nobody Said It Would Be Easy*. Toronto: Irwin, 1987.

Hamilton, Mary. *The Tin-Lined Trunk*. Illustrated by Ron Berg. Toronto: Kids Can, 1980.

*Harris, Christie. *Raven's Cry*. Illustrated by Bill Reid. Toronto: McClelland & Stewart, 1966.

*———. *Secret in the Stlalakum Wild*. Illustrated by Douglas Tait. Toronto: McClelland & Stewart, 1972.

———. *Once Upon a Totem*. Illustrated by John Fraser Mills. New York: Atheneum, 1963.

———. *Sky Man on the Totem Pole?* Toronto: McClelland & Stewart, 1975.

*Harris, Dorothy Joan. *The House Mouse*. New York: Warne, 1973.

Harrison, Ted. *A Northern Alphabet*. Montreal: Tundra, 1982.

*Hart, Julia Beckwith. *St. Ursula's Convent; or, The Nun of Canada*. Kingston, Ontario: Thomson, 1824; reissued, edited by Douglas Lochhead, Maritimes Reprint Series. Sackville, New Brunswick: R.P. Bell Library, 1978.

Hayes, Clair. *The Boy Allies: with Haig in Flanders*. New York: Burt, 1918.

Hayes, John. *Treason at York*. Illustrated by Fred Finley. Toronto: Copp Clark, 1949.

———. *Rebels Ride at Night*. Illustrated by Fred Finley. Toronto: Copp Clark, 1953.

Hawkes, Clarence. *Shaggy Coat, the Biography of a Beaver*. Illustrated by Charles Copeland. Toronto: Musson, 1906.

Heaton, Hugh. *The Story of Professor Porky*. Illustrated by H. E. M. Sellen. Toronto: Heaton, 1937.

Henty, G. A. *With Wolfe in Canada; or, The Winning of the Continent*. London: Blackie, 1887.

Herbert, Agnes. *The Moose*. London: Black, 1913.

Hewitt, Marsha, and Claire Mackay. *One Proud Summer*. Toronto: Women's Press, 1981.

Hieatt, Constance. *The Sword and the Grail*. New York: Crowell, 1972.

Hill, Douglas. *The Huntsman*. Toronto: Macmillan, 1982.

*———. *Warriors of the Wasteland*. Toronto: Macmillan, 1983.

————. *The Caves of Klydor*. London: Gollancz, 1984.

Holbrook, Frances. *The Hiawatha Primer*. Illustrated by Elmer Boyd-Smith. Toronto: s.n., 1898.

Houston, James. *Frozen Fire*. London: Penguin, 1979.

*————. *River Runners: A Tale of Hardship and Bravery*. London: Penguin, 1981.

*————. *The White Archer*. Toronto: Longmans, 1967.

*Howard-Gibbon, Amelia. *An Illustrated Comic Alphabet, 1859*. Toronto: Oxford University Press, 1966.

*Hudson, Jan. *Sweetgrass*. Edmonton, Alberta: Tree Frog, 1984.

*Hughes, Monica. *Hunter in the Dark*. Toronto: Irwin, 1981.

*————. *The Keeper of the Isis Light*. London: Hamish Hamilton, 1980.

*————. *The Guardian of Isis*. London: Hamish Hamilton, 1981.

Hume, Ethel. *Judy of York Hill*. Boston: Houghton Mifflin, 1923.

Hunter, Bernice Thurman. *That Scatterbrain Booky*. Toronto: Scholastic-TAB, 1981.

An Hymn to be sung in St. Paul's Church on Sunday, December 7th, 1788, when a sermon will be preached for the benefit of the Sunday schools, and of the poor in Halifax. Halifax, Nova Scotia: Anthony Henry, 1788.

*Jamieson, Nina. *The Hickory Stick*. Toronto: McClelland, 1921.

Jefferys, C. W. *Canada's Past in Pictures*. Toronto: Ryerson, 1934.

*Johnson, Pauline. *Legends of Vancouver*. Vancouver: Thompson, 1911.

————. *The Mocassin Maker*. Toronto: Briggs, 1913.

————. *The Shagganappi*. Toronto: Briggs, 1912.

Johnston, Basil. *Tales and Elders Told*. Illustrated by Shirley Cheechoo. Toronto: Royal Ontario Museum. 1981.

Johnstone, C. L. *The Young Emigrants: A Story for Boys*. London: Nelson, 1898.

Katz, Welwyn. *Witchery Hill*. Vancouver, British Columbia: Douglas & McIntyre, 1984.

————. *Sun God, Moon Witch*. Vancouver, British Columbia: Douglas & McIntyre, 1986.

————. *Third Magic*. Vancouver, British Columbia: Douglas & McIntyre, 1988.

*————. *The Prophecy of Tau Riddoo*. Edmonton, Alberta: Tree Frog, 1982.

*————. *False Face*. Vancouver: Douglas & McIntyre, 1987.

Kavanaugh, Bridget. *The Pearl Fountain and Other Fairy Tales*. Toronto: Belford, 1872.

Kennedy, Howard. *The New World Fairy Book*. New York: Dutton, 1904.

Kenyon, C. R. *The Young Ranchmen*. Toronto: Musson, 1891.

*Khalsa, Dayal Kaur. *The Baabee Books*. Montreal: Tundra, 1983, 1984.

*————. *I Want a Dog*. Montreal: Tundra, 1987.

*Kidd, Bruce. *Hockey Showdown*. Toronto: Lorimer, 1979.

Kingman, Lee. *Pierre Pidgeon*. Boston: Houghton Mifflin, 1943.

Kingston, W. H. G. *The Trapper's Son*. London: Gall and Inglis, 1873.

Kirby, William. *The Golden Dog. A Legend of Quebec*. Montreal: Lovell, 1877; authorized edition. Boston: Page, 1896.

*Kirkconnell, Watson. *Titus the Toad*. Illustrated by Davina Craig. London: Oxford, 1934.

Kogawa, Joy. *Naomi's Road*. Illustrated by Matt Gould. Toronto: Oxford University Press, 1986.

Kong, Shiu and Elizabeth Wong. *Fables and Legends from Ancient China*. Illustrated by Michele Nidenoff and Wong Ying. Toronto: Kensington Educational, 1985.

————. *The Magic Pears*. Illustrated by Wong Ying. Toronto: Kensington Educational, 1986.

*Korman, Gordon. *I Want to Go Home!* Toronto: Scholastic-TAB, 1981.

————. *Who is Bugs Potter?* Illustrated by Dino Kotopoulis. Toronto: Scholastic-TAB, 1980.

*Kurelek, William. *A Northern Nativity*. Montreal: Tundra, 1976.

————. *A Prairie Boy's Winter*. Montreal: Tundra, 1984.

*Kushner, Donn. *A Book Dragon*. Toronto: Macmillan, 1987.

————. *Uncle Jacob's Ghost Story*. Toronto: Macmillan, 1984.

*————. *The Violin Maker's Gift*. Illustrated by Doug Panton. Toronto: Macmillan, 1980.

"A Lady." *A Peep at the Esquimaux*. London: Thomas, 1825.

Lancaster, Muriel. *Jingles for Juniors*. Toronto: Nelson, 1920.

Laurence, Margaret. *A Bird in the House*. Toronto: McClelland & Stewart, 1980.

————. *The Christmas Birthday Story*. Illustrated by Helen Lucas. Toronto: McClelland & Stewart, 1980.

*————. *The Olden Days Coat*. Illustrated by Muriel Wood. Toronto: McClelland & Stewart, 1982.

*————. *Six Darn Cows*. Illustrated by Ann Blades. Toronto: Lorimer, 1979.

*Lee, Dennis. *Alligator Pie*. Illustrated by Frank Newfeld. Toronto: Macmillan, 1974.

————. *Garbage Delight*. Illustrated by Frank Newfeld. Toronto: Macmillan, 1977.

*————. *Jelly Belly*. Illustrated by Juan Wijngaard. Toronto: Macmillan, 1983.

————. *The Ordinary Bath*. Illustrated by Jon McKee. Toronto: Magook, with McClelland & Stewart, 1979.

*————. *Lizzie's Lion*. Illustrated by Marie-Louise Gay. Toronto: Stoddart, 1984.

*————. *Nicholas Knock and Other People*. Illustrated by Frank Newfeld. Toronto: Macmillan, 1974.

Leighton, Robert. *Rattlesnake Ranch*. Toronto: Pearson, 1912.

LeRossignol, J. E. *Little Stories of Quebec*. Illustrated by Laura Miller. Toronto: Briggs, 1908.

Levert, Mireille. *The Train/Le Train*. Toronto: Lorimer, 1984.

Little, Jean. *Different Dragons*. New York: Viking Kestrel, 1986.

*———. *From Anna*. Illustrated by Joan Sandin. New York: Harper and Row, 1972.

———. *Mine for Keeps*. Illustrated by Lewis Parker. Boston: Little, Brown, 1962.

———. *Mama's going to Buy You a Mockingbird*. New York: Viking Kestrel, 1984.

———. *Look Through My Window*. Illustrated by Joan Sandin. New York: Harper, 1971.

Long, W. J. *Following the Deer*. Illustrated by Charles Copeland. Toronto: Copp, 1901.

———. *Way of the Wood Folk*. Illustrated by Charles Copeland. Boston: Ginn, 1899.

*Lunn, Janet. *Double Spell*. Toronto: Irwin, 1983; as *Twin Spell* in USA.

*———. *The Root Cellar*. Toronto: Lester & Orpen Dennys, 1981.

———. *Shadow in Hawthorn Bay*. Toronto: Lester & Orpen Dennys, 1986.

———. *The Twelve Dancing Princesses*. Illustrated by Laszlo Gal. Toronto: Methuen, 1979.

Lyntonville; or, The Irish Boy in Canada. New York: American Tract Society, 1867.

MacEwen, Gwendolyn. *The Honey Drum: Seven Tales from Arab Lands*. Oakville: Mosaic, 1983.

Machar, Agnes Maule. *Katie Johnstone's Cross: A Canadian Tale*. Toronto: Campbell, 1870.

*———. *Marjorie's Canadian Winter: A Story of the Northern Lights*. Boston: Lothrop, 1892.

*Mackay, Claire. *Exit Barney McGee*. Illustrated by David Simpson. Toronto: Scholastic-TAB, 1979.

Maclean, Flora. *True Anecdotes of Pet Animals*. Toronto: Blackett and Robinson, 1882.

Macmillan, Ann. *Levko*. Toronto: Longmans Green, 1956.

*Macmillan, Cyrus. *Canadian Fairy Tales*. Toronto: Gundy, 1922.

———. *Canadian Wonder Tales*. London: Gundy, 1918.

Macpherson, Jay. *The Four Ages of Man*. Toronto: Macmillan, 1971.

*Major, Kevin. *Hold Fast*. Toronto: Irwin, 1978.

———. *Far from Shore*. Toronto: Clarke, Irwin, 1980.

Maloney, Margaret. *The Little Mermaid*. Illustrated by Laszlo Gal. Toronto: Methuen, 1983.

*Marchant, Bessie (Mrs. Comfort). *Athabaska Bill*. Toronto: Sheldon, 1906.

————. *A Daughter of the Ranges.* London: Blackie, 1905.

————. *Juliette the Mail Carrier.* London: Collins, 1907.

Marquis, Thomas. *The King's Wish.* Toronto: Ryerson, 1924.

*Marryat, Frederick. *The Settlers in Canada. Written for Young People.* London: Longman, Brown, Green & Longmans, 1844.

*Martel, Suzanne. *The King's Daughter.* Illustrated by Debi Perna. Translated by S. J. Homel and Margaret Rose. Vancouver: Douglas & McIntyre, 1982.

*————. *The City under Ground.* Translated by Norah Smaridge. Vancouver: Douglas & McIntyre, 1982.

————. *Robot Alert.* Translated by Patricia Sillers. Toronto: Kids Can, 1985.

*Martin, Eva. *Canadian Fairy Tales.* Illustrated by Laszlo Gal. Vancouver: Douglas & McIntyre, 1984.

*May, David, ed. *Byron and His Balloon.* Written by the Children of LaLoche and Friends. Edmonton, Alberta: Tree Frog, 1984.

Mayo, Isabella ("Edward Garrett"). *A Black Diamond.* London: Home Words, 1899.

McArthur, Grace. *Sarah Jane's Bedtime Stories.* Hanna: s.n., 1936.

*McClung, Nellie. *Sowing Seeds in Danny.* New York: Doubleday, 1908.

McIlwraith, Jean. *The Curious Career of Roderick Campbell.* Boston: Houghton Mifflin, 1901.

————. *The Little Admiral.* Toronto: Hodder, 1924.

————. *Kinsmen at War.* Ottawa, Ontario: Graphic, 1927.

*McKend, Heather. *Moving Gives Me a Stomach Ache.* Illustrated by Bill Johnson. Windsor, Ontario: Black Moss, 1980; Illustrated by Heather Collins. Erin, Ontario: Porcepic, 1989.

McKishnie, Archie. *Dwellers of the Marsh Realm.* Chicago: Donohue, 1937.

McMurchy, Marjorie (Lady Willison). *Letty Bye.* (Toronto: Macmillan, 1937).

————. *The Child's House.* Toronto: Macmillan, 1923.

Melling, O. R. *The Druid's Tune.* New York: Viking, 1983.

————. *The Singing Stone.* New York: Viking, 1986.

Melzak, Ronald. *The Day Tuk Became a Hunter & Other Eskimo Stories.* Illustrated by Carol Jones. Toronto: McClelland & Stewart, 1967.

*Mitchell, W. O. *Who Has Seen the Wind.* Toronto: Macmillan, 1947.

A Mohawk Song and Dance . . . a Tune to an Indian Drum . . . Printed for Little Master Henry Caldwell. Quebec: William Brown, 1780.

Montgomery, L. M. *Anne of Avonlea.* Boston: Page, 1909.

*————. *Anne of Green Gables.* Boston: Page, 1908.

————. *Anne of the Island.* Boston: Page, 1915.

————. *Anne's House of Dreams.* New York: Stokes, 1917.

*————. *The Blue Castle.* Toronto: McClelland, 1926.

———. *Emily of New Moon*. Toronto: McClelland & Stewart, 1923.

———. *Kilmeny of the Orchard*. Boston: Page, 1910.

*———. *The Story Girl*. Boston: Page, 1911.

*———. *Rilla of Ingleside*. Toronto: McClelland, 1921.

*Mowat, Farley. *The Dog Who Wouldn't Be*. Boston: Little, Brown, 1957.

*———. *Lost in the Barrens*. Boston: Little, Brown, 1956.

———. *Never Cry Wolf*. Toronto: McClelland & Stewart, 1963.

*———. *Owls in the Family*. Boston: Little, Brown, 1961.

Muller, Robin. *Tatterhood*. Illustrated by author. Richmond Hill: North Winds, 1984.

Munro, Alice. *Lives of Girls and Women*. Toronto: McGraw-Hill Ryerson, 1971.

*Munsch, Robert. *David's Father*. Illustrated by Michael Martchenko. Toronto: Annick, 1983.

*———. *The Paper Bag Princess*. Illustrated by Michael Martchenko. Toronto: Annick, 1980.

———. *Jonathan Cleaned up—Then He Heard a Sound, or Blackberry Subway Jam*. Illustrated by Michael Martchenko. Toronto: Annick, 1981.

———. *Murmel, Murmel, Murmel*. Illustrated by Michael Martchenko. Toronto: Annick, 1982.

———. *Thomas' Snowsuit*. Illustrated by Michael Martchenko. Toronto: Annick, 1985.

Murray, W. H. *How John Norton the Trapper Kept His Christmas*. Illustrated by Frank Merrill. Toronto: Briggs, 1911.

*Nichol, bp. *Once, A Lullaby*. Illustrated by Ed. Roach. Windsor, Ontario: Black Moss, 1983; Illustrated by Anita Lobel. Toronto: Greenwillow, 1988.

*———. *To the End of the Block*. Illustrated by Shirley Day. Windsor, Ontario: Black Moss, 1984.

*Nicol, Eric. *The Clam Made a Face: A Play for Children*. Toronto: Simon and Pierre, 1975.

*Nichols, Ruth. *A Walk out of the World*. New York: Harcourt Brace, 1969.

*———. *The Marrow of the World*. Illustrated by Trina Schart Hyman. Toronto: Macmillan, 1972.

*Obed, Ellen Bryan. *Borrowed Black*. Illustrated by Jan Mogensen. St. Johns, New Foundland: Breakwater, 1989.

O'Brien, Jack. *Corporal Corey of the Royal Canadian Mounted*. Chicago: Winston, 1936.

*Oppenheim, Joanne. *Have You Seen Birds?* Illustrated by Barbara Reid. Toronto: North Winds, 1986.

Orton, Helen. *The Gold-Laced Coat*. New York: Stokes, 1934.

Outram, Mary. *The Story of a Log House*. Toronto: Musson, 1920.

*Oxley, J. M. *Bert Lloyd's Boyhood. A Story of Nova Scotia.* Philadelphia: American Baptist, 1889.

———. *Fergus MacTavish.* Philadelphia: American Baptist, 1892.

———. *Fife and Drum at Louisbourg.* Boston: Little, Brown, 1899.

———. *The Wreckers of Sable Island.* Philadelphia: American Baptist, 1891.

Pacey, Desmond. *The Cat, the Cow, and the Kangaroo.* Fredericton, New Brunswick: Brunswick, 1968.

Packard, Frank. *The Adventures of Jimmie Dale.* Toronto: Copp Clark, 1917.

*Paperny, Myra. *The Wooden People.* Boston: Little, Brown, 1976.

Parker, Gilbert. *The Seats of the Mighty.* London: Methuen, 1896.

*Patriarche, Valance. *Tag; or, The Chien Boule Dog.* Boston: Page, 1909.

Patten, Harris. *Wings of the North.* Chicago: Goldsmith, 1932.

Peate, Mary. *The Girl in the Red River Coat.* Toronto: Clark, Irwin, 1970.

Peterson, Len. *Billy Bishop and the Red Baron.* In *A Collection of Canadian Plays,* edited by Rolf Kalman. Toronto: Simon and Pierre, 1975.

Phillipps-Wolley, Clive. *Gold, Gold in Cariboo! A Story of Adventure in British Columbia.* London: Blackie, 1984.

Phillips, Ethel. *Gay Madelon.* Boston: Houghton Mifflin, 1931.

Pickthall, Marjorie. *Dick's Desertion. A Boy's Adventures in Canadian Forests.* Toronto: Musson, 1905.

———. *The Straight Road.* Toronto: Musson, 1906.

*Poulin, Stéphane. *Can You Catch Josephine?* Illustrated by author. Montreal: Tundra, 1987.

———. *Could You Stop Josephine?* Illustrated by author. Montreal: Tundra, 1988.

———. *Have you seen Josephine?* Montreal: Tundra, 1986.

*———. *A Beautiful City/Ah, belle cité!* Illustrated by author. Montreal: Tundra, 1987.

Pratt, Pierre. *The Fridge/Le Frigo.* Toronto: Lorimer, 1985.

Price, Margaret E. *The Angora Twinnies.* Rochester, New York: Stecher, n.d.

*Raddall, Thomas. *His Majesty's Yankee.* New York: Doubleday, 1942.

———. *Son of the Hawk.* Philadelphia: Winston, 1950.

Ray, Anne Chapin. *Janet: Her Winter in Quebec.* London: Frowde, Hodder & Stoughton, 1908.

*Razzell, Mary. *Snow Apples.* Vancouver: Douglas & McIntyre, 1984.

*Reaney, James. *Apple Butter and Other Plays.* Vancouver: Talonbooks, 1978.

*———. *The Boy with an R in His Hand.* Illustrated by Leo Rampen. Erin, Ontario: Porcépic, 1984.

———. *Names and Nicknames.* Vancouver: Talonbooks, 1978.

Reed, Helen. *Amy in Acadia.* Toronto: Morang, 1905.

*Reid, Barbara. *Sing a Song of Mother Goose.* Richmond Hill, Ontario: North Winds, 1987.

Reid, Mayne. *The Young Voyageurs.* London: Routledge, 1853.

*Richler, Mordecai. *Jacob Two-Two Meets the Hooded Fang.* New York: Knopf, 1975.

*Roberts, Charles G. D. *A Sister to Evangeline.* Boston: Lamson Wolffe, 1898.

————. *Barbara Ladd.* Boston: Page, 1902.

*————. *Reube Dare's Shad Boat. A Tale of the Tide Country.* New York: Hunt and Eaton, 1895.

————. *Earth's Enigmas.* Boston: Lamson Wolffe, 1896.

*————. *Eyes of the Wilderness.* New York: Macmillan, 1933.

————. *The Kindred of the Wild: A Book of Animal Life.* Boston: Page, 1902.

————. *Red Fox. The Story of His Adventurous Career.* Boston: Page, 1905.

Roberts, T. G. *The Red Feathers.* Boston: Page, 1907.

*Robertson, Margaret Murray. *Christie Redfern's Troubles.* London: Religious Tract Society, 1866.

*————. *Shenac's Work at Home. A Story of Canadian Life.* London: Religious Tract Society, 1868.

*Roper, Edward. *Icebound; or, The Anticosti Crusoes.* Toronto: Musson, 1900.

*Roy, Gabrielle. *Children of My Heart.* Translated by Alan Brown. Toronto: McClelland & Stewart, 1979.

*————. *Street of Riches.* Translated by Harry Binsse. Toronto: McClelland & Stewart, 1955.

————. *The Road Past Altamont.* Translated by Joyce Marshall. Toronto: McClelland & Stewart, 1966.

————. *Where Nests the Water Hen.* Translated by Harry Binsse. Toronto: McClelland & Stewart, 1950.

Sadlier, Mary Anne. *Willie Burke; or, The Irish Settler in America.* Boston: Donahoe, 1850.

Saltman, Judith. *Goldie by the Sea.* Illustrated by Kim LaFave. Vancouver: Douglas & McIntyre, 1987.

*Sandwell, Helen. *The Valley of Color-Days.* Illustrated by Alice B. Preston. Boston: Little, Brown, 1924.

San Souci, Robert. *The Enchanted Tapestry.* Illustrated by Laszlo Gal. Vancouver: Douglas & McIntyre, 1987.

Sandys, Edwyn. *Trapper "Jim."* New York: Macmillan, 1903.

————. *Sportsman "Joe."* New York: Macmillan, 1904.

Sass, Gregory. *Redcoat.* Illustrated by Pat Foote-Jones. Erin, Ontario: Pocupine's Quill, 1985.

*Saunders, Marshall. *Beautiful Joe: The Autobiography of a Dog*. Philadelphia: American Baptist Society, 1894.

*———. *Beautiful Joe's Paradise*. Boston: Page, 1902.

*———. *Bonnie Prince Fetlar: The Story of a Pony and His Friends*. Toronto: McClelland, 1920.

———. *Princess Sukey: The Story of a Pigeon and Her Human Friends*. New York: Eaton and Mains, 1905.

Savigny, A. G. *Lion the Mastiff*. Toronto: Briggs, 1904.

Saxby, Argyll. *Comrades Three!* Toronto: Musson, 1900.

Saxby, Jessie. *Snow Dreams*. Edinburgh: Johnstone, Hunter, 1882.

Saxe, Mary. *Our Little Quebec Cousin*. Boston: Page, 1919.

———. *Our Little Canadian Cousin of the North-West*. Boston: Page, 1923.

Scribe, Murdo. *Murdo's Story: A Legend from Northern Manitoba*. Illustrated by Terry Gallagher. Winnipeg, Manitoba: Pemmican, 1985.

Sellar, Robert. *Hemlock. A Tale of the War of 1812*. Montreal: Grafton, 1890.

———. *Morven. The Highland United Empire Loyalist*. Huntingdon, Quebec: Gleaner, 1911.

Seton, Ernest Thompson. *The Buffalo Wind*. Santa Fe: Seton Village, 1938.

*———. *Two Little Savages: Being the Adventures of Two Boys Who Lived as Indians and What They Learned*. Montreal: Montreal News, 1903; reprint, New York: Doubleday, 1959.

———. *Lives of the Hunted*. New York: Scribner, 1901.

———. *Wild Animals I Have Known*. New York: Scribner, 1898.

*Shackleton, Helen. *Saucy and All*. Toronto: Macmillan, 1929.

Sharp, Edith. *Nkwala*. Toronto: McClelland & Stewart, 1974.

Sheard, Verna. *The Golden Apple Tree*. New York: McCann, 1920.

Singer, Yvonne. *Little Miss Yes Miss*. Toronto: Kids Can, 1976.

Skelton, Henrietta. *Grace Morton*. Toronto: Irving, 1873.

Smucker, Barbara. *Underground to Canada*. Illustrated by Tom McNeely. Toronto: Irwin, 1977.

Spray, Carol. *The Mare's Egg: A New World Folk Tale*. Illustrated by Kim LaFave. Camden East, Ontario: Camden, 1981.

Stables, Gordon. *Wild Adventures around the Pole*. London: Hodder and Stoughton, 1888.

———. *Off to Klondyke*. London: Nisbet, 1890.

Stedder, Eleanor. *Lost in the Wilds: A Canadian Story*. London: Nelson, 1893.

Stefansson, Vilhjalmur, and Violet Irwin. *Kak the Copper Eskimo*. Toronto: Macmillan, 1924.

Stickney, J. H., and Ralph Hoffman. *Bird-Wood*. Toronto: Ginn, 1898.

*Stinson, Kathy. *Red Is Best.* Illustrated by Robin Baird Lewis. Toronto: Annick, 1982.

Strang, Herbert. *Rob the Ranger.* Toronto: Musson, 1907.

Stren, Patty. *I Was a 15-Year-Old Blimp.* Toronto: Totem, 1985.

Surrey, George. *The Shack in the Coulee.* London: Oxford, 1932.

*Tanaka, Shelley. *Michi's New Year.* Illustrated by Ron Berg. Toronto: Peter Martin, 1980.

*Taylor, Cora. *Julie.* Winnipeg, Manitoba: Western Prairie Producer, 1985.

Taylor, E. A. *Beatrice of Old York.* Toronto: Musson, 1929.

Thistle, Mel. *Peter the Sea Trout.* Toronto: Ryerson, 1954.

*Thompson, Dora Olive. *That Girl Ginger.* London: Religious Tract Society, 1931.

*Thurman, Mark. *The Elephant's Cold.* Illustrated by author. Toronto: NC, 1981.

Toye, William. *How Summer Came to Canada.* Illustrated by Elizabeth Cleaver. Toronto: Oxford University Press, 1969.

*———. *The Loon's Necklace.* Illustrated by Elizabeth Cleaver. Toronto: Oxford University Press, 1977.

———. *The St. Lawrence.* Toronto: Oxford University Press, 1959.

*Traill, Catharine Parr Strickland. *The Canadian Crusoes, a Tale of the Rice Plains.* London: Hall, Virtue, 1852.

*———. *Lady Mary and Her Nurse; or, A Peep into the Canadian Forest.* London: Hall, 1856; published as *Stories of the Canadian Forest; or, Little Mary and her Nurse.* Boston: Crosby & Nichols, 1861.

———. *The Young Emigrants; or, Pictures of Canada.* London: Harvey and Darton, 1826.

Trent, Martha. *Phoebe Marshall: Somewhere in Canada.* New York: Pearse and Hopkins, 1919.

*Truss, Jan. *Jasmin.* Vancouver: Douglas & McIntyre, 1982.

"Uncle Richard." *Northern Regions.* London: Harris, 1825.

Vernon, Dorothy. *A Fairy's Garland of B.C. Flowers.* Vernon, British Columbia: Vernon News, 1947.

Walker, Benson. *Scottie, a True Story of a Dog for Young Folks.* Ottawa: Graphic, 1927.

*Walker, David. *Dragon Hill.* Illustrated by Robert Hodgson. London: Collins, 1963.

———. *The Lord's Pink Ocean.* London: Collins, 1972.

———. *Pirate Rock.* Illustrated by Victor Mays. London: Collins, 1969.

Wallace, Archer. *Stories of Grit.* Toronto: Musson, 1925.

*Wallace, Ian. *Chin Chiang and the Dragon's Dance.* Vancouver: Douglas & McIntyre, 1984; New York: Atheneum, 1984.

Wallace, Paul. *Baptiste Larocque.* Toronto: Musson, 1923.

Walsh, Ann. *Your Time, My Time.* Erin, Ontario: Porcépic, 1984.

[Elizabeth Walshe] *Cedar Creek. From the Shanty to the Settlement.* London: Religious Tract Society, 1863.

*Waterton, Betty. *Petranella.* Illustrated by Ann Blades. Vancouver: Douglas & McIntyre, 1980.

*———. *A Salmon for Simon.* Illustrated by Ann Blades. Vancouver: Douglas & McIntyre, 1978.

Wathen-Fox, Marion. *Grandma's Party.* Little Folks Stories Series. Toronto: Nelson, 1926.

*Weaver, Emily. *The Only Girl: A Tale of 1837.* Toronto: Macmillan, 1938.

Weir, Joan. *So, I'm Different.* Vancouver: Douglas & McIntyre, 1981.

*Wheeler, Bernelda. *I Can't Have Bannock But the Beaver Has a Dam.* Illustrated by Herman Bekkering. Winnipeg, Manitoba: Pemmican, 1984.

*Whitaker. *Pernilla in the Perilous Forest.* Illustrated by Jetska Ironside. Ottawa, Ontario: Oberon, 1979.

*White, Stewart. *The Magic Forest.* New York: Macmillan, 1903.

Wilkinson, Ann. *Swann and Daphne.* Illustrated by Leo Rampen. Toronto: Oxford University Press, 1960.

Williams, Valentine. *Captain of the Club; or, the Canadian Boy.* New York: Kennedy, 1899.

*Wilson, Barbara, and Gisèle Daigle. *ABC & 123.* Erin, Ontario: Porcépic, 1980.

*Wood, Angela. *The Sandwich.* Illustrated by Ian Wallace. Toronto: Kids Can, 1985.

Wood, Frances. *The Old Red School House.* London: Partridge, 1913.

Woodruff, Ann. *Betty and Bob.* New York: Stokes, 1903.

Wynne, May. *Two Girls in the Wild.* London: Blackie, 1920.

*Wynne-Jones, Tim. *Zoom at Sea.* Illustrated by Ken Nutt. Vancouver: Douglas & McIntyre, 1983.

———. *Zoom Away.* Illustrated by Ken Nutt. Vancouver: Douglas & McIntyre, 1985.

Young, E. R. *My Dogs of the Northland.* New York: Revell, 1902.

———. *Three Boys in the Wild North Land, Summer.* New York: Eaton & Mains, 1896.

*———. *Winter Adventures of Three Boys in the Great Lone Land.* New York: Eaton & Mains, 1899.

Young Canada's Nursery Rhymes. Illustrated by Constance Haslewood. London: Warne, 1888.

Zola, Meguida. *My Kind of Pup.* Illustrated by Wendy Wolsak. Winnipeg, Manitoba: Pemmican, 1985.

Secondary Works

Bibliographies

Amtmann, Bernard. *Early Canadian Children's Books 1763–1840/Livres de l'enfance & livres de la jeunesse au Canada 1763–1840.* Montreal: Bernard Amtmann, 1976.
———. *A Bibliography of Canadian Children's Books and Books for Young People 1841–1867/Livres de l'enfance et livres de la jeunesse au Canada 1841–1867.* Montreal: Bernard Amtmann, 1977.
Aubrey, Irene. *Notable Canadian Children's Books: 1975–1979/Un choix de livres canadiens pour la jeunesse: 1975–1979.* Ottawa: National Library of Canada, 1985.
Canadian Children's Literature/La littérature canadienne pour la jeunesse. Guelph, Ontario: Canadian Children's Press. Annual Bibliographies, 1975–1990.
Gagnon, André and Ann Gagnon. *Canadian Books for Young People/ Livres canadiens pour la jeunesse.* Toronto: University of Toronto Press, 1987.
McDonough, Irma. *Canadian Books for Children/Livres canadiens pour enfants.* Toronto: University of Toronto Press, 1976.
———. *Canadian Books for Young People/Livres candiens pour la jeunesse.* 2nd ed. Toronto: University of Toronto Press, 1978; 3rd ed. 1980.
Our Choice/Your Choice Catalogue. Toronto: Canadian Children's Book Centre. Annual, 1975–.
St. John, Judith. *The Osborne Collection of Early Children's Books, 1566–1910: A Catalogue.* Toronto: Toronto Public Libraries, 1966.

Books

Atwood, Margaret. *Survival: A Thematic Guide to Canadian Literature.* Toronto: Anansi, 1972. Thought-provoking opinions about the motifs that characterize Canadian books, as viewed by a talented writer in the year she published her novel *Surfacing.*
Egoff, Sheila. *The Republic of Childhood: A Critical Guide to Children's Literature in English.* 2nd. ed. Toronto: University of Toronto Press, 1975. An essential comprehensive history of books published between 1950 and 1975, with a brief chapter on earlier books for children.
———. *Worlds Within: Children's Fantasy from the Middle Ages to Today.*

Chicago: American Library Association, 1988. Updates some comments on Canadian fantasy writers.

Frye, Northrop. *The Educated Imagination*. Toronto: Canadian Broadcasting Company, 1963. Professor Frye here presents a digest of his archetypal approach that has had a seminal effect on Canadian writers and critics of children's books.

Klinck, C. F. et al., eds. *Literary History of Canada*. Toronto: University of Toronto Press, 1965; rev. ed. 1975. Compiled by a constellation of scholars, this definitive history includes chapters on children's literature by Marjorie McDowell in the first edition, Sheila Egoff in the second.

Landsberg, Michele. *Michele Landsberg's Guide to Children's Books*. London: Penguin, 1985. A witty, readable guide to the best children's books in the English-speaking world, with a strong representation of Canadian children's books and "a good balance of books in which boys and girls play active central roles" (xii).

McDonough, Irma, ed. *Profiles: Authors and Illustrators of Children's Literature in Canada*. Toronto: Canadian Library Association, 1982.

Potvin, Claude. *Le Canada français et sa littérature de jeunesse*. Montreal: Editions CRP, 1981. Adds a Francophone perspective to considerations of the context and progress of children's literature in Canada.

Ricou, Laurie. *Everyday Magic: Child Language and Canadian Literature*. Vancouver: University of British Columbia Press, 1987. A stimulating innovative study of the intersection between the uses of child language in creative literature and psycholinguistic theory about child development.

Saltman, Judith. *Modern Canadian Children's Books*. Toronto: Oxford University Press, 1987. Evaluates picture books, fiction, oral tradition, and poetry produced during the "creative surge" of writing, illustrating, and publishing in the decade after Egoff's study.

Stott, Jon C., and Raymond E. Jones. *Canadian Books for Children: A Guide to Authors & Illustrators*. Toronto: Harcourt, Brace, Jovanovich, 1988. Effectively condensed biographical information and critical comment on 105 Canadian producers of English-language books, supplemented by a guide for choices and use. Unique in historical and critical range.

Toye, W. E., ed. *Oxford Companion to Canadian Literature*. Toronto: Oxford University Press, 1983. A national reference guide edited by a writer and publisher of significant books for children.

Articles

Canadian Children's Literature/La Littérature canadienne pour la jeu-nesse (abbreviated as CCL throughout). Available through the University of Guelph, Guelph, Ont., N1G 2W1. 1975–. Contains relevant articles in every issue.

Canadian Literature. Available through the University of British Columbia, Vancouver, B.C., V6T 1W5. 1959–. Presents occasional important articles on children's literature; see for example issue number 108 on popular culture.

Index

Alderson, Sue, 61–62
Allison, Dorothy, 16
Allison, Rosemary, 107
American influences, 2, 29, 43, 48, 49, 52, 61, 63, 82, 158; Alcott, Louisa May, 113; Baum, L. Frank, 62, 65, 68; Blume, Judy, 126; Burgess, Thornton, 97; Dewey, John, 48; Forbes, Esther, 153; Gesell, H., 48; Heinlein, Robert, 168; Howells, W. D., 49; Le Guin, Ursula, 168; Longfellow, H. W., 31, 114, 151; Poe, E. A., 163; Porter, Gene Stratton, 115; Rice, Alice Hegan, 115, 121; Salinger, J. D., 142; Sendak, Maurice, 63, 76; Seuss, Dr., 51; Twain, Mark, 43, 111; "Uncle Remus," 93; White, E. B., 73, 96, 107; Wiggin, Kate Douglas, 115; Wilder, Laura, 125
Anfousse, Ginette, 61
Aska, Warabé, 42
Atwood, Margaret, 11, 45, 52, 53, 57, 110, 123, 128
Aubert de Gaspé, Philippe, 36, 151
Aubrey, Irene, 177
Aubry, Claude, 36
authors briefly cited: Acorn, Milton, 23; Anastasiu, Stéphane, 14; Anderson, W. B., 137; Béha, Philippe, 14; Bennett, E. H., 138; Bindloss, J., 137; Brereton, Captain, 137; Cody, H. A., 152; Coleman, H. I. J., 48; Coté, Marie-Josée, 14; Dunham, Mabel, 86; Foster, Janet, 107; Frith, Henry, 134; Hoffman, Ralph, 98; Hume,

Ethel, 118; Kingman, Lee, 50; Layton, Irving, 23; Leacock, Stephen, 99; Leighton, Robert, 137; Levert, Mireille, 14; Muir, Alexander, 48; Revoil, Benedict, 129; Souster, Raymond, 23; Stickney, J. H., 98

Baird, Frank, 149, 152
Ballantyne, R. M., 3, 129, 131, 132, 139, 141, 147
Barbeau, Marius, 36
Bayley, Diana, 65
Beck, Christopher, 137
Beissel, Henry, 77
Bennett, Mary, 112
Berg, Ron, 92
Berton, Pierre, 68, 74
Bice, Clare, 139
Bilson, Geoffrey, 159
Bishop, William, V. C., 137
Blades, Ann, 56, 57, 59, 142
Bonnefons, Amable, 2
Bonner, Margerie, 120
Bourgeois, Paulette, 108
Bowman, Anne, 134
Boyd-Smith, Elmer, 19, 20
Boylan, Grace Duffie, 48
Boyle, David, 19
Brandis, Marianne, 159
Buchan, Susan, 67
Buchan, John, 67, 141
Burkholder, Muriel, 32
Burnford, Sheila, 105
Burrace, E. H., 137
Butler, W. F., 3, 129, 132, 134, 139, 141

205

Index

The Author

Elizabeth Waterston is professor emeritus and former chair of the Department of English, University of Guelph, Ontario. She is a former national president of the Humanities Association of Canada and of the Canadian Association of Chairmen of English. Born in Montreal, Dr. Waterston was educated at McGill University, Bryn Mawr College, and the University of Toronto and has taught at Concordia University in Montreal and the University of Western Ontario in London. In 1975 she helped found *Canadian Children's Literature* and is still coeditor of this magazine. She is the author of *Survey: A Short History of Canadian Literature* and *Canada to 1900: The Travellers* and is coeditor, with Mary Rubio, of *The Selected Journals of L. M. Montgomery.* She is the mother of five children and has nine grandchildren.

The Editor

Ruth K. MacDonald is a professor of English and head of the Department of English and Philosophy at Purdue University. She received her B.A. and M.A. in English from the University of Connecticut, her Ph.D. in English from Rutgers University, and her M.B.A. from the University of Texas at El Paso. To Twayne's United States and English Authors series she has contributed the volumes on Louisa May Alcott, Beatrix Potter, and Dr. Seuss. She is the author of *Literature for Children in England and America, 1646–1774* (1982).